I Have Iraq in My Shoe

a memoir

MISADVENTURES OF A SOLDIER OF FASHION

Gretchen Berg

 sourcebooks

Published by Sourcebooks, Inc.
P.O. Box 4410, Naperville, Illinois 60567-4410
(630) 961-3900
Fax: (630) 961-2168
www.sourcebooks.com

Library of Congress Cataloging-in-Publication Data

Berg, Gretchen.
  I have Iraq in my shoe : misadventures of a soldier of fashion : a memoir / Gretchen Berg.
     p. cm.
  Includes bibliographical references and index.
  (pbk. : alk. paper) 1. Berg, Gretchen—Travel—Iraq—Irbil. 2. English teachers—
Iraq—Irbil—Biography. 3. English language—Study and teaching—Iraq—Irbil. 4.
Irbil (Iraq)—Social conditions—21st century. 5. Irbil (Iraq)—Biography. I. Title.
  PE64.B47A3 2012
  956.7044'3092—dc23
  [B]

                              2011046365

            Printed and bound in the United States of America.
                    BG 10 9 8 7 6 5 4 3 2 1

To all my students in Iraq

Q: Recent polls have shown that a fifth of Americans can't locate the U.S. on a world map. Why do you think this is?

A: I believe that our education like such as South Africa and, uh, The Iraq, everywhere like, such as and…I believe that they should, our education over here in the U.S. should help the U.S., er, should help South Africa and should help The Iraq…

—Miss Teen South Carolina, 2007

Part 1

....

Opportunity Knocks

....

Chapter One

Fiddle-Dee-Dee

I hate the word recession. *Recession* was what happened to unlucky men's hairlines. *Recession* was very bad news for your gums. *Recession* meant "no new shoes" in 2008.

My job as a website copywriter was set to end in December, a very short two months away, and I had been sending out résumés since July, with a myriad of nothing to show for it—like when my dad would say to me, "You want to know what you're getting for your birthday? Close your eyes. What do you see?" and then he would chuckle to himself. *Nothing.*

Oh, the woes of impending unemployment. Why couldn't potential employers recognize my amazing potential? Why? *Why?* In a perfect world they would coordinate with my grade school teachers and sort things out:

> **Mrs. Vivian, First-Grade Teacher:** Gretchen is not working up to her potential...
>
> **Christian Louboutin, CEO of Christian Louboutin Shoes:** Oh, so this Gretchen has potential? Let's bring her in for an interview!

Something like that. Not having my amazing potential recognized was horribly discouraging. Other things to file under Horribly Discouraging were nagging credit card bills, rent, automobile insurance, health insurance, food, the inflated cost of gas…these were the reasons I found myself metaphorically clad in a dingy old dress, sitting crumpled on the dry, barren ground, a la Scarlett O'Hara, sobbing into my apron.

I fancied myself a modern-day Scarlett. Margaret Mitchell began her wildly romantic, sweeping epic with "Scarlett O'Hara was not beautiful," and I love a heroine I can relate to.

Scarlett was also "strong and unscrupulous, passionate and earthy."

- **Strong:** I once assembled a mini-trampoline by myself, when the directions called for *three* people to do the job. *Three.*
- **Unscrupulous:** I ordered a ski bag from a big online retailer, and instead of one ski bag they sent me two ski bags. I didn't return the second ski bag; I gave it to my sister Jessie. Returning Second Ski Bag would have required boxing and taping the bag up, getting in the car, driving to UPS, driving home from UPS. Oh God, I'm exhausted just telling you about it.
- **Passionate:** Ask any of my friends how I feel about Humboldt Fog or truffle cheese.
- **Earthy:** Sometimes I go to the store without makeup.

Scarlett and I also shared similar views on the topic of war: "Fiddle-dee-dee. War, war, war. This war talk's spoiling all the fun at every party this spring. I get so bored I could scream." This was precisely my inner monologue when party talk turned to war in the Middle East, politics in general, or whatever was on the news last night. *No, I did not see that special report.* Project Runway *was on. I'm bored! Tell me my dress is pretty!*

And Scarlett was highly inventive when it came to fashion. I haven't yet turned my living-room curtains into a dress, but I did cut the ankle straps off a pair of platform peep-toes because they felt too restrictive.

You know what else was restrictive? *The recession.*

ⅇ∽ⅇ∽ⅇ∽

One day, in the middle of October, I was checking my voice mail, in the hopes that one of the résumés I had sent out had garnered some proper attention:

> **Voice mail:** *Beep,* "GERRRRRRTS, it's Warren, and no, I'm not drunk."

I hated it when my friend Warren called me "Gerts." I had made the mistake of telling him that "Gerty" was a nickname unfortunately bestowed upon me in junior high by a group of mean boys whose main extracurricular activity was tormenting. *"Gerty Gertruuuuude!"*

Eeeesh. The sound of that name sent me reeling back to seventh grade, when I went home from school crying almost every day. Warren was the kind of person who assigned unflattering nicknames to nearly everyone he met as a way of subtly bully-ing them (like "Ham Hocks" for a girl who had saddlebags). I had saved him the trouble of conjuring a label for me—he just borrowed "Gerty." Of course no one would know "Gerty" was offensive except me, but it takes a while to rid yourself of junior high torment. I'll probably be over it by the time I'm eighty. I only tolerated Warren's use of the nickname because he was really funny, and he made me laugh out loud.

We met back in 1995 while teaching English at a language academy in Seoul, South Korea, and clicked immediately. He was the brother I never wanted. Teaching fussy adolescents was often a challenge, and having Warren there for comic relief made it infinitely more bearable.

Fast forward to early 2007, twelve years after Korea, when I was working for a travel company in Seattle and Warren was back to teaching English again, this time in Dubai, United Arab Emirates. Dubai had the reputation of being the Vegas of the Middle East, and Warren made his life there sound like a dream: "tons of cash, private villa, Jet Skiing to private islands," etc. He would always casually throw out a "You should come out here and teach! It's great!" He was prone to wild exaggeration, but from his Facebook photos, it looked like he really was enjoying himself in the style in which he was perpetually yammering. Warren on a Jet Ski, Warren feeding camels, Warren posing in front of the famed Burj Al Arab—that last one was in sepia, which really added a touch of class to the album. He seemed to be in his element in the Middle East.

That was nice for him, but it was somewhere I had no desire to go.

My extremely limited knowledge of the Middle East, juxtaposed with reasons I should absolutely not go there:

- FACT: Women, typically, do not live alone.
- FACT: I had lived in my own apartment for eight years.
- FACT: Conservative Muslim women wear black fabric covering their heads and entire bodies.
- FACT: Black makes me grumpy.
- FACT: It is illegal (at least in Saudi Arabia) for women to drive.
- FACT: I started driving when I was twelve years old.

Living, dressing, and driving were all very important things to me, a girl born in the era of Gloria Steinem. I was raised on *Free to Be You and Me* and *Our Bodies, Ourselves* and, as far as I know, neither of those has been translated into Arabic. But you know what has been translated into Arabic?

Gone with the Wind.

Chapter Two

Knock-Knock, It's Iraq!

In August of 2007, Warren randomly showed up at my office in Seattle, totally unannounced—like any good stalker would—and greeted me with a "GERRRRRRRRRTY!" and a sternum-crushing hug. I was wearing a heavy, metal-plated necklace that is now kind of imprinted on my chest, but I was more annoyed with the revival of the nickname.

I hadn't seen him in over ten years, but he looked almost exactly the same, with his stocky, barrel-chested frame, short militaryesque crop of blond hair, and big friendly grin. When I say "friendly," I mean "shit-eating." Warren was always up to something.

He had moved on from Dubai and was on a break from his latest "living the dream" opportunity, according to him: teaching English and coaching soccer in Iraq.

> **Me:** Hanh? Whaaaaa? You're in Iraq now?
> **Still me:** Iraq?
> **Still me, again:** Why?

He said it was a great opportunity; he was acting as educational director or some such thing, blah blah, inconsequential details, whatever. My brain couldn't get beyond the "I'm living and working in Iraq" thing to actually absorb any of his explanation.

Iraq? Like Iraq, Iraq? Like, the Iraq that was the setting of the war? The Iraq that was hosting some-odd thousand of our troops in some sort of reconstruction effort but was still plagued by violence and bombing and other manner of grave danger to which I'm generally averse? That Iraq? Or was Iraq the name of a posh suburb in, maybe, Vancouver?

If I separated my friends into categories (and I do) like "good for coffee dates," "fun to shop with," "only in small doses," or "always with a grain of salt," I would put Warren firmly in the latter. Most of what he says is caked in embellishment.

Warren (again): It's a great opportunity…
Me: IN IRAQ?

In Warren's brain our brief, shared overseas teaching extravaganza must have somehow translated into a globe-trotting life plan. Last year he wanted me to go join him in Dubai, and now he wanted me to teach in Iraq. That was all kinds of crazy. IRAQ. No one voluntarily goes there. They are *deployed*, or *sent on assignment*, or *exiled to*. I am a self-diagnosed mild claustrophobic, and in the CNN footage, the local women of these Middle Eastern countries were all covered, head to toe, with billowing black tablecloths. I'm no psychiatrist, but I could not see "burka" being a sartorial recommendation for the mildly claustrophobic. Even for those of the self-diagnosed variety.

I loved to travel. I had made it to all seven continents. Some considered this quite an accomplishment, although I knew it was just a matter of booking plane tickets and boarding when your group number was called. Despite my love of traveling, I remembered being utterly relieved upon discovering that the Middle East was considered part of Asia. I had already been to Asia! I wouldn't have to go to the Middle East to complete my continental tour!

No, there would be no Middle East for me.

That was my state of mind pre-recession. In the Good Old Days. When I had job security and knew where my next pair of shoes was coming from.

$$e \sim e \sim e$$

So, with the recession hovering over me like Death in a burka, I listened to Warren's allegedly nondrunk message, which arrived in my voice mail in August of 2008, almost one year to the date after he had ambushed me in Seattle, a year during which I told everyone about my friend Warren the lunatic who was living in Iraq. In said allegedly nondrunk voice mail, he slurred things about how I never had my phone turned on, blah blah, but didn't really say anything of great importance. I assumed he wanted to discuss Iraq. I responded by email[*]:

> I got your messages, but I'm not coming to Iraq to teach.

---

[*]All emails, text messages, and other written communications in this book have been copied as they were written, including spelling, grammar, and syntax errors.

He responded shortly after:

> **Hey** Gerrrrrty *[dear God, why did he insist on calling me that?]*,
> That's fine about you but if you know anyone please let me know. We are in Kurdistan—Northern Iraq. Its very safe here so if someone is interested in the adventure let me know and I can take a look at them. Lots of time off and great pay in the safest part of Iraq…

Here he inserted a link to a story CNN had done on the university, complete with contrived "casual" footage of Warren jocularly interacting with a few Iraqi students.

> Great link with some really good-looking people that work here…. ;)
> W

I replied:

> No thanks, but send me the details and I'll see if anyone I know might be interested.

> Hey, Gerts *[ucchhh]*,
> I have teaching and admin jobs. I am the Director of this unit and hire them myself. A teacher will make $70,000 and pay no taxes. We pay for a new villa (no roommates in a 4 bedroom house), transportation, security, etc…the only thing not paid for is food which is around $300 a month. I've been

here a while and saved about 96% of what I made. Plus crazy travel opportunities… when we leave here for all these breaks we go to Amsterdam, Greece, Italy, Turkey, Vienna, Germany, London, and home.

So to wrap up, it is 100% safe here in the North, crazy cash, no expenses, and lots of travel opportunities. I respect you don't want to come, but when you are talking to people, tell them I feel it was the best decision I ever made—how else can you save a ton of money in one year and also travel the world?

Take care, Gerts, and thanks for the help (or effort anyway).

W

He had a point there. He actually had several points: seventy grand, no taxes (there is some fantastic law or decree that U.S. citizens may work overseas and make up to $86,000 a year, tax-free), close proximity to Turkey, Greece, and the rest of Europe. I wanted to go to The Rest of Europe. Plus, Miss Teen South Carolina had vehemently stressed that our education over here should help The Iraq. Or something like that.

Supercrap.

I was starting to consider it.

I had been unemployed before, and it was not a good color on me. (In my mind unemployed was a pukey shade of rust, which totally washes me out.) The Harry Potter books had saved me from becoming completely suicidal, but those were still some dark times. December, and the end of my copywriting contract, was fast approaching, and there was nothing else on the horizon, except the credit card bills, which were hovering around $39,000.

Yep, that's a lot.

Please don't tell Suze Orman.

My credit card debt was not a result of reckless shoe shopping, which is probably what you're thinking. *You're so mean.* I had started a travel-planning business in 2002, which was *expensive.* Expensive, and ultimately unsuccessful. Reckless shoe shopping would have at least produced something tangible and wearable. I was unemployed, paying $1,000 per month in rent, and spending exorbitant sums on things like brochures and flyers and hospitality booths at trade fairs, not to mention automobile insurance, health insurance, food, and gas, and *look what you've done*, now I'm crumpled on the floor again, sobbing into my Scarlett O'Hara apron.

After a year of hoping and struggling, I had given up on the travel business dream but was so exasperated from living hand to mouth that when I finally got a paying job, I thought, "Cannot. Eat. Cereal. For dinner. Anymore!" I wasn't willing to tighten my belt to pay down the debt. My belt had been tight for a year, and belts, like ankle straps, were just so restrictive. Suze would have been positively livid and would have spent several years screaming "YOU CAN'T AFFORD IT!" at me.

I was still carrying a weighty credit card balance that mocked me, monthly, from my statements. Neener, neener, neener— you owe us money! I had watched Suze patiently, but forcefully, explain how you needed to come up with a debt-elimination plan—you were supposed to sit down and plan how long it was going to take you to get out of debt. With $39,000 of debt, I couldn't bear the thought of even trying to figure that out. It was paralyzing. A lot of debt, and no jobs on the horizon. The deafening cricket chirping was making my ears ring and my brain hurt.

With this new opportunity I was envisioning my crushing debt being swept away, me flying off wherever I wanted to go, and NEW SHOES! And I might even be able to finally start a savings account. That should probably come before the new shoes, but it probably won't.

I wiped my eyes with my Scarlett O'Hara apron, pulled those sorry, few carrots out of the barren earth, shook them at the sky, yelled something about not liking vegetables, then emailed Warren:

I can't start until March.

Chapter Three

Details, Details

I chose March because I wanted to make sure I was mentally prepared. I needed holiday time with my family and mental time for myself, but in the meantime, I began grilling Warren about anything and everything related to The Iraq. Warren explained a bit about the location of the university, which was in a city called Sulaimaniah*, in the middle of the Kurdistan region of Iraq.

Warren said Kurdistan was the "safest" part of Iraq and was far from Baghdad and other violence-filled locations. So I was Googling "Northern Iraq weather," mainly because I wanted to know what kind of clothes I should pack. Along with various weather reports were other kinds of reports:

18 hours ago: Gunmen kill 4 police officers in Northern Iraq.

Now wait just a minute, that doesn't sound safe. The story detailed the growing unrest in the city of Mosul (a city in

---

*You will see "Sulaimaniah" spelled in a variety of different ways. The Kurds can't seem to agree on one particular way to Anglicize the spelling, and neither can I.

the allegedly safe Kurdish region of Northern Iraq) and how Christians were being killed. Another story popped up about the increase in female suicide bombers. I decided to stop reading. Ignorance really is bliss. Or, in my case, ignorance will help you proceed with your plan to get out of debt, start a savings account, and travel to places like Turkey, Greece, and The Rest of Europe.

᭙᭠᭙᭠᭙

Warren had said I would be able to start in March, and then asked me to send him an email with "what I wanted" in my contract. I had no frame of reference for this, so I asked him, "What do you *mean*, what I want?" He continued to speak cryptically and said, "Just email me with what you want—you know, like salary, etc." But he had already explained to me the salary and vacation, hadn't he? I was confused, so I just sent this:

> Okay, ideally I would like:
> A contract for 1 year
> $75,000
> July/August off (plus the standard time off you mentioned: 2 weeks in October, month of December off)
> 2 weeks off after each term (how long are the terms?)
> A pony
> How's that?

I had always wanted a pony.

Warren responded:

> Gerrrrts,
>
> Now, the money—okay, extra time off between sessions—maybe okay depending on starts of upcoming programs, and we already have a pony here for you.
>
> The pony is a big responsibility. As the main means of transportation in and out of the city, you will have to care for "Tyrone" every day and make sure he is happy. I am sure you will do fine.
>
> So, let's wait and see now. Maybe a repeat of 1995/1996? Hope this works!
>
> W

I responded:

> No repeat of 1995/1996. I don't want you skipping out two months after I get there.

(Warren had broken his one-year teaching contract in Korea and left after two months without telling anyone.)

> Will you be able to send an actual contract before you go home for break?
>
> PSYCHED ABOUT THE PONY!

No one names their pony Tyrone though. Honestly.

❧❧❧

Warren called me to discuss the many, many details and answer my many, many questions. He explained that he could "get me a better deal" if I signed a two-year contract. Sharp inhale of breath. Two years in Iraq? Then, he also explained that there was a caveat in the contract that stated something like, "At any time employee or employer may give sixty days written notice, and the university will fly you home." Well, that sounded almost like the two-year contract part was somewhat unnecessary, but it also sounded like precisely the kind of escape hatch with which I would feel quite comfortable.

I then set to work, asking Warren the same types of hard-hitting questions Christiane Amanpour probably asked rebel freedom fighters about their living conditions:

"Do the apartments have TV?"

TV makes me feel more connected to the world. I could press the nice, red power button and see what was happening in Washington, D.C., or New York, or London, or the Land of Make-Believe. (When I say "see what's happening," I mean see what sitcoms or movies are playing.)

Warren confirmed I would have TV. "Yes, you can get a few regular channels for free, including CNN, movie channels, or for $70 a month you can get the full range of stuff you get at home."

I was sold. Go ahead and book my ticket. Okay, not really, but that small bit of information did make me feel better.

Me: How do you get around?

Warren: Convo…well, I don't want to say convoy, but that's kind of what it is.

Hmmm, that sounded covert and exciting. I was imagining tanks.

Me: What do you eat?
Warren: Lots of lamb.

Meh. I could eat lamb, I guess.

Me: Where do you grocery shop?
Warren: We get groceries at the local market, and it's all fresh produce—no preservatives, you have to eat it right away.

This confused me, as it sounded like Warren was unfamiliar with how fresh produce worked. Of course you'd have to eat it right away. Otherwise it would mold or rot, right? I mean, I didn't cook, but I did eat, and I felt like I knew a thing or two about fruit.

Me: What about…um, drugstore stuff?

Warren thought I meant medicine and started discussing various medications, which was not what I needed to know.

Me: Um, no, you know, *drugstore* items…like… sunblock…

Warren: Yeah, I'm not sure about that.

Me: And *other drugstore* items...

Warren: (Confused silence)

Me: Tampons. Can I get tampons there?

I tried to say "tampons" in a Christiane Amanpour-ish British accent to make it sound less pedestrian and embarrassing, and by the time I finally blurted out the sentence it no longer sounded like a question. It was a flat statement.

> **Warren:** *(Laughing)* Oh! Yeah, you'll have to bring tampons—it's a Muslim country, and they don't do tampons at all.

Yikes. I wondered if they had to use those old-timey sanitary napkin belts, like in the Judy Blume books.

> **Me:** What is the year-round weather?
>
> **Warren:** Not humid, but it can get up to fifty Celsius in summer...

Warren was Canadian and forgot that we Americans foolishly cling to an entire system of temperature/climate measurement no one else in the world used. I would just double-check it on an online conversion website.

Crap, 50 Celsius was hot. It was like 122 in regular, American degrees.

Warren: It's hot between March and October. But bring
  about two months' worth of winter clothes.
Me: Is there a dress code?
Warren: Not really.
Me: Really?
Warren: Nah. It's Northern Iraq, Gerts. It's different,
  you'll see.

No dress code? In a predominantly Muslim country? That seemed odd, but at least I wouldn't have to wear the black tablecloth.

Me: How do you get exercise?
Warren: The compound is very safe. There aren't any
  weight machines or anything like that, but you can run
  or walk around.
Me: What is the electrical voltage?

At this point the rest of the Q&A could be considered travel guide fodder, so I won't bore you with the details. But, 220v.

Since Warren had said he was "doing all the hiring" and was the director, I had a moment of unease. I said doubtfully, "You're not going to be my *boss*, are you?" He paused and answered, "No…" Extended pause. "I mean, not really. Kind of—I mean, you'll report to me, but you're going to really be doing your own thing."

Warren knew me well enough to know that I would not want him to be my boss. In Korea we had been coworkers, and I never considered him someone I could take orders from. I had seen him dance.

Chapter Four

Joan of Arc & She-Ra Will Work for Shoes

I sent the following email to friends who I thought might react with confounded shouts of "Whaaaaaaaa?" if I didn't tell them before posting Facebook status updates from Iraq, like "Gretchen Berg is suffering in this fifty-degree (Celsius) weather."

This will seem completely crazy to all of you, and initially did to me as well, but I've given it some good thought over the past couple of weeks and am DOIN it:

In March I'm going to go overseas to teach ESL in Sulaymaniya, Iraq.

Go ahead and digest that. See? Not so bad!

Here is a CNN clip about the school, where my good friend Warren is Director of Something (he does all the hiring for the teachers and administrative staff):

[I included the same link Warren had sent me.]

Warren has sent me a bunch of info on the pay & benefits and both are great. We had a conversation this morning, and

I asked him all the important questions, like "Will I have TV?" and "Can I bring my shoes?"

I am signing a two-year contract, and will be able to pay off all my debt and such. Since Warren is in charge he's being REALLY flexible about the details, and I will have lots of time off to travel (I think all of July/August/December, plus several weeks here and there). This means I'll want people to come meet me in places like Greece, Turkey, Croatia...

Okay, you can keep digesting, but I'll also welcome your comments. ;)

And I did. I welcomed their comments, which were varied, hilarious, a little bit paranoid, and a lot ludicrous.

"Good freaking Lord. Go big or go home! This is beyond big!"

"Why not Korea? That was fun, no? Or Belize...good snorkeling without the bombing and such. Japan...good sushi and they love Americans. Seriously. No Iraq-y for Gretch-y!"

"Stay in the Green Zone."

"I think it is an amazing experience and think YOU are amazing for taking on this challenge. I mean, who does that? That is just incredible!"

"You're probably going to meet some hot Iraqi guy and fall in love."

And finally:

"VERY cool! I want to go!"

No one *really* wanted to go, though.

There were some people who reacted as if I were doing something noble and courageous. They used those words, which had me immediately imagining myself as a modern-day Joan of Arc, wearing a chain-mail tunic with matching headband, brandishing a sword high above my head. I may have had Joan of Arc confused with She-Ra. I thought to myself, *Well, it would be more noble and courageous of me if I weren't being paid enough to eliminate my sizable credit card debt, and if I weren't being given outlandish travel opportunities.* To me, it wasn't so much noble or courageous as necessary and self-serving. No one likes to have Suze Orman screaming at her.

I did not have as easy a time explaining the decision to my family. "No," "Absolutely not," and "You are NOT going to Iraq" were the respective responses of my mom, dad, and sisters when I broached the subject. My dad's was the most vehement, which was surprising—I had expected my mom to put up more of a fuss.

That my dad was so staunchly opposed to the idea was almost more of a selling point than anything else. Gordon Berg was perpetually criticizing my life choices. When I decided to do my student teaching in New Zealand, his response was "*Oh*, no. How much is *that* going to cost me?" When I wanted to teach English in Korea, he questioned the legitimacy of the hiring company. When I wanted to quit my dead-end sales job to explore my talents as a copywriter, he could only point out the instability of the new company and the lack of medical benefits. When I wanted to buy a car while living in Seattle, he waxed poetic about the city's public transportation system and lambasted the soaring costs of auto insurance and car payments.

He loves me and means well, but my dad and I have extremely opposing views on how to live life. My dad subscribes to the "work at the same job for sixty years, never spend your money, never take any risks" life plan. That plan sucks. The longest I have ever worked at any one company was three and a half years, I never met a balance-transfer option I didn't like, and I have indulged in behavior that could be considered risky, including bungee jumping, skydiving, and drinking tap water in Indonesia. And now I was going to Iraq.

I had to remind everyone that I was a grown-up and could make my own decisions and that no one was the boss of me! And since I was technically unemployed, that was a very true statement: no one *was* the boss of me. After explaining the benefits of accepting the position, and relaying everything Warren had told me about the school and the region, my family reluctantly acquiesced. Jessie and my youngest sister, Ellie, agreed to try to figure out how to use Skype. My parents agreed to accept my mail, take care of my fat, furry kitty cat Herb, and store some of my shoes.

※※※

I hated the thought of leaving any of my shoes behind. As impractical as I could be at times, I was pretty sure my sojourn in Iraq would not present occasion to wear multicolored, silk Ferragamo cocktail sandals or brown suede Valentino rosette pumps. Those would have to stay in America, safely boxed up in the storage unit, and I would miss them. I was the single, cat-having, shoe-obsessed girl. Clichés and stereotypes exist for a reason. *Because they happen.* I loved my shoes. I loved them so much that I would often sit around my apartment, in pajamas or sweats, wearing various pairs of fancy high heels, occasionally holding them out to Herb for appraisal.

The obsession extended beyond shoes. I admittedly had a problem/issue/fixation with all kinds of clothing. I blamed this on my mom, who littered our home with issues of *Vogue*, *Bazaar*, and *Glamour* when I was growing up. Don't give girls fashion magazines in their formative years if you expect them to wear sensible shoes.

In high school I used to make lists of every outfit I wore (if Excel spreadsheets had been around in the '80s I would have been in *heaven*), and I would then review those lists to ensure I did not duplicate an outfit more than once in a month. *Why? That's ridiculous. Who would notice? Or care?* Me. I would notice *and* care. Variety is the spice of life. It is also the spice of wardrobe. That's a lesser-known idiom, sure, but just as true.

Different people have different passions for indulgence: video games, Cuban cigars, subwoofers, television sets the size of billboards, first-edition books, Fabergé eggs, art. My passion was fashion. Judge if you must.

Since I was going to The Iraq and *would* be making a substantial salary, I thought it would be okay to buy a new pair of boots. What?! They were on sale! I doubted that I would be able to do any shoe or boot shopping at all once I moved, and part of my mental preparation was making a point to do all the things I would have to give up. I went to Starbucks, I got together with my friends at the wine bars, I went out for sushi, and I bought new boots. They were Diane von Furstenberg tall, red suede boots with a two-and-a-half-inch heel, which almost made them sensible. They were my Wonder Woman boots, and I loved them so much. My mom did not. "Suede boots? Those will be practical in Iraq" was her official position. I packed them anyway.

$e \sim e \sim e$

There were other phone conversations with Warren leading up to my departure, during one of which he excitedly informed me that he had "hooked me up" with a unique situation. The main university was located in Suli (the lazy Western abbreviation for Sulaimani). However, Warren had opened up a sort of satellite campus, three hours north of Suli, in a city called Erbil.

Warren practically gushed about Erbil and went on and on about how all the other teachers would donate a dominant limb to be up there. "Seriously, Gerts, it's way more of an actual city. There's a German restaurant, with *real* German beer—they serve it in steins. There are all kinds of restaurants and places to go out and there are two five-star hotels on either side of the compound where you'll be living."

Me: Really? Five-star hotels?

I tried to picture a giant, shiny high-rise with a doorman welcoming me, but it didn't really work.

Warren: Yeah, one's a Kempinski. You've heard of Kempinski, right? The German hotels? And the other one's…well, I can't remember the other one right now.

Me: So, they might even have a good brunch I could go to!

Warren paused a second and then said, "Sure!"

This new development called for a readjustment of my expectations. I would no longer be at the main university, and I had to ask Warren an entirely new set of questions about what to expect in Erbil. He was, as usual, vague and unconcerned with details, which crippled my ability to create any type of visual to help me picture my upcoming life there. It was just a blurry unknown, *Erbil*. Meh, Iraq was Iraq. If Erbil was moderately fancier, with German restaurants and five-star hotels, all the better.

❧❧❧

While packing I came across an article I had saved from Oprah's *O* magazine (October 2005). I had been single for a long time. Yes, yes, quite possibly due to the combination of control issues, self-diagnosed claustrophobia, the shoe obsession, and the cat. There had been a couple of longish relationships in my early twenties, and then a handful of shortish dalliances into my early thirties, but nothing earth-shattering. I wasn't bitter, I wasn't jaded, but I also wasn't going to settle, and I would save anything in print that validated that stance. While some girls were clipping pages from bridal magazines, I saved Tish Durkin's 2005 article in *O* about "holding out for real love":

> …Thus I was always defending myself against the peculiar charge, leveled more frequently and frankly with each passing year, of insisting upon love as a prerequisite for marriage. And not sensible, better-than-nothing, he-respects-me love, either. I wanted great, big, core-connecting, fate-fulfilling, gotta-have-it earthquake love or a lifetime supply of soup for one…

Preach! I had attended at least two weddings that could have been mistaken for funerals and knew countless couples who I was certain were together more out of convenience than actual, genuine affection. I had friends who endured numerous awkward evenings of blind dates, and even more painful second and third dates, in the hopes something would work out and they would get to wave a big, shiny diamond around and excitedly chirp, "I'm engaged!"

It wasn't necessarily that I didn't want the big, shiny diamond (jewelry is fun) or the excited chirping (enthusiasm is always good), but I was bound and determined to have it be the real deal. As I reread Durkin's article, I sprouted goose bumps. She had met her "great, glove-fitting love" in Iraq.

I made the ridiculously incongruous mental leap to understand this meant all the tall, gorgeous, brilliant, and hilarious soul mates who had been mysteriously evading me must be clustered in some sort of Hot Man/Glove-Fitting Love Warehouse in the middle of Iraq. WMD didn't stand for Weapons of Mass Destruction. It was the Warehouse of Men we've hidden from you in the Desert.

I thought, *Oh, now, wouldn't that just figure. That I would have to go all the way to Iraq to meet The One?* Like everyone else who searches for metaphysical road signs, I thought maybe the article was at least an alert. Your love alert level is now at orange.

So that was one more thing to add to my List of Reasons to Go to The Iraq:

- Eliminate debt
- Travel
- Buy shoes (or at least have enough money to do so)
- Meet soul mate

And while we're at it, I should probably attempt to increase my cultural tolerance of the Middle East, shouldn't I? They say, "Don't knock it 'til you try it." *Who? Who says that?* Probably members of a 1940s barbershop quartet, but it was still a saying that stuck in my head. I had never been to any Middle Eastern country and may have been unfairly judging.

My new List of Reasons to Go to The Iraq:

- Eliminate debt
- Travel
- Buy shoes
- Meet soul mate
- Increase cultural tolerance

While I was busy making lists and imagining a wildly romantic, fateful encounter in Iraq, my mom sent me this email:

Just want you to be as informed as possible about the cultural challenges for women in Iraq even in Kurdistan.

Love, Mom

"Iraqi women—attacked and fighting for a voice

Iraqi activists are trying to counter the rising influence of religious fundamentalists and tribal chieftains who have insisted that women wear the veil, prevented girls from receiving education and sanctioned killings of women accused of besmirching their family's honor…"

This continued in an MSN.com story I decided not to read. I loved the word "besmirching," but "religious fundamentalists" and "tribal chieftains" were not things I wanted to think about. They would only make me second-guess my decision to go. I was normally not a big fan of ignorance; however, I was a big fan of bliss. The road to bliss went straight through The Iraq, and I would be taking it, apparently in some sort of convoy, while wearing my chain-mail tunic and matching headband.

Chapter Five

Hockey Bags, Eh?

The frequency of my phone conversations with Warren increased as March drew closer. I was still feeling apprehensive about such a monumental life change. I loved to travel. It made the world seem a much more manageable place. Being surrounded by a culture—the sounds, smells, and general feel of a place—allowed me to really see how other people lived, and I could weather a mild-to-moderate case of culture shock for brief periods of time (two weeks in China, a month in Nepal).

One whole year had been a struggle for me. I was in Korea from 1995 to 1996, when email was a radically new form of communication. Most people were still writing actual letters, with pen and paper, and using the abacus for financial transactions. Very few people used email regularly. Keeping in touch with friends and family back home was a challenge, which made Korea an isolating experience. There were many Crying Days in Korea. Ergo, I publicly declared I would *never* live overseas again. *Never say never.* There's a reason Justin Bieber is so popular. He's very wise.

I would be living overseas again, which meant schlepping stuff.

I needed to know how much stuff I could or should bring, and whether or not it could be shipped, to avoid unnecessary schlepping.

> **Warren:** Gretch [not "Gerts"—we were making progress], I just came back here from Canada, and I had five hockey bags, each about ninety pounds, and I had no problem.
>
> **Me:** Hockey bags?
>
> **Warren:** Yeah! Get a couple of hockey bags, and just load 'em up! Bring everything!

Canadians. I didn't know what hockey bags looked like, but I was assuming they were sturdy enough to carry big ice skates and hockey sticks, the Stanley Cup, and maybe a goalie. That actually sounded like a good idea. Some of my shoes bore a faint resemblance to ice skates, in both structure and weight.

I ordered two "medium" hockey bags online at Amazon, and two bags were delivered (unlike the ski-bag experience, which I'm still saying was not my fault). When they arrived, I opened them up and discovered they could sleep two people, comfortably. I don't know how everyone else likes to pack, but I want the bags to be completely full, practically bursting. No empty corners or pockets; just keep stuffing them. Did I really need to bring forty-six pairs of socks? Probably not, but they fit into those empty corners so nicely.

I packed everything. Warren had transported five ninety-pound hockey bags with "no problem," and I only had two ninety-pound hockey bags (so I thought) and two suitcases, which were probably around seventy pounds each. By my crafty powers of deductive reasoning, the airline would practically be thanking me for packing so light.

My mom went to the Delta Airlines website to look up their weight/baggage restrictions. She came to me with a worried look on her face and said, "Honey, they say you can only take two bags, at fifty pounds apiece." I rolled my eyes in typical childish exasperated fashion and said, "Mom, Warren said he brought five hockey bags that were ninety pounds apiece. I'll be *fine*."

Mothers. They could be so meddlesome sometimes.

It is possibly my least favorite thing to be standing at the Delta Airlines counter, at 5:00 a.m., listening to the agent say, "You can't take any bags over seventy pounds." I had four bags, two of which were one hundred pounds each (stupid hockey bags with their stuffable corners, and my inability to balance them on the bathroom scale at home); the other two were seventy pounds. I was told there'd be no math at the airport.

If you're saying, "I'll bet you're regretting packing all those socks now, aren't you?"... you're right. If you're a mom, you're probably also saying, "I'll bet you're wishing you had listened to your mom now, aren't you?" Yes, ma'am.

From Portland's PDX to New York's JFK, I paid a staggering $1,530 to get *almost* everything to travel with me. I got the hockey bags down to ninety pounds each, and the baggage agent took pity on me and let them go through. I had my mom take a few things back to the house, like the heavy Lonely Planet guides for Greece and Sweden (both part of The Rest of Europe, and potential vacation destinations) and a few pairs of shoes (dammit!).

I had arranged to have a weekend stopover in New York, to visit friends and my favorite cousin, before taking the final plunge and leaving the United States for the unknown. This did not work in my favor. I ended up having to pay extra-baggage charges twice: once in Portland and once in New York, rather than just the one time, had I flown straight through. Do not listen to airlines that are whining and complaining about being bankrupt. I am supporting many of them solely through my overweight baggage fees.

Dante's Eighth Circle of Hell was Fraud. My Eighth Circle of Hell was the Royal Jordanian Airlines counter at JFK's international terminal. Royal Jordanian apparently only allowed two checked bags, at a maximum of seventy pounds each. That should not have been surprising to me, as it was similar to Delta's policy, but those details were back in Portland, days ago, and it had been 5:00 a.m. then. The Royal Jordanian desk agent informed me that it was impossible for the airline to accommodate my two (agreeably colossal) hockey bags of now-ninety pounds apiece, two suitcases, and one small duffel bag. He explained that I could bring all one hundred eighty pounds of hockey-bag-what-have-you, but it had to be distributed among three bags, not just the two hockey bags. That was not logical. It was not efficient. It was not flier-friendly.

But if I had to use various adjectives to describe Royal Jordanian Airlines, those adjectives would not include logical, efficient, or flier-friendly. Also not flier-friendly was the $850 in additional charges to get my luggage from JFK to Sulaimani, Iraq.

Wasn't there some special loophole for people *moving* overseas? I was *moving* overseas. For two years. I wouldn't bring all this stuff if I were just going for a week in Amsterdam, come on! Nope. No special loophole. I was forced to purchase another duffel bag, which was conveniently sold a mere eighty feet from the Royal Jordanian counter.

> The monster Geryon transports Virgil and Dante across
> a great abyss to the Eighth Circle of Hell, known as
> Malebolge, or "evil pockets"...

> —From a Spark Notes summary of Dante's *Inferno*

I assume these "evil pockets" are where Royal Jordanian keeps the money I pay them for the duffel bags.

I parted with still more money ($40 for my new duffel bag) and was then forced to use a vacant luggage scale to redistribute 180 pounds of stuff between the two hockey bags and the new duffel bag. By this time I was frustrated and hot and stressed and frantically zipping and unzipping bags, while yanking items out of one, then shoving them into another. Pillows, sheets, bottles of mouthwash and shampoo and Woolite, jeans, sweaters, DVDs, books, magazines. I was trying my very best not to pull out anything like the Costco monster-box of Tampax, or any other humiliating accoutrement, as there were roughly forty other Royal Jordanian passengers standing in line, waiting to check in and observing me. I so wished I were just having a nightmare and at any moment my alarm clock would begin its stuttered beeping, but no, there was my alarm clock, next to the monster-box of Tampax. Quiet as could be.

The rest of the procedure was a blur, but I know that I was eventually relieved of my two stupid hockey bags, two suitcases, two duffel bags, and $890. I was then ushered to the security line to enter the ticketed-passenger part of the terminal. After clearing security, and huffily re-dressing myself (shoes, belt, etc.), my mood shifted. I saw a bright light and could almost hear angels singing.

I pledged my undying gratitude to the gracious Korean masseuse at Xpress Spa, who prevented me from crying by guiding me to one of the leaning massage chairs and then prodding and kneading me into a state of "Now I don't care about the $890 anymore" for thirty minutes. It was a half hour of Relaxy Time, in between the nightmare of flight check-in and the dreaded twelve-hour flight in the ever-shrinking economy class on the very unfamiliar, illogical, inefficient, flier-unfriendly Royal Jordanian Airlines. I almost stayed for another thirty minutes, but I would have missed my flight. I signed my credit card slip, and the gracious masseuse handed me an Xpress Spa pen, with a slight bow and a smile. She must have known there would be something to write about on my flight.

Chapter Six

As the Dude Turns

We all have friends and acquaintances who are one-upper downers.

One-upper downer (n.): Someone who tries constantly to outdo your bad personal experiences with their own bad stories, which in their eyes, is always worse.

—Urban Dictionary

You had the flu? I had swine flu. Your kitchen remodel cost two thousand dollars? Mine was forty thousand. You had reconstructive knee surgery? I had every single bone in my body replaced with titanium rods. Sometimes it's fun to one-up down *yourself*. Yes, the flight check-in was bad, but it was nothing compared to the first half hour on the airplane.

I was seated across the aisle from an American guy, probably in his early thirties, with that scruffy, disheveled, "I do Bangkok, frequently" look. I called him "Dude," but just in my head. He wasn't the moderately entertaining kind of Dude who takes twenty minutes to make your coffee because he's slightly stoned and subsequently engrossed in all those wavy lines that appear on the surface of the latte, but rather the more repellent kind of Dude who, while seated on a crowded airplane, pulls out a plastic cup for his chewing tobacco spit.

While most of us were patiently waiting for takeoff, on the ground at JFK, Dude used the wait time to make some phone calls. We waited, and he talked for about an hour.

Dude: Babe, are you coming?

(Pause for Babe responding.)

Dude: No, no, whatever. I'm already in Jordan.

What? No, you're not—you're still at JFK. We're sitting on the tarmac, but whatever, it's not my phone call.

Dude: So, you're not coming.

(Pause for Babe.)

Dude: Whatever, Lisa.

We will stop calling her "Babe" now.

Dude: You didn't bother to call me for the last three days, and now you're not coming.

Dude's tone was becoming more aggressive, and I was becoming much more invested in this conversation. *Lisa was supposed to go with him! But she's not here!*

> **Dude:** Well, have a good time with your BOYFRIEND, you fucking whore—you're such a fucking whore, and have you ever even been out of the COUNTRY or out of California before?

OH MY GOD! "...*you fucking whore...*" I mean, we were on an international aircraft, not a Greyhound bus. (Also, my personal guess was Lisa had possibly been to Mexico. It's just right there, below California.)

> **Dude:** Who is that? Is that that military fuck?

Ooooh, a love triangle. I like it. (Here is where I deduce that Military Fuck takes the phone from Lisa.)

> **Dude:** Oh, YEAH? Oh, YEAH? Is this the Marine? Please tell me this is the Marine—you sorry son of a bitch—what do you call yourself? G-Funk?

Hey! Sometimes my friends call ME G-Funk! Not the right time, though, I know, I know.

Here, Dude lowers his voice, slightly, and hisses "nigger!" into the phone while muttering threatening-sounding expletives.

OH MY EFFING GAWD! PEOPLE DO NOT SAY THAT!

I very badly wanted to move to another seat far, far away from Dude, but I was also dying to hear how this played out.

Lisa or Military Fuck must have disconnected because Dude began dialing again. He muttered something into the phone, then looked at the phone and dialed a bit more.

> **Dude:** Well, have a nice life. Yeah. And oh, I gave that guy I know? That guy who does things? Yeah, I gave him your address, so have fun with *that*. Have a nice life!

This kind of thing really only happens on *CSI*—you know, in those blurry flashback scenes.

Dude was dialing again.

> **Dude:** Lisa, do you even give a flying fuck about me?

Lisa, you needn't have traveled outside of California and Mexico to have the common sense to answer no to this question.

There were a few more instances of Dude looking at his phone, then redialing. I had no idea if anyone was even answering on the other end anymore.

> **Dude:** *(in a soft, inside voice)* Are you gonna marry me?

I must admit this was the best soap opera I had ever witnessed in my life.

> **Dude:** When? September? Gimme a kiss.

Wait a minute. Is this Lisa, or someone new? These soaps are so hard to follow!

Dude: Where do you wanna do it? Lebanon?

This couldn't possibly still be Lisa. She'd never been anywhere other than California and Mexico. She would never agree to a Lebanese wedding. Who was this mystery fiancée?

Dude: Uh-huh. Gimme a kiss.

I began wondering if this soap was on cable or just regular TV. Dude dialed again.

Dude: Whatever, Lisa—you don't tell someone you're going to meet them and then not meet them. God, you're such a fucking whore, and...who's that? Is that Kristy? She's a fucking whore too. What?

Dude dialed again.

Dude: So you're going to marry me, right? Gimme a kiss.

(I am not making any of this up. I was so floored by Dude's initial phone manner that I whipped out my tiny notebook and began documenting this verbatim with my new Xpress Spa pen. Some of the writing got pretty squiggly because I was writing so fast; for example, it took me several minutes to work out

"Lebanon" as I was reading my notes. I was squinting and think-ing: *That doesn't say "Leinenkugel" does it? I don't think you can get married in Leinenkugel*.)

We were finally given the announcement that requested we turn off all electronic equipment and cell phones. It was right about this time, while Dude was arguing with the flight attendant about his right to a spit cup during takeoff, when I remembered Warren saying something about a fellow teacher who would be on the Royal Jordanian flight with me. I blanched. *Please, please, PLEASE don't let Dude be That Guy. PLEASE! That would just be unusually cruel. Oh, please.* All the hard work that masseuse had done on my clenched-up muscles was now wasted. I was all clenchy again.

I glanced over in Dude's general direction. Another guy, sitting two empty seats away from Dude, had struck up a conversation with him about where they were going. I couldn't hear exactly what they were saying, but I did happen to notice that Other Guy was black. I was dying to know if Other Guy had overheard Dude's use of the N-bomb during his absurd cell phone tirade.

This soap is fantastic!

I opened a magazine in an effort to appear to be minding my own business while trying to hear if Iraq was mentioned. It was! And then Dude started to talk about being "picked up at the airport in the helicopter," and I thought, *Hmmm, Warren didn't mention a helicopter*. Then Dude said, "My name is Brandon," and my brain started racing. *Brandon. Brandon? Was that the guy's name? Brandon? DAMMIT! I can't remember what Warren said! Oh God, oh God, oh God. This cannot be one of my coworkers. Please let the*

coworker guy's name be Matt, or Dave, or Something Else That Is Not
Brandon. I cannot fathom having to be within spitting distance (sorry,
no pun) of this person on a regular basis. Please please please, NO!

If I had to land in Iraq, and then be introduced to Dude/
Brandon as a coworker, I would have most likely lost my shit. My
shit was partially lost already, as I had undoubtedly unpacked and
repacked it into several different bags.

‿❧‿

Twelve hours later, I had more or less forgotten about Dude
when we landed at the Amman, Jordan, airport. I was to have a
brief overnight at the airport hotel. When I spoke with a man at
the arrivals counter to arrange transporting my luggage on the
flight from Amman to Sulaimania, I was informed that I would
have to pay another overweight baggage fee. The rotten liars at
JFK had told me that the $850 (plus $40 for the duffel) would
cover the fees all the way to Iraq. The man at the Amman airport apologized and said, no, I would have to pay another $500.
Unbelievable. I had now spent a total of $2,920 on overweight
luggage. Go ahead and add it to the $39,000, but Suze is going to
be pissed.

The Amman airport was thankfully small, so it was easy to
locate the hotel shuttle. I boarded the little bus, just shaking my
head. While my brain was spinning with the gargantuan sums
that were crushing my poor, abused credit card, I pulled my
phone out of my purse, just to see if I had service in Amman,
Jordan. Can you hear me now? Shockingly, yes! My little phone

powered to life and then beeped to alert me that I had a new voice mail! Oh, that would be nice, hearing a familiar, happy, friendly voice from home.

As the shuttle bumped along, I heard, "Hey, Gretch, it's Jessie," and then her voice cracked and the rest of the message was convulsive sobbing from my sister, who was crying because she hadn't had a chance to talk to me before I left New York and thought I was going to die in The Iraq and was absolutely not helping me adjust to being in a strange new place after going through travel trauma and spending thousands of dollars I did not have. This was the thanks I got for giving her a free ski bag.

The hotel was called the Golden Tulip. That sounds pretty, doesn't it? Yeah, it wasn't. There was a metal detector just behind the front doors to the lobby, which did not instill me with a sense of warmth or, ironically, security. Welcome to the Middle East. I did not see one other woman between the time I checked in and the next morning when I checked out. The hotel employees were all men, and the other hotel guests were all men. My room had a very grotty feel to it, and I was pretty sure the stains on the curtains and carpet were blood. *What am I doing here?*

Bloodstains and slight unease aside, my night was uneventful. After using the hotel's business center to send an email to Warren that screamed, "I AM HEMORRHAGING MONEY," I was actually able to sleep for a few hours before reboarding the shuttle to the airport.

My mood improved perceptibly upon discovering that the Amman airport had both a Starbucks *and* a Cinnabon. I loved Amman! Welcome to the Middle East! It was 6:00 a.m., and I was insanely hopped up on sugar and having a jolly, hyper time waiting for the flight to Suli. It was amazing what familiarity and carbs could do to put me at ease.

Upon boarding the plane, I took my seat next to a young, apprehensive-looking, sandy-blond-haired American guy wearing a newsboy cap. He introduced himself and said that he was going to Sulaimani, to teach English at the university. His name was Steve.

Steve! That was the guy! Oh, thank God, it wasn't Brandon! I was so relieved that Steve was not Brandon and still very hyper from the Cinnabon and Starbucks. I told Steve the whole Dude story, which he found amusing. Steve was the exact opposite of Brandon-the-Dude. He was like a little lost puppy you wanted to just pat on the head. He wasn't spitting chewing tobacco or ranting at alleged whores or hissing the N-word under his breath, and that made the short flight to Suli quite pleasant. We landed, and I looked over Steve's shoulder out onto the barren tarmac. We were in The Iraq.

❧ ASTOUNDING ❧
ACCOMPLISHMENTS OF PART 1

Running total spent on overweight luggage: $2,920 (okay, maybe "accomplishments" is the wrong word)

Debt eliminated: $0 (and now it's closer to $42,000, thanks to the overweight luggage)

Countries traveled to: ½ (I really don't count airport/airport hotel as a country visit, but the Jordan stamp will still be in my passport)

Pairs of shoes purchased: 0 (I'm not counting the red suede boots, and you can't make me)

Soul mates met: 0 (Steve was not Brandon, and he was also not The One)

Cultural tolerance level (on a scale of 1 to 10): 6 (I feel it is fair to start at a midpoint of 5, and Jordan gets an extra point for Starbucks and Cinnabon. That is not particularly cultural, I know, but it did make me more tolerant.)

Part 2

··

Everything!
Exciting & New!

··

Chapter Seven

The Iraq—Welcome to Smell

The Sulaimani airport was small and stark but still managed to be a complete mess of people, fierce body odor, and many heavy bags. Granted, most of those heavy bags were mine. Steve Who Was Not Brandon graciously helped me push them over to the customs area. The Iraqi customs agent looked wide-eyed from my voluminous luggage to me, pointed at the luggage, and said in halting English, "What is here?" Mentally recalling all the packing, dragging, repacking, and near sobbing, I just gave him a wan smile and said, "Everything." He didn't ask to look inside.

Warren met us just outside of customs, with his easy manner, big grin, and ridiculous Terminator sunglasses, and I waffled back and forth between wanting to hug a familiar friend and wanting to slap the jackass who recommended hockey bags. I went with the hug. He was the only person I knew in Iraq. Plus, I'm not really a slapper.

Warren loaded Steve, me, and the luggage into two non-tank, non-Hummer, very ordinary Nissan Pathfinder SUVs. This was anticlimactic. It was like the supermarket tabloids: Iraqis—they're just like us! They drive Nissans! Not tanks. At this point though, the more familiar, the better. The smell was familiar—rank body odor—courtesy of Warren's driver Rizgar.

"Yeah, breathe it in, Gerts!" Warren crowed. "They all smell like this."

I balked and hissed, "He can hear you!"

Warren responded with a dismissive wave of his hand, "He can't understand a word I'm saying."

Warren said he wanted to take us to the local grocery store, for a little orientation, before going to the university. My first Iraqi supermarket! It was called Zara. Exciting and exotic: *Zara*! This was not the international women's retail store Zara, where nothing ever fits me and they have fat mirrors, and I always leave feeling bloated and unfashionable. Stupid Zara. This was a better Zara, I was sure, and I was crossing my fingers that there would be Diet Coke and no fat mirrors.

We walked into the exotic Iraqi Zara through the double glass doors and I thought, "Well, hmmm." The supermarket was totally normal and looked exactly like any small, local grocery store you might find in the United States. It was clean, brightly lit, and organized into a maze of aisles. It was the Iraqi Piggly Wiggly. (They don't allow pigs in Iraq, though, so maybe the Goatly Woatly? Sheeply Weeply? They eat a lot of lamb here, so the Lambly Wambly? Never mind. Jet lag makes me loopy.) It had food, toiletries, and a functioning escalator that led upstairs, where you could buy clothing, toys, and linens, like towels and sheets. Why had I needed to "bring everything"? They had plenty of everything here. And what's more, the towels I brought from home said "Made in Turkey" on the tag. Guess which country borders Iraq to the north? Turkey. Sure enough, I checked one of the tags on a towel at not-so-exotic Zara and it had been made in Turkey.

> **Me:** Warren, I totally could have just bought stuff here! Why did you tell me to "bring everything"? Look, they even have Crest toothpaste!
>
> **Warren:** Yeah, but it's not real. It's the fake stuff. That stuff probably has cyanide in it.
>
> **Me:** What?
>
> **Warren:** It's not the real stuff. Trust me, Gerts.

I had to take Warren's word for everything, as he had been living in Iraq for close to two years, and I had been there less than two hours. But the Crest looked exactly like it did at home, except for the Arabic writing on the package. Warren didn't seem at all concerned about the authenticity of the Pringles and bought two cans for himself. Steve and I didn't buy anything, as Zara did not have Diet Coke, and Warren seemed to be in a hurry and sort of rushed us around the store. He said he would send the driver back with us later to get the groceries we needed. I suspected the Zara "orientation" was less of an orientation and more of an errand to get Pringles for Warren.

From Zara we drove to the university. The passing scenery was all very beige and very muddy. Sulaimani sits in the mountains of Kurdistan and enjoys a healthy amount of rainfall, particularly in March. We drove down narrow, unpaved roads that were flanked by numerous dilapidated storefronts that seem to be ubiquitous in underdeveloped countries. Coca-Cola? Sprite? Orange Fanta? Hubcaps? Yes. But no Diet Coke. Swarthy, mustached men stood on the sidewalks underneath tangles of overhead telephone wire, smoking cigarettes and gesturing to other swarthy, mustached men. We passed two- and three-story homes that were mostly obscured by high concrete walls, but every so often you could catch a glimpse of heavy burgundy velour curtains or gold-leaf adornments covering balcony doors. I would describe the interior décor as faux-luxe, or understated Trump.

The university building was a modern, angular, three-story structure with large greenish windows and was set back behind the ever-present cement wall. When we approached the car entrance, we saw an armed guard, bedecked in camouflage and a jaunty beret, who stopped the car to be checked.

> **Me:** What's he checking for? Drugs?
> **Warren:** Bombs.

Warren's "safest part of Iraq" speech was still ringing in my ears while the guard ran a long stick with a large mirror attached to the end underneath the vehicle before stepping back and removing the row of guard spikes so the SUV's tires wouldn't be punctured.

In front of the building lay a large gravel parking lot that was mostly occupied by eight trailer-sized "cabins," where the classes were held. The new university building was under construction, at a separate site five miles away, and this was the temporary facility, Warren explained.

"This is Iraq," I kept saying to myself. "I'm in Iraq."

We walked up the front steps and into the lobby of the main building, where Iraqi students, both male and female, were milling around and chatting with one another. No one was wearing a black tablecloth. All were dressed in Western clothing, with some of the girls wearing colorful headscarves. I was too jet-lagged and bewildered to notice much more than what people were wearing. *I'm in Iraq. This is weird.*

Steve and I had to meet with the university's human resources director, Rana, a very pretty Kurdish woman around my age who had spent roughly ten years living in the United States and was fluent in both Kurdish and English (I quickly learned that the Kurds were the main ethnic group, and Kurdish, not Arabic, was the local language). She welcomed us to sit in the chairs in front of her desk and said to me, "Oh, you're the one who will be in Erbil, right?" I nodded, still not really knowing what that would entail. Rana's office was like the rest of the building: it was fairly stark with high ceilings and heavy dark furniture. After sitting down, Rana handed us copies of our contracts, and we reviewed the details. My pony was not discussed, nor could I find mention of it anywhere in the paperwork.

Rana had a small pamphlet titled "Cultural Awareness" for us to review and keep for reference. Number one on the pamphlet was "Dress Code."

Dammit, Warren.

1. Female: Please do not wear:
    - Shorts
    - Low-cut tops
    - Short tops

- Short skirts and dresses
- Tank tops

I exclaimed, "Yikes, I'm wearing a tank top right now!" (Although it was under a cardigan sweater.)

"Just don't take your sweater off," Rana replied.

Okay, crisis averted. I noticed that Rana's ensemble followed the code, technically. Nothing was short or low-cut, but everything seemed awfully snug. I then asked, "Does Warren know about this pamphlet?" and she smiled tightly and said, "Yes, we give these to everyone who is employed here."

For men, it just said, "Male: No Shorts." God, that was so typical. I recalled Warren telling me he wore shorts here, you know, because it gets up to 50 degrees Celsius—122 normal, American degrees.

The "Cultural Awareness" pamphlet was more than just dress code recommendations, though. Much, much more.

2. Jokes and Comments
   - Avoid making in-appropriate jokes and comments.

   Want to make joke about how no one had edited pamphlet for grammatical errors.

3. Personal behavior
   - No hugging, touching, or kissing in public.

   Should have slapped Warren at airport. Hug was mistake.

   - Avoid shaking hands with Hijab (veiled) girls.

   Pretend they're all sick and germy.

   - Avoid patting anyone on the back.

   But how to show congratulations or appreciation in kickball tournament?

4. Religion

- Religion is a very delicate subject.

Am already culturally aware of this. Do not need this pamphlet.

- Avoid making fun of Islam under any circumstances.

Imagine Islam as messy kid with long stream of toilet paper stuck to his shoe.

- It's probably best not to discuss your religion and beliefs unless asked by curious locals.

Am enjoying visual of "curious locals"—gnarled, elderly people in cloaks, peering at and poking me.

- If you find yourself involved in a conversation on religion, be aware that it is a delicate subject.

Am envisioning curious locals circling and attempting to trap me in conversation on religion.

- Avoid visiting any Mosque unless it has been converted to a museum or if you have been invited by another practicing Muslim. (It is a restricted area for Muslims.)

Curious locals have escalated religious conversation and have surrounded me and are leading me to a Mosque.

- Please cover your hair when going to a Mosque.

Curious locals refusing to let me shop for a headscarf on way to Mosque—as if they want me to fail test!

I'm in Iraq. This is weird.

5. Pets

- Keeping pets is not that common here.

Missing my little, fat Herb.

- Do not touch homeless animals on the streets in order to avoid diseases as the animals are not immunized.

Sad at idea of homeless street animals. Now want to hug them.

- If you have a pet, please do not take it with you to houses you visit, the shopping malls, or government department.

Have sudden urge to buy dog-in-small-purse and bring it everywhere with me.

6. Security
- Do not ride in strangers' cars.

Not even if they offer candy?

7. Dating
- Please be conservative while dating a local.

Am wearing red 1990s Nancy Reagan Adolfo power suit, sporting tight smile, and ranting about family values.

- In public do not show overly physical affection to your spouse or girl/boyfriend.

In red Nancy Reagan suit, am climbing on top of imaginary Iraqi boyfriend on public park bench.

- If you ask a local person for a date, or establish a relationship with a local person, be mindful of the cultural differences and be guided by your partner. Being conservative is a good general attitude to practice.

Need more Adolfo suits.

8. Relationships
- Often you may see same-sex people holding hands, kissing, or hugging each other in public. This is a normal way for Iraqis to express friendship and affection and should not be interpreted as homosexuality or stigmatized in any other way.

Picturing Iraqi men climbing on top of each other on public park bench.

9. Homosexuality
   - It is against the Islam religion. As it is a forbidden practice, please avoid talking about that subject with locals.

Must ignore men on park bench.

10. Tips
   - Tipping is not common or required here. It's at your discretion in hotels, restaurants, airports, etc.

Common sense. Taking an order at Starbucks, then calling order over to coworker who pours tea and milk into cup is not going above and beyond call of duty. Put that tip jar away.

11. Events
   - If you want a local to attend a dinner, party, or other gathering at your house or in a restaurant, try not to add alcohol to the event.

Am not being encouraged to mingle with locals.

   - Due to cultural differences, local women won't feel comfortable being invited to men's houses or apartments, but that does not mean they won't accept invitations for restaurants or public places.

Just plain smart. See original programming on Lifetime network, starring Tori Spelling or Meredith Baxter-Birney, for emphasis.

   - Do not show physical affection (kissing, hugging, etc.) when you visit a local and vice versa.

High fives?

12. General
  * Do not take alcohol as a gift.

Sad face.

  * Pork is taboo in Islam; do not expect to find pork on menus or in private homes.

No bacon?

  * Expect to receive presents or gifts from locals during Eid, Nawroz, Christmas, birthdays, and New Year. Giving gifts in appreciation and friendship is also always appropriate.

Must communicate that I really don't mind receiving alcohol as gift. I had some difficulty with the "rules" in this pamphlet but blamed my jet lag for my completely inappropriate imagined responses. I was a sort-of guest in this country and would have to keep my mouth shut.

Bacon, I miss you already.

⁊⁊⁊⁊

Later, sitting in Warren's office, I turned to him and said, "Listen, you have got to stop calling me 'Gerts.'"

He looked shocked. "Why?"

I reminded him that I was the one who had told him about the nickname in the first place and that I hated it. Not only did it put me into a retro, junior high tailspin, but Gerts rhymed with "squirts." No one gets a positive visual from "squirts." He promised to stop saying it but then seemed desperate to find a replacement nickname. "What can I call you?!" he practically wailed.

I didn't know why a nickname was necessary. My name was only two syllables; it wasn't as if it took *that* much energy to say it. What was his hang-up with nicknames? Nicknames should never be forced. Look at Sean Puffy P. Diddy Diddy Combs. It has to come naturally. However, Warren seemed bound and determined to call me something other than Gretchen.

I began suggesting alternatives: Gretch (the obvious choice, just stop short of saying my entire name and save yourself a whole syllable), Gretta (created by college roommates, although still with two syllables), Gretel (really only used by my friend Joli, and that hungry witch who lives in the woods), G-Funk (just like I was saying on the airplane!), G (for rappers), Princess Jasmine, or Princess Buttercup, or Princess... Anything that started with "Princess" was usually okay and might have reminded him that I was still due one pony. None of these seemed to satisfy him.

His nickname obsession was puzzling. When he was whisking Steve and me around the school that day, rushing through introductions, he would say, "This is Gretchen, who's going up to Erbil, and this is Steve, Joe's brother." Joe had been working at the university for a year, and everyone knew him well. One Kurdish staff member said, "Ahhh, Joe's brother! Same, same!" So Steve's nickname became Same-Same. There was an instructor at the school named Ryan Bubalo, who was apparently Warren's nemesis for reasons that were never entirely clear to me. Warren called him "The Boob" behind his back. Rizgar, who had picked us up at the airport, was Warren's designated Kurdish driver, and Warren had nicknamed him Turd Ferguson, from *Saturday Night Live*'s *Jeopardy!* sketch:

> **Will Ferrell as Alex Trebek:** "Apparently Burt Reynolds
> has changed his name to Turd Ferguson."
> **Norm MacDonald as Burt Reynolds:** "Yeah, Turd
> Ferguson; it's a funny name."

My least favorite nickname was given to poor Jen, a great Canadian girl who was the kind of person who put you immediately at ease. She was genuinely warm and friendly, with a quick smile. Warren inexplicably called her Skank. "Hey, Skank! You'd better snatch up some guy soon; you're gettin' to be Cougar-age! Heh heh heh." Jen was twenty-nine and about as far from Skank as you could get.

Given The Boob, Turd, and Skank as alternatives, I guess I should have been grateful for Gerts.

ᕒᕲᕒᕲᕒ

After the HR orientation, and what seemed like hours of waiting in Warren's office for him to finish up whatever he was doing, he said he wouldn't have time to escort me back to Zara, and I should just have one of the drivers take me and then drop me off at the hotel, which would be my temporary home in Suli for the next three days. Wow, he was really just throwing me into the swing of things. By that time my eyes were at half-mast from exhaustion, and my stomach was gurgling in protest of the emptiness.

I swung my bag over my shoulder and clomped down the two flights of stairs to the main level, passing several female students on the stairs. (Skinny jeans and heels were "in" here? Tablecloths, you're out.) I reached the main level, where the drivers' room was, and knocked on the door. A short, Kurdish man with beady eyes blinking behind wire-rimmed glasses answered, and I looked past him to where three other Kurdish men sat, drinking tea and talking. The stench of unwashed armpit was unbearable. I tried not to breathe through my nose and said, "Um, I need someone to take me to Zara and then to the Bayan Hotel."

The man who had answered the door looked me up and down and then said, "Yes, I am Sabah. I manage drivers. Hello. Ahhh, there are no drivers now. You must wait until four o'clock."

I looked at the three men drinking tea, then at my watch which said it was 2:30, and I gasped. I had to wait there for another hour and a half? Weren't those guys drivers? Tired and hungry! I halfheartedly thanked Sabah and clomped back up the stairs to Warren's office.

I relayed the Sabah conversation to him, and he smacked his hand down on the desk and threw his head back with an exaggerated eye roll. "Fucking Sabah. Gerts—sorry, Gretch—go back down there and tell him I said someone needs to take you *now*. They're lazy, and if you don't yell at them, they won't do anything."

Oh, for crying out loud. I really didn't have the energy for this. But I went back, clomping down the two flights of stairs I had just clomped up again and back to the drivers' room. I knocked on the door again, and when Beady-Eyes opened the door, I just took a deep breath and said, "Warren says someone needs to take me right now" and waited for a reaction.

Sabah made a "pfft" sound with his teeth, then yammered something unintelligible at one of the tea drinkers, who slowly stood up, finished draining his cup, and slowly made his way over to the door where he motioned for me to follow him.

Welcome to Iraq, woman.

The driver waited in the car while I went into Zara, where I wandered up and down each aisle of the store, looking for edible items that did not require cooking. I didn't cook. I just needed a few things to tide me over for the next two days until I was taken up to Erbil. I settled on some kiwi, a container of yogurt, a small jar of honey, and a can of dolmas. I knew dolmas! I used to get them at Trader Joe's! These were all familiar things: nothing that would involve me standing over a boiling pot of water, staring at a box with instructions written entirely in Arabic, and ultimately starving.*

Zara had four checkout counters, which were just like any other grocery store checkout counters. The cashier passed my items over the scanner, just like any other grocery store scanner. The bagger prepared to bag my groceries, just like any other bagger, except that I had brought one of my super eco-friendly cloth shopping bags with me from home (I brought everything), which I handed to him. I paid the cashier with my new beige and blue bills of Iraqi dinar and then turned back to the bagger, only to find that he had put my groceries into a plastic bag and my cloth shopping bag into another plastic bag. I had to say, "No, no," and took the cloth bag out of the plastic bag, then placed my groceries inside the cloth bag while the cashier and bagger looked at me curiously. This was Zara's inconvenient truth. I guess you're

---

*This country confused me. While Kurdish was the main language, the grocery items were brought in from Turkey or the surrounding Middle Eastern countries, so the labels were either in Turkish or Arabic, not Kurdish.

less concerned about the environment when your country is in a constant state of turmoil.

❦❧

My temporary accommodation in Suli was a room in the Bayan Hotel. The lobby was a small room with a thick Persian rug, a cheap-looking pleather couch, and a low desk where the manager sat watching a small television set. Despite Warren telling me that the manager was "a great guy" and he'd get me anything I needed, I still felt apprehensive about being there. Were people noticing that I was a single female staying at a hotel alone? Was I just being completely paranoid? It was *Iraq*. I couldn't avoid paranoia on my first night there. Of course, there was also the problem that my incessant television watching contributed to a completely overactive imagination, and I was envisioning insurgents (or cave trolls, or vampires, or Dementors) lurking around every corner.

The entrance to the lobby of the hotel was in the front, but to access the hotel rooms you had to walk around to the side of the building. Two diminutive, pungent Bangladeshi boys dragged my luggage from the lobby up to the third floor, where my room was located. *Was Bangladesh an even worse place to live than Iraq?* I wondered. *Why would they be here?* These were the questions that were popping into my head as I followed my hockey bags up the stairs. Also popping into my head was the woefully ungracious "Oh my God, I will never get used to the smell of body odor." I just have a really sharp sense of smell.

The room was a suite, with a small kitchen, bedroom, bathroom, and living room with the requisite heavy dark furniture. The suite was dark, even after I flipped on every possible light switch I could find. I loathed darkness. This stemmed from a childhood where my dad was obsessed with saving electricity. So much so that he would turn off any lights in any rooms in the house, even if those rooms were occupied by offspring who might have been reading, watching too much TV, or just enjoying the happy brightness. My overwhelming need for bright light may also be related to my self-diagnosed claustrophobia, in my entirely nonmedical opinion.

I couldn't find a can opener for the dolmas, so I enjoyed a very skimpy dinner of kiwi, yogurt, and honey and felt decidedly healthy and self-sufficient after all the airplane food, snacks, and Cinnabon I had consumed in the past twenty-four hours.

In the dimly lit bedroom, I unpacked a few of my clothes and toiletries, surveying all the stuff I had dragged over several continents. So much stuff. What if I needed to get out of here in a hurry? What if this was a huge mistake?

I brushed my teeth (with the cyanide-free Crest I brought from home) and checked that the front door was locked. I then closed myself into my bedroom, locked that door, and checked to make sure the windows were securely locked. I felt a sudden kinship with OCD sufferers and checked the locks again.

I collapsed on the bed and groggily reviewed my initial observations of Kurdistan, Northern Iraq.

- Kurdish was the main language, not Arabic.
- Diet Coke/Diet Pepsi was nowhere to be found, and I had a severe caffeine headache.

- Wine and beer were to be found—there were liquor stores.
- The national bird was a plastic bag.
- It was mountainous. Not desert-ous.
- The electricity went out several times a day, but only for about ten seconds at a time.
- Many of the men bore a striking resemblance to Borat.
- Many of the men wore body odor like a badge.
- There was a dress code. The dress code I saw for women? Revealing clothes: not okay. Extremely tight clothes: perfectly acceptable. Lots of skinny jeans and high heels. Some covered their heads with a scarf, some didn't.
- Everything was in a state of disrepair.
- The dim lighting made everything seem kind of dirty and sad.

I finally gave up willing the light bulbs to grow brighter, turned them off, and went to sleep, hoping the locked doors and windows were secure. Why hadn't my friends and family protested more? They let me come here! Scarlett left Tara for new opportunities in Atlanta. Why couldn't Iraq be more like Atlanta? I hope the body odor smell doesn't stick to my stuff...

Chapter Eight

I'm an Immigrant

I was awakened around 4:00 a.m. by the sound of faraway wailing. As soon as I figured out where I was and had a few more pangs of "What have I done?", I listened to what I assumed was the Call to Prayer. I had heard about this: loudspeakers were placed all over the city and broadcast a man wailing a somber, eerie-sounding tune that was the reminder it was time to pray. I prayed that I would be able to fall back asleep.

I decided I needed some added strength when getting dressed later that morning. After wrapping myself in a chunky wool cardigan sweater and scarf and pulling on a pair of brown Capri-length pants, I drew my red suede Diane von Furstenburg boots out of the hockey bag and said, "Okay, boots, Wonder Woman me." They cheered me a little and reminded me of home, online shopping, and my mom. She said they wouldn't be practical here, but HA! It was cold! It was like eight degrees. Celsius, but still. That's only forty-six American degrees.

With all the hectic craziness of the previous day, I had forgotten about how rainy and muddy it was. There was a sidewalk from the hotel door to where we loaded into the SUV, so I didn't notice the mud until we arrived at immigration and I stepped out of the car in my pretty Wonder Woman boots. I cursed my poor short-term memory. Wonder Woman needed to go get her residency card so she could be a legitimate resident of The Iraq, and now she also needed to have her boots professionally cleaned. The only thing that helped me feel less ridiculous was that Carey, the school's new director of finance, who just arrived from Washington, D.C., hadn't anticipated the mud either, and her sleek ivory trousers now had an interesting splatter pattern covering the back side. Steve, who probably put the least amount of thought into his outfit, appropriately wore brown shoes and jeans.

Carey, Steve, and I were taken to immigration by a university-employed bodyguard who looked exactly like a Middle Eastern Buddy Hackett. He was not tall, muscular, or imposing, but he did carry a gun. The immigration "complex" was behind a barricade and down a muddy road, where one of our stops was a couple of wooden tables set under the same kind of plastic coverings we used for our sandbox when I was little. It was like registering for Coachella or Glastonbury, except they shuffled our paperwork around, then sent us on our way, without lanyards or drink tickets.

The paperwork was just the first step. We were also required to do the following:

- Participate in a sassy photo shoot for our residency card photos
- Have blood drawn (to check for HIV, according to Warren)

- Be fingerprinted four different times—or, rather, thumbprinted

I was thumbprinted four times with my left thumb only. I noted that smart criminals could literally get away with murder here, if they were just careful not to use their left thumb.

There was one building where we spent most of the morning, and the scene was surreal. There was a small waiting room lined on all sides with plastic chairs, which were filled with swarthy men who just sat and openly stared at us (we were later told they were mostly Turkish Kurds).*

From my chair I could see into one of the adjacent rooms, where there was a thirty-two-inch television set on the floor, tuned to a channel showing three slight Asian women in colorful aerobics gear doing pelvic raises. This made me snicker. Carey had a better vantage point from which to view the rest of the room. I whispered, "Are there men in there watching the TV?" She craned her neck a bit then resettled in her seat and said, "Yep. Two of them." We were then called into that very room to have our blood drawn.

Our doctor (nurse? physician's assistant? who could say?) was a very casual-looking man, just hanging out in a sweater and khakis. He was obviously an enthusiastic aerobics fan, who I hoped had some sort of medical background. At least the needles came out of brand-new wrappers for each of us. That was reassuring.

After the thumbprinting, and the blood drawing, and the

---

*The Turkish government made it illegal to speak Kurdish in Turkey. The region that borders Turkey and Iraq was said to be quite dangerous and very unfriendly for the Kurds, so it was no wonder they were trying to immigrate to Iraq.

ubiquitous shuffling of papers, and more waiting, we were finished and could go to lunch.

We ate at the Warren-approved Assos Restaurant. He liked it because it was a Lebanese restaurant and was "safe," which I assumed meant they did not use cyanide as a cooking ingredient. Warren also had yet to say anything complimentary about the Kurds. Assos was decorated in faux-luxe/understated-Trump with dark wood and gold leaf everywhere. We ordered hummus, baba ghanoush, fatoush (cucumber, tomato, onion, and crouton salad), and chicken kebab. Carey explained that she had a really weak stomach and had already been having some intestinal difficulties. She only ate the chicken. I was starving after my paltry meals of kiwi, yogurt, and honey (and am conversely blessed with a constitution like an InSinkErator garbage disposal), and I ate everything.

It was fantastic. The chicken kebabs were tender and juicy, the hummus was tangy and smooth, and the bread was fresh and piping hot. I loved Middle Eastern food. In Seattle there was a restaurant called Mediterranean Kitchen, and my friends and I used to go for shawarma and hummus and all that stuff. This came as somewhat of a surprise to Warren, who had really begun to relish his new role of Knowledgeable High Priest of The Iraq. He informed me that I would undoubtedly get sick here, everyone gets sick here, and then grandly attempted to explain baba ghanoush to me.

Warren: Ger...sorry, *Gretch*, baba ghanoush is...
Me: I know, it's basically pureed eggplant.

Warren: You've had baba ghanoush before?

Me: Yes.

He seemed disappointed. And I was *not* going to get sick.

e~e~e

The evening before I was to go up to Erbil, Warren hosted an informal dinner, again at Assos. I had a hard time believing this was the only acceptable restaurant in a city of close to a million people. This was now my third visit to Assos. More hummus? More baba ghanoush? More chicken kebab? Fine. It really was good, and my kiwi-yogurt-honey combination had lost its allure after three days.

The dinner was just for Warren's department, which was known as CED (the Continuing Education Division). It was sort of a "welcome to the new semester" situation. There were ten of us at the table, and as I looked around at everyone, who seemed to be slightly in awe of Warren, I thought, "Oh, that piece of crap. He really *is* my boss." So much for my autonomous experience here. I *will* have to report to him.

There was really no getting out of this now. I was thousands of miles away from home and thousands of dollars in debt—even more now, thanks to the stupid hockey bags.

Warren pushed back his chair, stood up, puffed up his chest, and looked around the table. He seemed nervous when he began his speech, which started out with him saying this was a casual dinner, and then took a slightly awkward turn as Warren made a crass, toilet-related joke at the expense of one of the teachers at the table, and everyone gave polite, awkward laughs (or coughs). Erf, I was uncomfortable.

I felt like I didn't know this Warren very well, and I really wasn't sure if I liked him. Was I just PMS-ing? Was I still jet-lagged? Was there something wrong with the hummus? He was much more aggressive than I had remembered. Earlier, I had seen him get into an argument with Turd Ferguson about the true meaning of a specific Kurdish word. I was thinking since Turd was Kurdish, he was probably right, and watched in mild horror as Warren completely lost his temper. His face burst into a brick-red balloon as his eyes bulged out of their sockets and a temple vein popped out on his forehead. I finally yelled, "Stop arguing with him! Your head is going to explode!"

He seemed like he was trying too hard to assert himself in the boss role, or maybe he felt like he had to put on some sort of show for me. I had never seen him in a position of authority. In Korea we had been coworkers, and he had been really easygoing and fun. This New Warren was an only slightly more charming combination of Rush Limbaugh and the Great Santini.

Again, the nagging question surfaced. *Was this a mistake?* Ohhhhhhhh, *laws*, I hate mistakes. Especially those of the uprooted-your-entire-life-and-are-now-stuck-in-scary-Middle-Eastern-country variety. Warren was the one and only person I knew here, and I felt like he was a complete stranger.

What happened to him? Maybe my expectations were unreasonable. This was, after all, someone who idolized Vin Diesel. God, maybe I was just old. I felt a tiny wave of relief that I would be leaving Suli to move up to Erbil. I wouldn't have to be around New Warren, with his obnoxious nicknames and his Terminator sunglasses and his swaggering and insane need to exaggerate everything. I was ready for some much-needed me-time and me-space and also ready to see all there was to see in Erbil.

Chapter Nine

"E" is for "Erbil" and "Embellishment"

The morning after the Assos dinner, my new coworker Adam (who strangely did not have a nickname from Warren) and I loaded my hockey bags and suitcases and Adam's lone backpack into one SUV, then climbed into a second car to be driven three hours north to Erbil, the alleged wonderland: home of a real German restaurant (with real German beer) and five-star hotels! The two of us would be the lone employees of the CED satellite campus. Again, no tanks and no Hummers, not even the H3. Warren's idea of a convoy was apparently the trusty Nissan Pathfinder, and something called a Prado. This was not exciting. According to Warren's definition of the word, I had taken a convoy to go skiing in Canada, visit the wineries in eastern Oregon, and camp out at a Dave Matthews concert at the Gorge in the late 1990s.

While uneventful, the drive was visually stunning. Northern Iraq had some surprisingly beautiful mountain scenery, which reminded me of eastern Oregon, with its broad expanse of green, rolling up into the craggy, brown mountain range. We passed the odd goat shepherd with his flock, and several donkeys pulling large wooden carts of various things, and a handful of small farm villages that were seemingly crafted out of brown Play-Doh and straw.

We also passed a vast compound, set a few miles back from the road, which, our gleeful driver Karwan informed us, was an infamous prison. Chemical Ali* was held there. It was creepy. Less creepy when Karwan pointed at the prison and laughingly crowed, "Hotel five star! For terrorists! Ha ha ha! Eat, sleeping, hotel!" The five-star terrorist hotel passed quickly, as we were going 150 kph. In American, that's around 93 miles per hour. My photos of the scenery were blurry.

Between Suli and Erbil there were five military checkpoints, complete with gun-toting Iraqi soldiers. The soldiers appeared mostly bored and young, many of them joking with one another, with guns casually slung over their shoulders. Karwan would roll his window down and greet the checkpoint guard with "Choni, bash, bash, choni" (which was sort of "hello, how are you, good") and a few other Kurdish greetings thrown in, which all sounded like the same two words over and over again. Depending on the mood of the guard, we would either be waved through, or asked for our Iraqi residency cards, at which they would squint and look from Adam to me to the cards and back again. I had no idea what the card said. It was my smiling photo and a lot of indistinguishable squiggles. I sat in the backseat, watching each exchange,

---

*According to Wikipedia, Ali Hassan al-Majid, military commander and chief of the Iraqi Intelligence Service, was dubbed "Chemical Ali" by Iraqi Kurds for his use of chemical weapons against them.

and curiously wondered what would happen if they wouldn't let us pass. Would we have to sit there at the remote outpost until someone from the university called one of the politician-overlords and demanded our release? Warren had said we (university employees) were "treated like royalty" in and around the region. But he said a lot of stuff that wasn't necessarily true.

I really wanted to take tourist pictures at one of these checkpoints, but Adam said, "Nooo, no. You don't want to do that. One of the other teachers took a picture once, and a guard came and yanked his camera out of the car." But I needed photographic evidence for my friends. I just didn't feel like it was *real*. It was like being in some Disneyland or Universal Studios simulation: It's a Small Iraq after All.

As we drew closer to Erbil, the roads improved visibly. There were finally painted lines marking separate driving lanes (although no one paid much attention to them), and one stretch of road was dotted with solar-powered streetlights, which I found impressive. The Erbil compound was called English Village, and when we approached it from the main road, I saw that it was flanked by two similar-looking construction sites, complete with two comparable tall concrete skeletons of buildings. There was a sign in front of the nearest one, which had a sophisticated computer-generated image of a grand, impressive-looking hotel with "Kempinski" splashed across the lower left-hand corner. When Warren had said there were two five-star hotels next to the compound, I had sort of assumed they were finished. If I planned to have brunch at the Kempinski, I would need to bring my picnic basket.

English Village, on the other hand, was thankfully completed, although it was nothing like a charming hamlet in Britain. It was more like a gated community you'd see in Orange County, California. Maybe just a little less opulent, but the villas looked very nice. Limestone maybe? Cement, probably. I wasn't a builder, I didn't know. I thought those farmhouses were made of Play-Doh.

The "village" part was not an exaggeration. English Village was indeed a village. There were 420 villas connected by winding streets, and all of them, save the entrance and exit, ended in cul-de-sacs. As we drove in I counted the passing of seven blocks before we reached the university's "campus," which consisted of two identical side-by-side villas, #69 and #70, connected by a wooden deck. I was in #70, and Adam was in #69. Sixty-nine, har har har, Warren thought that was hilarious..

My villa was an open floor-plan spacious five-bedroom manse. Sort of. Downstairs there was one small bedroom, two bathrooms, two classrooms, and a large kitchen. Upstairs there were four bedrooms, one bathroom, and a living room. It was really too much for just me, and after we had unloaded all my bags, I learned it wouldn't be just me. Apparently the downstairs bedroom was set up for the Suli drivers to stay overnight. They wouldn't have enough time to turn around and drive back to Suli that same day, so the gleeful Karwan and the disrespectful, beady-eyed Sabah would be sleeping in my house that night.

My sense of wonder at the new accommodations quickly melted into a combination of astonishment and prickly defensiveness. I was tired of picking things out of my suitcase and exhausted from the tornado of activity from the past few days. I had been *so* looking forward to finally arriving in Erbil so I could fully unpack, regroup, and let my brain unwind and process everything, and I thought I would be able to do that in peaceful solitude. "The drivers sleep in my villa?" I asked Adam, my voice heavy with trepidation. He just shrugged and said, "Yeah, I didn't think that was logical, but that's how Warren set it up."

I have no idea why Warren thought this was an acceptable situation. It was as if he were creating his own exploitative reality show: We take a single American female, drop her into a house in an extremely conservative Muslim region, and then allow Kurdish Muslim men to sleep over. Watch what happens! Sure! Why not have random Kurdish men sleeping in the same villa? Furthermore, Adam then explained that Warren kept one room in the upstairs of "my" villa for himself, when he came up for weekly visits. I liked Adam. He had a mellow, easygoing presence and a wicked sense of humor. But he kept telling me things I did not want to hear and casually shrugging at my bewilderment.

Back in November Warren had said, in one of his enticing emails, "four-bedroom villa, no roommates." You all saw the email! I couldn't have cared less about the four bedrooms; it was the "no roommates" part that I wanted. I was an occasionally reclusive Hobbit who craved privacy and had been living by myself in a one-bedroom apartment for the past eight years. For me to make a profound life change, like moving to Iraq, I really needed to be sure I would at least have my own little private living space. My astrological sign was Cancer, and according to horoscope and astrology information everywhere, "a secure home base is important to all Cancers, where they can crawl into their dens and find welcome and comfort as a respite from the workaday cares of the world." Hobbit, hermit crab, same-same.

I had a very specific conversation with Warren about the living situation and what my expectations were. The conversation went like this:

Me: Tell me about the living situation.

Warren: Your villa is attached to the classroom and conference room—those are downstairs. Your living quarters are upstairs.

Me: The classroom is *in* the villa?

Warren: Yeah, but it's totally separate. There's a door that locks that part off.

Me: Is the kitchen upstairs?

Warren: Uhhh, no.

Me: So the students have access to my kitchen?

Warren: Well, technically yes. We need to have it available for them to have tea and coffee during the class breaks.

Me: But how do I keep my food separate? I don't want the students getting into all my stuff and eating my food.

(I may have been imagining them as naughty, hungry squirrels.)

Warren: Oh, they won't do that!

Me: Um, okay. And the other person who will be up there—they have their own villa, right? I don't want a roommate.

Warren: No, no, they have their own villa. Gerts, it's totally up to you, whatever you want. If you want a roommate, you can have a roommate. If you don't want a roommate, you don't have to have one.

Me: I don't want a roommate.

Warren: No problem. But if you decide later that you want one, you can have one.

Me: I DO NOT WANT A ROOMMATE.

Warren: No problem!

In the ten years between his Korea teaching stint and his job in Dubai, Warren had lived in a bucolic eastern Canadian province town and dabbled in several different careers, one of which was selling used cars. I desperately wished I had remembered that when adding details to my contract. I didn't want the pony anymore. I wanted my privacy. No roommate. No room for random Kurdish men, regardless of their employ with the university, sleeping in my villa. Honestly. I said no god damned roommate! I don't know how I could have been any clearer with Warren. A neck tattoo? "I Don't Want a Roommate" in Broadway bold font?

Upon inspection of the upstairs of #70, I discovered that Warren had taken the larger, brighter room for himself. Surprise, surprise. Several of his jackets hung in the closet, his shoes were on the floor, keys were on the dresser, and next to the bed was a huge full-length mirror. Definitely Warren's room. The other available bedroom, opposite his, was darker, smaller, and just sadder. I wondered if someone had died in there. There was a tiny balcony outside the room that was a mere five feet from the next-door neighbor's balcony. I did not know the next-door neighbors and wasn't in a commune-with-the-neighbors kind of place just yet. I was still getting used to the idea that I was in Iraq and needed as much of a figurative security blanket as I could get.

I called Warren on my new, university-issued cell phone and asked, "Can I have the room that your stuff is in?" He paused for a second, but then responded with the usual, "No problem!" I didn't even care if he didn't mean it. That fucker owed me. I quickly moved all of his stuff to the sad, dark, foreign-neighbor–balcony room. Why didn't he just have his room in Adam's villa? Adam was a boy! I wasn't! I didn't understand this. Adam didn't understand it either and, again, just shrugged when I asked him about it.

My mood brightened a little when I pulled my bags into my new, bigger, brightly lit room. Adequate lighting, hooray! And a full-length mirror! I dug around in the hockey bag to find my fancy Bose iPod docking station, plugged in my iPod, and began the Herculean task of unpacking. The combination of my music and the sight and feel of my clothes, magazines, toiletries, and general crap bumped my mood from brightened to brilliant, and I was truly happy for the first time since arriving in Iraq. As Janet Jackson sang, "Everywhere I go, every smile I see…" I lined up all my shoes in a little parade in front of the closet, so they were all there, smiling back at me.

I went to sleep that night having unpacked enough to make me feel much more at home, but the villa was still very foreign. Knowing the two drivers were downstairs, I made sure not to drink any water before going to bed, so I wouldn't have to go

to the bathroom in the middle of the night. To reach the bathroom I had to walk out of my room and down the L-shaped hallway, which was nakedly visible from the downstairs entryway. I
double-locked my bedroom door with the key and stuffed a dirty
shirt along the crack at the base of the door.

In the moments before drifting off to sleep, I had massive
pangs of homesickness, and I missed my kitty cat, Herb. He
was a seventeen-pound black Maine Coon mix, a very affection-
ate breed, and he would always press his fat, furry little body up
against my torso, sigh deeply, and settle in for the night. I didn't
have anything other than a small, squishy pillow to snuggle up
with, and the pillow didn't purr.

Herb had managed to express his vehement displeasure at my
leaving. He was a smart little guy and any time I pulled out the
suitcases, he knew I was going away. The second I turned away
to pull something from the closet, Herb would jump into the
middle of the suitcase, or bag, and park himself there, in a fuming
manner. I could tell he was angry because his eyes were slightly
narrowed. Herb couldn't talk, but he was a master of communicating in bodily elimination.

As I had unzipped one of the hockey bags while unpacking,
a faint waft of urine passed under my nostrils. Dammit, Herb!
Bending closer to the top part of the hockey bag, I confirmed
that Herb had indeed peed on top of the bag. I panicked, thinking that the urine may have soaked through to the clothing that
was packed on top. I didn't want to be the new English teacher
who smelled like cat pee. The hockey bag material was pretty
industrial, though. Sure, they needed to be sturdy to carry all that

hockey crap, but I'll bet a few of those hockey players had vengeful kitty cats at their houses too, and no one wanted to be the pro hockey star who smelled like cat pee.

Chapter Ten

Attempted Assimilation

Immediately after the drivers left my villa that first morning, my anxiety just evaporated. It was as if I had been holding my breath all week and was finally able to let it whoosh out. I unpacked and put everything away in proper places, and it felt like home.

It's amazing what a familiar down comforter and fragrant candles can do for a place.

Adam came in to look at my room, out of the sheer curiosity of seeing where all the crap would go, took one look at my homey bed, and enviously wailed, "Aww, a comforter!" He was stuck with the shiny, garish, standard university-issue polyester top blanket. I grinned at him and shrugged.

Every morning I would wake up, unlock my bedroom door, pad down the hallway and down the cold stone stairs to the kitchen. There was a large picture window over the sink that displayed our small front yard, immaculately manicured by the Kurdish septuagenarian gardener, who worked in his traditional costume. The traditional Kurdish costume was essentially an MC Hammer jumpsuit with embroidered cummerbund and rolled-scarf head wrap. The little old man was always crouched over the short rosebushes, picking at something while various small birds chirped and flitted from our eaves to the neighbors'. Ahh, domestic life in Iraq.

Classes hadn't started yet, and Warren was being vague about the start date, which just meant I was being paid to hang out and wait. I was really good at doing nothing, so it was a win-win.

The Erbil campus came equipped with both a gardener and a driver, Chalak, to whom I referred as our Man-About-Town. Chalak didn't really speak English, but he understood most of what Adam and I said, and would take us on errands and help us with household needs when he wasn't busy sitting on the porch swing, smoking his cigarettes. Chalak was also really good at doing nothing. He wore jeans and plaid button-down shirts, had light-colored hair and blue eyes (unusual for a Kurd), sported the ubiquitous Kurdish-man mustache, and loved his cigarettes. He lived somewhere else in Erbil and would drive his trusty old pickup truck to English Village Sunday through Thursday to work for the university.

One day our Man-About-Town informed us we had to go to Security. That was all Chalak could explain in his extremely limited English. "We go Security."

One of my biggest frustrations was the absence of maps or organizational material for the city of Erbil. I had asked Chalak for a map, and he said there was none. Warren was also unable to assist in my endeavor and said there really just weren't any maps or many marked streets. At home I was so used to driving myself everywhere, but here I was stuck in an unfamiliar city, chauffeured from place to place, and completely dependent on

Chalak and his knowledge of Erbil. I had no bearings, no sense of the city at all.

Chalak said Security was "around corner," so Adam and I thought it was the little booth at the entrance to English Village. Chalak, however, kept driving out of the village, onto the main road. We drove about six or seven miles before reaching our destination. Security was a small three-story building with many random employees who stopped and stared at Adam and me as we walked up to the second floor, down the hall, and into a large office. The office was furnished with several couches and armchairs upholstered in a rough, textured fabric. I imagined the catalog offering the set as their Loofah Collection. Opposite a large, clunky desk sat a large, clunky television set showing a Turkish soap opera. Perhaps the security employees didn't know about the Asian-woman aerobics show? It was funny that I had felt slightly silly and shallow, asking Warren if I would have TV there. The Kurds clearly loved their TV as much as I did.

The man behind the desk didn't look particularly official or businesslike in his Members Only–ish jacket, with his hair greased up like Danny Zuko, the Fonz, or one of the kids from *Jersey Shore*.

The greasy man spent the first five minutes chatting with Chalak in Kurdish while Adam and I just sat there shrugging at each other and trying to figure out what was happening on the Turkish soap. It looked very dramatic. All of a sudden the questions began. Greasy Man asked if Adam and I were married, what our jobs were, what our parents' names were, what our fathers' jobs were, the names of our siblings, the occupations of our siblings, and our previous jobs. We answered all the questions as straight-faced as was possible, and after much note taking, paper-shuffling, and another five-minute Greasy Man/Chalak conversation, we were permitted to leave.

What was that all about? Why did Kurdistan need to know if I had siblings, or what my father did for a living? I'm thirty-eight.

 ⌒⌒⌒

Being an official, registered immigrant in Kurdistan was one step toward assimilation, but I also wanted to assimilate on a more personal level. I wanted to feel comfortable in my new surroundings. I wanted to have a routine.

I really wanted to work out.

Adam had discovered a men's gym where he could do all his heavy lifting, and there was a women's fitness center adjacent to the men's. I was kind of amazed that there even *was* a gym (that women could go to). I decided I could have a little look-see one day while Adam was working out.

Chalak drove Adam and me to the gym. When Adam took his gym bag and went off to the testosterone arena, Chalak walked with me to the estrogen entrance. Men weren't allowed past the front desk, so Chalak explained to the man behind the desk that I wanted to go to the gym for a trial day. I walked past the front desk and around the corner into what seemed like an enormous, musty garage. The floor was covered with squishy floor mats that fit together like jigsaw puzzle pieces. There were a few weak, caged light bulbs that hung from the rafters, and broken windows so the birds could fly in and out and poop on the exercise equipment as they pleased. Oh, sad place. This was where crippled exercise equipment came to die.

There were around twenty Kurdish women, all in some form of full covering, mostly velour sweat suits. A few wore head scarves, and some were just wearing turtleneck sweaters and pants. They were all in the middle of a 1970s aerobics class, where there was a lot of arm-flapping and calisthenics-type exercises. When I walked in, all heads turned toward me and I froze. I smiled politely and carefully sidestepped over to an empty exercise bike, climbed on, and started pedaling. There was no danger of my overexerting myself—the bike wasn't plugged in. In fact, the only machine in the entire room that was plugged in was one of those vibrating things that you stand on and it just jostles you around.

The women continued to flap their arms and do waist bends and, every once in a while, turned to look at me, sitting quietly on my broken exercise bike. Without warning, one older headscarved woman, arms still flapping up and down, marched over to me and shouted in (unfortunately) understandable English, "You join class!"

Me: Ohhhh, no, no, thank you.
Headscarved lady: (yelling) WHY?

(Panic setting in. Everyone staring.)

Me: Oh, I just…um…need to…work up to it?
Headscarved lady: *(inexplicably still yelling)* OH, OKAY!

She nodded curtly and marched back to her spot, still flapping her arms. I thought that was really quite nice of her to invite me to join them. However, I was still in my state of awed observation and was not prepared to be the main feature in the Kurdish version of a Jane Fonda flashback.

The fitness center was kind of like a combination gym/party room/day care, with colorful "Happy Birthday" banners (in English) hanging from the ceiling and sticky children running around shrieking and playing on the weight machines. Yes, there were weight machines. Most of them still had plastic wrap on the seats, anointed with the occasional plop of bird doody.

The aerobics class took a pause, and everyone went running around the room in circles to some very loud, wailing Arabic music. The women were still staring at me, even as they jogged. I slowly crept over to the elliptical machine, which also was not plugged in. I had to somehow pass the time, because Chalak wasn't due to pick us up until Adam finished his workout, which lasted for an arduous ninety minutes. Ninety minutes of my pretend exercise had to burn at least a few calories, so I climbed back on the unplugged exercise bike and pedaled away.*

e~e~e~

Friday is the Islamic holy day, so the Middle Eastern weekend is Friday and Saturday. Chalak didn't work on those days, and

---

*Adam was not to become the Love of my Life—in case you were thinking about that Tish Durkin article. He was engaged to a really adorable girl back in Canada, and I just wouldn't want you reading too much into our interactions. Adam was absolutely hilarious and fun to be around, though. Warren was the brother I never wanted, and Adam was the awesome brother I never had.

Adam and I were left to fend for ourselves, sans car, sans driver, and sans direction. Adam had been to Erbil a few times before, and one sunny Friday he felt confident that he could find a good restaurant where we could have lunch. It was something to do.

We started out walking around 10:30 a.m. wearing long pants and long-sleeved shirts in the ninety-degree heat. We were totally culturally aware. We walked five minutes to the entrance of the compound, crossed the threshold out into the real world, and turned left. There were no other pedestrians on our route, and we were the object of much attention from the drivers. There was a great deal of horn honking as the cars whizzed past. It could have either been because Erbil was like L.A., and the drivers were so surprised to see people walking, or just because Adam and I were so sexy in our pajamalike outfits. I started yelling, "Thank you!" after each horn honk. I told Adam, "You know, I get that we're supposed to be covering up the sexy here, what with all the stipulations on the Cultural Awareness pamphlet and all, but the sexy really comes from the inside. You can't cover up this sexy," and I gestured wildly up and down my frame. That made Adam laugh pretty hard, and then another horn honked. "You can't cover up this sexy" became my new motto.

We passed several armed guards along the way, just guarding random cement-walled buildings, and as the guards would eye us suspiciously, Adam and I would smile and wave. Nearly all the guards would respond with genuine smiles and waves themselves. People really are the same everywhere, I thought. It was nice to see that the men with big guns still spoke Friendly Smile.

We walked and talked about how Adam used to live with

Warren down in Suli, but Warren had kicked him out of the villa for no apparent reason, and he had to stay with another teacher for a couple of months right before moving up to Erbil. Adam was one of the most mellow, unaffected guys I had ever met, and I couldn't imagine anyone not getting along with him or having a reason to dramatically kick him out of a living arrangement. Adam said, "Yeah, I mean it was kinda weird, but he just wanted me out and I was like, 'Okay, man' and moved out of the villa." That first day in Suli, when we were hanging out in his office, Warren had said to me, "Gretch, keep an eye on your food. If you let Adam into your kitchen, he'll eat everything, seriously," and then he went on to complain that Adam was a huge slob who never did the dishes and that he "left shit all over the place" and that their villa was always a "fucking pigsty."

I had been over to Adam's villa a number of times since we had moved to Erbil, expecting a mosh pit of filth, and it was always disappointingly clean. He did his dishes regularly and picked up after himself. He definitely wasn't a slob. On the other hand, I had stopped in to Warren's villa in Suli during that first week, where he was living by himself after having kicked Adam out, and there were piles of dirty dishes and shit left all over the place, and it was pretty much a fucking pigsty. Warren's words, not mine.

We had been walking for an hour, in ninety-degree heat, when we finally reached an area that looked as if it might have restaurants. It was a busy street with basic buildings that included dusty storefronts for furniture stores, a produce market, and a couple of hotels. Adam had been hoping to get us to Bakery & More, a Lebanese restaurant with a bakery on the ground floor. He thought we were headed in the right direction, but we had been walking a long time and were both losing steam, and my stomach was starting to eat itself. We stopped in front of something called the Darya Hotel and decided to see if it had a restaurant.

We entered the lobby, where there were several men sitting on leather couches, smoking shisha pipes. They all turned and stared as we approached the front desk.

With my previous traveling and experience living in a foreign country, my pantomime skills were pretty good, and Adam and I were able to mime "menus" and "eating," so the manager led us to the restaurant area. It was empty, which usually isn't a good sign, but then the manager motioned for Adam to go into the kitchen to take a look. For once, I welcomed the role of lowly female and collapsed into a chair, just relieved not to be walking and sweating profusely anymore.

Adam came back from the kitchen, shrugging, and said, "Yeah, looks good. Clean." We had a delicious meal of (da-da-da-dum) chicken kebab, hummus, and fatoush. I was noticing a distinct lack of variety in the cuisine. But here, I could completely ignore variety, if the trade-off was Diet Coke. *Diet Coke!* I had been look-ing for it since I got here! I squealed as the waiter brought it to the table.

The waiter at the Darya Hotel was a lively young man who told us he came to Erbil to avoid the unrest in Mosul. Mosul was the notoriously dangerous city two hours west of Erbil; it was discussed in one of those Internet news stories I had carefully ignored prior to coming to Iraq.

This waiter was the first one who had asked me what I wanted before asking Adam. Over the past couple of weeks, I had been ignored in most interactions with locals (even with Man-About-Town Chalak), and I was the last to be acknowledged and served at restaurants. The waiters at Assos, in Suli, spoke to and waited on the men first. The manager at the Bayan Hotel spoke to me only after conversing with Warren and the male drivers. When we were getting settled in Erbil, the university's drivers directed all inquiries and comments to Adam. It was no surprise that men were treated better here, but it was a little unsettling to experience it, repeatedly, firsthand.

One day, I was thinking out loud that it was annoying that they *really* didn't respect women here. I was certain that Warren had been thoroughly brainwashed when he countered, "Gretch, they *totally* respect women here. They're treated like gold." Gold is a commodity. "They are like prized *flowers*." Flowers, also a commodity, just slightly less valuable than gold. "That's why they have to keep their heads covered, to shield their beauty..." Blah, blah, blah. I couldn't believe he actually bought that. I later heard him say, "Yeah, they [Muslim men] basically think all women are whores. It's why the women can't be left alone. The men think they'll just screw anything that walks." I'm sorry, what?

My brain veered off on a tangent, and I considered the likelihood of Muslim women *really* wanting even to have intercourse with their husbands, much less "screw anything that walked." Female genital mutilation was still practiced in many of the smaller towns and villages in this region (probably the ones we passed, made out of brown Play-Doh), and if I had experienced a horror like that, I would demand a chastity belt made out of granite, equipped with biometric fingerprint and retinal scan, that only my gynecologist could access, so that nothing could get close to that area. And the women who didn't have their lady flowers brutally maimed? I had serious doubts that they even enjoyed sex. Did conservative Muslim men go down on their wives?

I had too much free time (when would classes start?!), much of which I spent scouring Google, typing in phrases like "oral sex and the Koran." I'm sure this was sacrilege, but Islam dictates all areas of life for the Muslim, and my curiosity was killing me.

The first link I clicked on said that oral sex is permitted, according to the Koran. But then it had this paragraph about women and "their courses," with an opening quote from the Koran.

> They ask thee concerning women's courses. Say: They are a hurt and a pollution: So keep away from women in their courses, and do not approach them until they are clean. But when they have purified themselves, ye may approach them in any manner, time, or place ordained for you by God. For God loves those who turn to Him constantly and He loves those who keep themselves pure and clean. (The Noble Quran, 2:222)…
>
> It is obvious from the Noble Verse that intercourse is prohibited during the woman's period. Oral sex is also prohibited because the vagina would contain germs in it, and any physical contact with it, whether through the penis, tongue or finger, will not only bring pain to the woman, but also could and would hurt the

man through the harmful bacteria. Allah Almighty in Noble Verse 2:222 clearly ordered men to stay away from any physical contact with the women's vaginas during the monthly period.

This was fascinating, not to mention valuable information. I didn't need a handgun, or mace, or pepper spray, or even that fancy granite chastity belt to protect myself here. All I had to do was tell any potential attacker that I was experiencing the diabolic menses and they'd go screaming into the woods, a la Scooby Doo when faced with an evil, wax-faced villain. I would be smug in the knowledge that the diabolic menses was just my highly efficient self-cleaning uterus, and that the wax-faced villain was really just Old Man Murphy trying to protect his property from those meddlesome kids.

Chapter Eleven

Assimilation Speed Bumps

Two weeks had passed. I was working on my assimilation, but it was still a very strange, unfamiliar place. When one finds oneself in a very strange, unfamiliar place, and one is female, in a female-unfriendly region, one is not terribly inclined to open one's door should one's doorbell ring at 10:30 p.m.

My doorbell rang at 10:30 p.m., and it stopped me in my tracks. Suddenly, I was Scarlett again, sitting alone in the living room knitting (watching TV) while menacing Union soldiers pounded on the door. The doorbell startled me into a state of wide-eyed paralysis. I mentally ran through my new, standard defensive opener, "I am totally having my period right now!" The doorbell rang again, and I was finally able to mobilize myself, and crept to the stairwell and yelled, "ADAM?" A muffled voice from behind the door answered, "No, it's Tom Pappas from the university."

Who?

I opened the door to find one middle-aged, bespectacled American man, one short Kurdish man smoking a cigarette, and one short Kurdish Buddy Hackett bodyguard (who had escorted me to immigration and now stood outside my front door with a rolling suitcase). I was one startled, bespectacled girl, and I was in my pajamas.

Bespectacled American Man held out his hand and said, "Hi, I'm Tom Pappas, you must be Gretchen." I had no idea who Tom Pappas was, why he knew who I was, or, most importantly, why he had brought his suitcase to my house. In situations where I'm bewildered, my reaction times are a bit slower than usual, but I did manage to extend my hand for a greeting, all the while looking from Tom Pappas, to Buddy Hackett, to the cigarette, to the suitcase, then back to Tom Pappas.

Tom Pappas said he was the chancellor of the university. He then asked if anyone had told me he would be coming, and I slowly responded, "Noooooo…" while wondering if I was supposed to invite him in for a slumber party. *I'm sorry, but we can't have a slumber party, because I'M TOTALLY HAVING MY PERIOD RIGHT NOW!* Although, I wondered if that diversionary tactic might not work on American men the same way.

I had not been briefed on this type of situation. What was the protocol when the chancellor of the university showed up on your doorstep at 10:30 at night, while you were wearing your jammies and he was toting a rolly suitcase and an entourage? After an uncomfortable silence, he finally asked, "Is this the girls' villa?" and with relief I answered, "Yes, Adam is next door." I was still in slow-motion bewilderment as the trio turned to walk to the next villa and I closed the door.

Then it sunk in: Tom Pappas was the chancellor of the university, and I had just had my first meeting with him in my pajamas, and it had been extremely awkward. And once they had gotten the chancellor situated in Adam's villa, the two short entourage members would be returning to spend the night in my villa.

Adam came over ten minutes later, looking for an extra towel for his slumber party guest. My language gets really bad when I'm angry, and I blurted out, "WHAT THE FUCK?" to which Adam just shrugged. "Did you know they were coming up here?" I asked it as an outraged rhetorical question, in a conspiratorial manner, as I was sure no one thought to let either one of us know what was happening.

Adam said, "Oh. Yeah. Warren sent me an email a few hours ago."

My eyebrows were scraping the ceiling at this point. "And you didn't tell me because…"

Adam just shrugged again and said, "I didn't think they'd come to your villa." I thought Adam could probably skip the next few gym workouts with all the shrugging he was doing.

An exasperated "Pffft!" came out of my mouth. Our villas were on a dead-end street. There was one villa at the very end (that belonged to some oil company), then Adam's villa, then mine. If you were driving to the villas, mine came first. Of course they would go to my villa first. I had to explain to Adam that he needed to tell me things like this, so I would be *prepared* for them and would not be wearing *jammies* the next time someone came up from the university. If Adam were actually my brother, I would have demanded our parents ground him for a week. Honestly. It was times like those when I really could have used a drink.

‿‿‿

Adam did not agree with my shrugging-as-workout idea and went to the gym every day at 10:00 a.m. The next morning I decided to hitch a ride with him and Chalak, and then have Chalak help me track down some wine and hopefully Diet Coke. I was given reason to hope during our adventuresome lunch at the Darya Hotel.

Adam had thus far been the one doing all the communicating with Chalak. If Chalak had questions about anything, including my villa, he would ask Adam. It was like I was invisible. I was convinced it was the Middle Eastern man/female-aversion thing, and Chalak didn't want to deal with me directly. So I thought this excursion would be interesting. We dropped Adam off at the gym, and as I climbed into the front passenger seat, I said, "Okay, so the liquor store?" Chalak looked confused and I had to run through other ways to say "liquor." "Wine? Wine and beer? Alcohol?"

"Alcohol" was the magic word, and Chalak's eyes registered recognition. He drove me to a small, shabby-looking shop that was markedly different from the nice little liquor store Warren had shown us in Suli. The Suli shop had a really nice Chilean Sauvignon Blanc; this shop had only Chateau Kefraya. I guess we would be indulging in some Lebanese wine. It was worth a try. They did have a lot of "spirits" at the shop, but I really wanted wine. "Spirits" seems like a misnomer for hard liquor. "Spirits" seems light and sparkly and fruity, much like wine. I never describe Jim Beam or Captain Morgan as "light," "sparkly," or "fruity."

Chalak could sense my disappointment at the shabby shop and said, "Okay, I take you better place. Ainkawa." I thought Ainkawa must be the name of another liquor store, but apparently Ainkawa was a neighboring town. Exciting! New Iraqi town! My mom would be wringing her hands at the idea of a new Iraqi town. She had seen one of my photos of the road signs that said "to Baghdad—to Mosul" and had declared, "No exploring, Gretchen!"

Chalak explained, "Here? Liquor store? Only two. Ainkawa? Two hundred!" Ainkawa sounded like my kind of town. It was a short five-minute drive from English Village. It took less time to drive to Ainkawa than it did to drive to the Erbil grocery stores. Ainkawa was predominantly Christian, and as we turned off the vast, wide roads of Erbil onto Ainkawa's narrow residential streets, we passed at least one church and many beloved liquor stores. God bless and praise Jesus. I bought Jacob's Creek Chardonnay, and Chalak bought cigarettes. All the men here smoke like their mustaches depend on it for growth, and he was no exception.

Back in the car I asked, "Can we find Diet Coke? Or Diet Pepsi?" Chalak looked confident and said, "Yes!" We were having such a fun errand day! And I had been worried about communicating with him. We stopped at five different stores with no luck though. The last place we tried, Chalak spoke to the store manager, who said, "Don't even bother looking." He meant anywhere in Ainkawa. I thought I might have to drown my sorrows in Jacob's Creek.

I then had a caffeine epiphany and told Chalak about the hotel/restaurant where Adam and I had eaten the previous week, explaining that they had Diet Coke. So we found our way back to Erbil and the Darya Hotel. I approached the front desk and with a friendly smile and a pantomime asked if they had Diet Coke. The woman behind the desk did speak a little English and gradually understood what I wanted, so she called the manager over. They agreed to sell me some Diet Coke from their restaurant supply. They loaded twelve cans of Diet Coke into a plastic bag while I clapped my hands in sheer glee. The manager was the same man who had helped Adam and me and recognized me as the shrieking crazy. Both the manager and the front-desk receptionist were totally amused with how excited I was about Diet Coke, and I had to explain, "You just can't find it anywhere here! Thank you so much!"

I wasn't so much assimilating into Iraqi life as bringing some of my culture to Iraq.

ᕮᕬᕬᕬ

My "culture" was brought to me via the Diet Coke and the TV. We had five stations that broadcast a myriad of Americana: syndicated sitcoms, dramas, and even *Jeopardy!*, as well as movies. One night, Adam indulged me and we watched *27 Dresses*. He agreed to forgo *Call of Duty* or *Warcraft IV* or whatever testosterone-y video games he had been playing, and have some good girl time with me. I was so excited about watching *27 Dresses*, which I had already seen, and remembered there were very attractive people, bright colors, and excellent New York locations, not to mention all the dresses. I needed a frothy, froufy escape.

It was guilty-pleasure satisfying, up until the point where I realized (and Adam confirmed) that they cut out all the kissing scenes in movies.

Me: WHAT?

How can they not show kissing on TV? How were these people ever going to learn how to kiss properly if they had no TV or movie kissing references? Wasn't that how everyone learned? I suppose the no-kissing rule made sense, as #3 on our Cultural Awareness pamphlet did specifically say "no kissing," but I didn't realize that would extend to the pretend world of television.

I loved watching movie kissing, so this was a devastating development for me. James Franco and Sophia Myles in *Tristan & Isolde*; Keira Knightley and James McEvoy in *Atonement*; Heath Ledger and Jake Gyllenhaal in *Brokeback Mountain*—all good kissing. I found myself wondering if the spaghetti scene from Disney's *Lady and the Tramp* would be cut.

Not even *The Simpsons* was safe. One of the English-language channels was Fox Series, which showed back-to-back episodes of *The Simpsons*. There was one episode where Apu, the Kwik-E-Mart owner, has an affair with the Squishee lady. The Middle Eastern, romance-hating censors cut that scene. If I hadn't seen the episode before, I would have been really confused as to why Manjula was so pissed at Apu. Here, even animated infidelity had to be hushed.

The more time I spent here, the more I was convinced it was exactly like Victorian England:

- No public affection was allowed.
- Women had to be covered from neck to ankle.
- Unmarried women and men could not be seen in each other's company without a chaperone.
- No kissing on TV.

Exactly like Victorian England.

꧁꧂

One night, about a week after Chancellor Tom Pappas's unannounced visit, Adam and I were hanging out and attempting to drink the horrible Lebanese wine. I was finding notes of Borax and hints of turpentine, and Adam was laughingly relating the details of how Tom had accidentally walked into Adam's room while clad in his sassy tighty-whities. I shrieked a loud "Noooooooo!" both in regards to the story and the mental image that mercilessly burned itself on my delicate brain. Then Adam said, "Yeah, I probably shouldn't tell you this, but Tom asked if you were whiny."

> **Me:** What?
>
> **Adam:** Yeah, he was talking to Warren and said, "So, is Gretchen kind of whiny?"

I was whiny because I wasn't Little Miss Welcome Wagon when a strange man showed up at my door at 10:30 at night, in Iraq, two weeks after I had arrived. It might be more of a challenge to assimilate into the university culture than into the Middle Eastern culture.

Chapter Twelve

Escaping Erbil

When I signed my contract, back in November, I was given a calendar of the school's upcoming breaks. The Kurdish people celebrated Nawroz, which was a sort of New Year/Welcome to Spring celebration, and this equaled a ten-day paid holiday at the end of March. Even before I left the United States, I thought, "It would probably be smart of me to go somewhere Western, to alleviate the inevitable culture shock of the Middle East." So I coordinated a trip with my old college roommate, Ellie, and picked what I considered to be the absolute polar opposite of Iraq: Paris, France.

Ellie said, "Seriously, you arrive there, work for three weeks, then get ten days off, paid?" Yes, and I absolutely deserved that, because I had committed to spending two years living in Iraq. I hadn't known it would be more like "I arrive here, pretend to work for three weeks, then get ten days off." The start date for my classes kept getting pushed back.

I had been putting off traveling to France because of all the clichéd stories about how the French hate Americans and mock them and treat them poorly. Given the option, I would choose not to be mocked or treated poorly on vacation. But considering I would be traveling from a place where women were treated poorly in general, being mocked by the French might not be all that bad. I am okay with mockery if it occurs while I'm comfortably lounging at a sidewalk café, drinking wine and eating brie.

෧෮෧

Erbil had an international airport, as Warren had explained to me, from which a number of different airlines provided service. None of them was familiar. I was still not speaking with Royal Jordanian and had no desire to test out anything called Zozik Air, or Zagros Air, or, God forbid, Iraqi Airways. Although I desperately wanted a boarding pass from Flying Carpet Airlines. That was a real airline; I'm not kidding. In my mind Aladdin was the captain, and they flew straight onto Ali Baba's property and employed the forty thieves as ground crew and baggage handlers…so, on second thought, maybe no.

One of the dangers of flying with an airline with devout Muslim pilots was their commitment to "inshallah." Warren explained to me that all Muslims subscribed to the idea of "inshallah," which means "If God wills it." He claimed that the Muslim pilots, when faced with violent turbulence or sudden aircraft malfunctions, would simply release their grips on the controls, throw their hands heavenward, and cry, "Inshallah!" assuming that if it was God's will for the plane to crash, they shouldn't try to interfere.

I chose Austrian Airlines. It was the most comforting-sounding of the options. Arnold Schwarzenegger was Austrian, and who wouldn't feel safe and secure with…okay, maybe not Schwarzenegger. Ferdinand Porsche was Austrian! The guy who created both the Volkswagen and the Porsche. Reliable *and* sexy.

Austrian Airlines had figured out, though, that Westerners in Iraq would want to fly with them, and therefore felt justified in charging $1,400 for a round-trip between Erbil and Vienna, a four-hour flight. Yes. Escaping from The Iraq, in a modern aircraft, with a civilized, professional flight crew who knew they had the ability to avert an unnecessary crash, would cost you. I didn't even care. Just to have the option of getting to Europe, in just a few hours, was absolutely worth it to me. The retail price of one week of freedom and glee was $1,400 (plus a little $200 flight from Vienna to Paris).

Before rolling around in all that freedom and glee, I would have to actually get there. Enter the Erbil International Airport security maze. Chalak, with cigarette dangling from lower lip, loaded my suitcase into the car and then drove me to the airport. The drive was approximately five minutes from English Village; however, there was another five minutes of driving once we turned onto the airport property. The airport road narrowed to an almost-tunnel, with low cement walls that jagged left and right before reaching the first armed checkpoint. Chalak yammered, "Choni, bash, choni" at the guard, gestured to me, and we were waved through. He then pulled up to a small, one-story brick building, got out of the car, and unloaded my suitcase. "Oh, is this it?" I asked hesitantly. This couldn't possibly be the airport. I couldn't even see any airplanes or a runway or… Chalak, nodded and gestured toward the building and to my suitcase. "Um...okay then, thanks!"

I was so excited to be going to Paris that I was grinning and giddy, and the Kurdish airport officials smiled right back. They may have thought I was mentally disabled. Who cares? I was off to Paris! I had to put my suitcase on a conveyor belt, which ran through a standard-issue luggage scanner, while I walked under the metal-detecting arch. The arch beeped, because I was wearing my boots, belt, watch, and all the other clangy crap I usually place in the tray in other airport security lanes. I had been carefully observing the people in line ahead of me, and the women did not remove any boots, belts, or clangy crap. Rather than having to arduously remove all of those things, and walk through the arch again, I was directed toward a door, which led into a tiny room where there was a female airport official, sitting at a desk, looking bored.

She gave me a physical once-over—and basically felt me up—to determine I wasn't packing any ammunition. It was the most action I had had in a few years. I didn't enjoy being molested, she actually cupped both breasts, *hello*, but it was convenient not to have to take off all the accessories and then put them on again. I made a mental note to wear an industrial-weight bra the next time I flew. My frisky date finished looking through my purse, smiled, and said in halting English, "Have a nice flight." Handsy, but friendly.

From that building I had to climb into a small shuttle bus, dragging my suitcase behind me, to be driven the additional two miles to the main building of the airport. "Rigamarole" is not a word I frequently use, but it was the only one that came to mind during this experience. The shuttle bus dropped me at the front entrance to the airport, which did look like an airport, and I entered through the sliding glass doors only to be confronted with yet another security lane, another conveyor belt, another metal-detecting arch, and another cringe-inducing molestation. I did not want anyone else touching me after this. But, again, all the airport security people were as nice as pie—or, as nice as baklava (which was, thus far, the only local dessert I had encountered— very flaky and tasty).

You would think that would be the end of the detecting and searching, no? No. After checking in at one of the two counters, and releasing my Tumi to the Gods of Baggage Handling (inshal- lah, they would not rummage through my belongings), I had to take my boarding pass, passport, and residency card through the customs window, where I was squinted at and photographed by a small webcam. "Have a nice flight," the customs agent said. I really did like this airport, aside from all the mistrust and inap- propriate touching.

But there was more.

After sitting in the smoky waiting room with a bottle of water and peanut M&Ms, the Austrian Airlines flight number appeared on the television screen suspended from the ceiling, and people began to line up to go through another metal-detecting arch, after placing their carry-on luggage on a small conveyor belt. This was exhausting. And what could I possibly have acquired between the last checkpoint and this one? And I had to go into the little pri- vate room for my third date of the day. *No more touching, please!* I decided, at that point, to invest in a steel tank top and matching girdle. I was sure Paris had a lingerie shop with something similar.

I was finally in the last waiting room; the final resting point, where I could sit and ponder if I had done anything to somehow invite the advances of the groping security officials. Was it my fault? Had I inadvertently winked? Raised my eyebrows suggestively? I longed to have a sympathetic psychologist sitting next to me, telling me, "It's not your fault. It's *not* your fault." I felt so dirty.

The final phase of the extraordinarily involved process of departing the Impenetrable Fortress of Erbil was boarding a large shuttle bus, which transported everyone fifty feet out to the Austrian Airlines 737. Upon summiting the metal staircase and entering the aircraft, I half expected the flight attendant to strip-search me and was greatly comforted when she simply smiled and said, "Hello."

✺✺✺

I said "Bonjour!" to Paris. Bonjour croque monsieurs (ham!), chocolate, cheese, wine, shopping, and my old roommate. It was so nice to see a familiar face and to be surrounded by so much opulence. We went a little crazy with the shopping. Rhett went to Paris and bought Scarlett dresses and hats. I went to Paris and bought myself Azzedine Alaïa animal-print booties and Christian Louboutin peep-toe sling-backs. When in Rome, you know. *Oh, now I want to go to Rome.* And really, once you've spent $1,600 on airfare, Alaïas and Louboutins seemed almost reasonable.

After a week of *indulgence française*, it was back to The Iraq. I sadly realized I would not, and should not, wear my fancy new shoe purchases in The Iraq if I wanted them to remain fancy. The sloppy combination of unpaved walkways and excessive dust and mud would just ruin them. I had not forgotten immigration, and neither had my Wonder Woman boots. I tucked both boxes into the back of my closet until I could take them back to the United States where they would be safe.

It was strange to think that Paris was a mere hop, skip, jump, and two short plane rides from Iraq. It was like hopping, skipping, and jumping from a trampoline of decadence and landing in a desolate sand trap. That was unfair. I mean, even my warm, adorable, welcoming hometown of Glen Ellyn, Illinois, would not be favorably compared to Paris. Paris was arguably the most beautiful city in the world and was constantly drawing comparisons to other places. Prague was the Paris of Eastern Europe. Beirut was the Paris of the Middle East.

I decided, based on my entirely limited time there, that Erbil could be the Paris of Iraq. You should always focus on what you *do* have rather than what you don't. Erbil probably had plenty to offer, and it was up to me to find out exactly what that was.

Chapter Thirteen

We've Got Students, Convenience, and Hookers

Since the Erbil campus was a relatively new project for the university, things had been a bit slow to start, and Adam and I didn't begin teaching until several weeks after we arrived. The Kurds were proving to be a fairly noncommittal people, and although Warren claimed to have ten students signed up for a class, I only ended up with two. Adam ended up with zero, so his duties were reduced to "coordinating" until more students signed up for classes. My new class would meet Sunday through Wednesday, the standard university schedule, for three hours each day. Not exactly taxing.

Dalzar and Renas were my two students, and they were quite the pair. Frick and Frack. Chip and Dale. Sonny and Cher. Renas actually did look like Sonny, with a mustache and lively eyes. Dalzar was bald, with a medium build, and had some fierce eyebrows that marched across his forehead in a pointy M. They were both bright, friendly, funny men in their late twenties/early thirties. From what I had seen, the Kurdish people tended to appear ten years older than their actual ages, so my initial guesses were slightly off. I think the premature aging had a lot to do with them having to live through disaster and atrocities that we only read about or see in movies or on TV. And the incessant smoking probably didn't help.

Dalzar and Renas were my very own Odd Couple. Anytime we had a discussion, those two disagreed. Dalzar was a bit more of a bulldozer and would loudly talk over Renas (and occasionally me) and had the irritating habit of going "uhhhhhhhh" in between words. It was as if he thought that still counted as English, just as long as he was making noise that wasn't distinctly Kurdish or Arabic. Renas was infinitely more articulate and would politely wait for Dalzar to finish his ranting and "uhhhhhhhhs" before stating his point.

One assignment in the textbook asked the students to "rewrite the sentence using 'may' or 'might' and 'be able to.'"

The sentence was: *Maybe you can buy an antihistamine in the gift shop.*

The correct answer would be: *You may be able to buy an antihistamine in the gift shop.* Or: *You might be able to buy an antihistamine in the gift shop.*

This may (or might) seem like a random, odd sentence, but we had just finished a unit on health issues, so the students were freshly familiar with ailments and medications. Dalzar's answer, which he read aloud, was: "You might not be able to buy an antihistamine in the gift shop."

I corrected him and said, "You *might* be able to buy an antihistamine in the gift shop."

Dalzar said, "No. You *might not* be able to buy an antihistamine in the gift shop."

We went back and forth in this manner for about a minute. Then I finally gave up and asked, "Why not?" Because Dalzar didn't think gift shops would sell antihistamines. Never mind that the assignment was merely to revise the sentence; Dalzar wanted to revise the potential offerings of the gift shop because the scenario just didn't make sense to him. I tried to explain that many gift shops, particularly those in hospitals, would likely offer both gifts *and* medications. Dalzar didn't seem convinced.

Later on, in class, the subject of weddings randomly came up.

> **Renas:** There is Steve Martin movie, I think, *Father of Bride*, Steve Martin movie about daughter getting married. I think is nice when he play basketball with daughter.
>
> **Me:** Oh, yes! *Father of the Bride*! That was very sweet. Did you cry?
>
> **Renas:** *(chuckling)* Yes.
>
> **Me:** Dalzar, did you see that movie?
>
> **Dalzar:** Yes, very good when many people…Gladiator, uhhhhhh, and the people, uhhhhhhh…
>
> **Me:** Dalzar, did you see *Father of the Bride*?
>
> **Dalzar:** Uh, no.

Dalzar may not be able to understand the topic matter at hand, but you really had to appreciate his willingness to participate in the discussions.

⌒⌒⌒

After finishing class, I went over to Adam's villa to see if he was ready for another *Sex and the City* marathon. He had never seen the show, and I had brought all six seasons with me. You know, in the hockey bags. Basically, if anyone dropped by my villa and asked, "Do you have any…" I would say, "Yes" before they could finish the question. All six seasons of *Sex and the City*? Yes. Giant vats of Bumble & Bumble shampoo and conditioner? Yes. Jars of Trader Joe's peanut butter? Yes. Enough sheets, comforters, and towels to stock my own white sale? Yes. Stupid hockey bags.*

> **Adam:** Do you want to walk to the store real quick first?
> I need some candy.
> **Me:** What store?
> **Adam:** The one, just a couple of blocks down.
> **Me:** What? We have a store? A couple of blocks down?
> What?

Adam may not be able to share pertinent information with me, *but we may be able to buy antihistamines at the new convenience store!*

Chalak was only available to drive us on errands Sunday through Thursday, 9:00 a.m. until 4:00 p.m. After that, we were sort of stuck. What happened if I had a sudden relentless urge for

---

*Adam became an instant fan of *Sex and the City*. He would burst out laughing every time Samantha said anything. At one point he asked me if I had any friends like Samantha, and I told him, "No one does. She's not real." He seemed disappointed.

chocolate, around 8:00 p.m.? Or on a Friday or Saturday? What would become of me? Now I knew.

Our villas were at the south end of the street. When Chalak took us out and about, we would drive to the middle roundabout and turn right to exit the compound. Had he continued north, two blocks past the roundabout, we would have run into the store. The "store" was a tiny, dusty shack at the end of our compound, with a flashy neon "open" sign, and blocks of soda cans (still no Diet Coke) stacked up right outside the door. Inside the store? So much more. It was a very tiny space, maybe around fifteen square feet, but this was the place to go if you needed peanut M&Ms (yes, please), Baghdad-brand potato chips, cigarettes, toothbrushes, diapers, phone cards, ice cream, cowboy hats, and spangled belt buckles. This place was our very own 7-Eleven, and I was practically shrieking with joy. There is no substitute for close proximity of snacks. PMS is a merciless mistress, and she does not cotton to the MacGyver'd snacks of your almost-empty cupboards. Butter doused in sugar packets and cocoa powder does not a cookie make.

Proximity of convenience store = convenient. Even more convenient? When the store comes to you. "The produce truck is here! The produce truck is here!" I would shout, to no one in particular, when the low-riding fruit-and-vegetable-laden pickup rolled down our street in the Village. The produce truck would stop right across the street in front of the neighbor's villa (she was a regular), and while it didn't have the lilting "Do your ears hang low..." song churning out of a crackly megaphone, the honk of the truck's horn elicited the same ice cream truck reaction I used to have when I was eight.

I would run out, wave to the produce man, then point to the fruits and vegetables that I wanted, and the nice man would put them on the scale with a half-kilo weight, then put them into a small blue plastic bag that smelled faintly of body odor. I would have to scrub the produce after taking it out of the blue plastic bag, but other than that the produce truck was awesome.

The first time I went out to the truck, the nice produce man looked surprised. I don't think he expected Westerners here. He realized I probably didn't speak Kurdish, and we had to muddle through the transaction with charades. The next time, when handing my 1,000-dinar notes to him, he said, in halting English, "Three. One, two, three," indicating that my total was 3,000 dinar (which is around $3.50). I exclaimed "Ah!" to indicate my grateful surprise that he spoke a little English.

The convenience was overwhelming. The truck drives right onto my block and the driver speaks a little English? This was fantastic, as I was not making any kind of effort to learn the local language. So much for assimilating. I learned "Thank you" ("Spass"), and that had served me well so far. In fact, I could say "thank you" in thirteen different languages, as I found it to be the absolute most useful phrase. Everyone loves "thank you." Plus, remember, I also spoke fluent Friendly Smile.

Reasons I was not learning Kurdish:

- I am lazy.
- I am terrible with languages (other than English).
- I wouldn't have been able to use Kurdish anywhere else.
- The Kurdish language differs from city to city.

Most languages have dialect differences for different regions, but several Westerners here had confirmed that there were actually different Kurdish words for the same things, depending on the city. A Swedish woman, who lived in English Village and worked for a nongovernmental organization, told me how she had been studying Kurdish and was very proud of herself for finally learning how to order a cup of tea. She took a weekend trip down to Suli, where she attempted to order tea in her newly learned Kurdish tongue and was met with confused looks. She was eventually told that the word for spoon was something totally different than what she had learned. I just didn't want to risk that kind of frustration. And also, as noted, I am lazy.

I truly did appreciate the struggles that my students went through. Learning a language is hard. In addition to my multilingual capacity for "thank you," I spoke Vacation Spanish and Menu French, and even still struggled with those on occasion.

ᘒᘓᘒ

Lazy loves convenience. I would wake up every day around 10:30 a.m., watch a little TV, occasionally run out to the produce truck, eat lunch, and spend some time on the Internet until I had to prepare for the three hours of evening class. That was my extremely demanding schedule. When I told my family and friends at home about it, they would gasp indignantly, then cry, "That is not fair!" before remembering where I was, and then say, "Oh, yeah."

Being able to communicate with people at home was such a luxury. Facebook and Skype were making up for that horribly lonely year in South Korea, where I was in a state of perpetual desperation for any phone calls or letters from home. Having access to the Internet was excellent, and at the same time, kind of scary. I discovered that, even all the way in The Iraq, I could shop online. I had unfettered access to Barneys, Bergdorf Goodman, Net-a-Porter and the Outnet, and my favorite Italian high-end discount site, YOOX (which my mom consistently, and incorrectly, pronounced "Yocks").

After successfully transferring two monthly paychecks into my bank account, back in the United States, I was ready to reward myself with a new pair of shoes. I mean, another new pair of shoes, in addition to the shoes I had purchased in Paris. Those were specific vacation shoes and didn't really count. I was on the slow climb out of my personal recession, and it was shoe time. Over the past couple of years I had begun to turn up my nose at affordable shoes in my tax bracket in favor of any ridiculously overpriced, high-end brand I could find: Gucci, Burberry, Ferragamo, Prada (but only if I could find them on the clearance rack—I did have some boundaries). I would still blame my mom and the fashion magazines for this.

When I discovered that I could shop online in The Iraq, I was both "Wheeee!" and "Oh." I had to resign myself to the reality that I would have to have the shoes delivered to my parents' house in Oregon. The mail system in Iraq was far too sketchy to expect anything, especially anything of value, to show up as requested. "Isn't that kind of anticlimactic?" my friend Sally asked, "I mean, you will buy something, and then you won't get to wear it right away." I thought about this, and yes, she did have a point.

However, I planned to fly home for summer vacation in July, and would then get to open any and all boxes that had been delivered. So it would really be like a second Christmas.

The aforementioned YOOX, my favorite site, was an Italian company that sold overstock and past-season pieces from the widest variety of designers. Everything in the company's standard inventory was marked down 50%, and the site would increase the fun periodically by reducing the prices even more—all the way down to 90% off. I loved % off, especially with "90" in front of it. My shoe-addict friends back home would email me photos of their latest shoe coups, and I would try not to cry about having missed out on the massive clearance sale at The Nordstrom Rack.

I had introduced Sally to YOOX, as she was a high-end label whore herself, but she said YOOX gave her a headache. "There's just too *much*." She was right. In the designer index there were approximately two hundred labels, for each letter of the alphabet. But I loved a challenge, and YOOX made the whole experience fantasylike by offering a Dream Box, where you could put up to fifty items over which you were drooling, but you wouldn't actually have to buy them. I liked to think of it as my virtual closet. I could wear the things in my virtual closet to imaginary events held in my head, and being isolated in a gated community in Northern Iraq meant there were many, many imaginary events. But the online shopping was mostly like therapy for me. It really just relaxed me to log on, forget the world outside, and click through the pages and pages of beautiful things.

One pair of beautiful things made its way from my Dream Box into my shopping cart, and I am now the proud owner of handmade, gray leather Golden Goose riding boots. I could see someone snarkily asking, "Oh, riding boots? So you *ride*?" Yes, I ride. I ride bikes, and I ride in cars, and I ride on subways and trains, and those boots normally retailed for around $1,000, and YOOX let me have them for $390. Ride that.

Oh my God, I finally had money! I could actually buy things! Granted, $390 was not parking-meter change and was the second-highest amount I had ever paid for a pair of footwear (see: Paris trip and Louboutin purchase). But they were handmade. And so, so, SO pretty. And I didn't have to justify my shopping to anyone. I was the boss of me! As I pointed out to my reproachful mother, in addition to a large salary increase, I was no longer paying $1,000 each month for rent. My rationalization was, I should at least have been allowed to spend that amount on shopping. Suze Orman may have disagreed with this logic.

∽∾∽∾∽

After our initial restaurant excursion, Adam and I rarely left the gated compound, what with our newfound über convenience and all. We did still have the need for weekly Chalak-escorted trips to the grocery store for nonconvenient-store fare or to pick up other necessities (wine and beer), but otherwise we kept to ourselves in the compound. This was disappointing to my dad, who really wanted me to "get out and mingle with the locals."

On the few occasions that I had been in a car at night, I noticed that the streets were lit up and lively, with people sitting out at sidewalk tables and walking around. It looked fun and social!

Upon closer inspection I realized these people were all men, and it was no longer fun and social. It was eerie and creepy. It was post-pubescent *Lord of the Flies*, you know, before they all lost their minds and started eating one another.

Apparently, if women here were out and about at night, unaccompanied by a man, they were assumed to be, to quote Dalzar and Renas, "bad women." Of course they were. Women were all whores and would, I think I'm remembering Warren's words correctly, "screw anything that walked." I explained to my dad that I was perfectly happy just mingling with my students. They were local enough.

I had wondered about actual prostitutes and whether they had them in Northern Iraq. I was sure they did; it was the oldest profession in the world, and we were in one of the oldest cities in the world.*

I had seen groups of Ethiopian women walking around English Village and had learned they were employed as villa cleaners by many of the businesses and families there. It was rumored that a few of them also moonlighted as prostitutes.

I found myself wondering, again, "Are things in Ethiopia worse than here? Really?" I tried to predict where my friends would go if the only options I gave them were 1) Bangladesh, 2) Ethiopia, or 3) Iraq. I am confident that Iraq would come in last. I'm also confident my friends would be pissed that those were the only options I was giving them.

---

*There is an ongoing debate among several Middle Eastern cities as to which one is the oldest continuously inhabited city in the world. Erbil is one of the contenders, as are Damascus, Syria; Varanasi, India; Byblos, Lebanon; and Jericho. Erbil residents were constantly reminding us of how it was one of the original civilizations. Okay, then, let's show some respect for your oldest continuously inhabited city and spruce up the squalor a little.

There was a handful of expats who lived and worked in English Village. A British attorney named Joanna told me about the time she went to Ainkawa for Chinese food. Joanna had been excited about the prospect of eating something other than hummus and chicken kebabs and had passed a Chinese restaurant one day while driving in Ainkawa, so she and a male coworker decided to try it for lunch. When they walked through the doorway of the restaurant, Joanna saw that there were several Chinese women standing around and every one of them just stared at her, wide-eyed. Joanna and her coworker were then seated and given menus, but the entire time the women stared at her strangely. They ordered, then ate their meals, paid, and left. She said the food was just okay, but the atmosphere was uneasy, and the Chinese women just stood off to the side, watching her.

Joanna was later talking about the experience to an American Army guy she knew, and he started laughing and then explained to her that the Chinese "restaurant" was actually a brothel.

e~e~e

I did not need a Chinese restaurant. Not only did I not like Chinese food, but I knew, coming here, that I would be doing without many things: Starbucks, wine bars, sushi restaurants, the Nordstrom half-yearly sale, a washing machine. Wait. I did not think a washing machine would be one of those things. But our Erbil villas did not come equipped with a washer or dryer. The teachers at the main university in Suli all had washing machines in their villas, but for some reason, no one thought we, up here in

Erbil, might want to have clean clothing. Warren's solution was "Take everything to the dry cleaner!" His blatant disregard for my finances was irksome. First the hockey bags, now the dry cleaners.

I had obviously not learned my lesson with his advice for the hockey bags, when I decided to have my clothes dry-cleaned. Everything but the dainties. I would hand wash my bras and underwear the same way everyone else living in developing nations did it: in the bathtub with Woolite. I could only imagine the potential confusion that would ensue if I sent twenty pairs of thong underwear to the Kurdish cleaners.

After my once-color-fast clothing came back from the Erbil dry cleaner in various stages of non-color-fastness (I am now fully stocked with pale pink T-shirts and socks that used to be white), I decided I would need to be the boss of *all* of my clothes and wash everything in the bathtub with Woolite. I also finally decided to stop listening to Warren's advice. Warren's advice was increasingly inconvenient.

Chapter Fourteen

Shopping, BBQing, and Santa Claus

Here I shop, there I shop, everywhere I shop, shop. The riding-boot purchase triggered my spending impulses. It made no difference that I was in a country whose name was synonymous with political turmoil and danger. No, no, I still managed to make it all about shopping, and when Adam and I took one of our monthly weekend trips down to Suli to do our bank transfers, I made certain I had time to shop.

When I traveled to Suli on those weekends, Warren arranged for me to stay in the spare room in Jen's villa, and we had subsequently become friends. She totally wasn't a skank. Warren should have nicknamed her Buddha: she did yoga and meditated and emanated a relaxing, Zen vibe. It was such a relief to have another female to talk to, and finally to have someone to shop with. On her way to school, Jen had seen a store with mannequins in the window, wearing Western clothing, so we had one of the drivers take us there one Friday.

They say first impressions are everything. As we entered the store, my first impression was, "Holy crap, this looks like Banana Republic." To my knowledge, the Banana had not yet opened a store anywhere in Iraq, but there was a lovely Kurdish salesgirl, assisting the customers, probably saying something like, "You can belt it! Cinch it!"

The sign above the entrance said "Istanbul Bazaar"; Istanbul was not in Iraq; it was in Turkey, but I was willing to overlook the seeming discrepancy if it meant new Capri pants.

"Istanbul Bazaar" was also emblazoned on the many festive balloons strung up in bunches around the store. During the shopping excursion one of these balloons popped, making a loud noise that sounded like a gun firing, which caused me to shriek and have a very small heart attack for a second, but I quickly recovered.

To engender the idea that the Iraqi people really weren't *so* different from you and me, I made note of the fact that the dressing room was littered with clothing, just as it would be at Banana Republic back home. That's right. Those bitches were just as lazy as we were, and wouldn't hang the clothes back up after trying them on. I was pretty sure I heard one of them say, "What? I don't work here," in Kurdish.

I am not only a claustrophobe; I am also a shopping savant. (Self-diagnosing is a very big thing with me.) And as shopping savants know, one of the most delirium-inducing symbols is the percentage sign. You know, our friend %. We loved %! Jen had seen signs around the store, covered in 50 percent, and assumed that everything in the store was 50 percent off. However, upon closer inspection, we recognized the fine print. I say "recognized" because it was in Kurdish, and we couldn't read it. In a nutshell, as translated to us by the nice cashier lady, it stated that we would receive 50 percent off our purchase, which would be "refunded" us in the form of Maximall Dollars. Maximall was the sister store to Istanbul Bazaar and conveniently offered locations in both Suli *and* Erbil. We were practically being ordered to shop more. The Iraq was a very strict place.

So, we left the store with a few cute, appropriately long-sleeved blouses and the aforementioned Maximall Dollars, which resembled U.S. currency, right down to Abraham Lincoln's picture. I was proud to be helping Iraq rebuild their economy.

I also continued to assist the economy of Italy. I bought silver Prada loafers at YOOX online.

ℯⁿℯⁿℯⁿ

That same weekend, there was a university barbecue held at one of the villas. Just like at Tara! We could wear our dresses and petticoats and ignore the talk about war! I suddenly wanted a big hat with a chin ribbon.

The barbecue gave me the chance to properly meet some of the staff and faculty, as my first few days back in March had been such a blur. It was so great to see so many Westerners milling around and so much barbecue fare on the picnic table. Potato salad, ribs, cheeseburgers, and no hummus or chicken kebabs anywhere. Chancellor Tom Pappas was there, and I thought, "Excellent, I can finally have a conversation with him while wearing something more appropriate than jammies, and hopefully produce a more positive impression than whiny jammies wearer."

I made polite, barbecue small talk with Chancellor Tom while waiting for the burgers to be cooked. We talked about the university, vacation time, and small-talky small talk, and I did an excellent job of ignoring the mental image of him bursting into Adam's room wearing tighty-whities, but then Chancellor Tom steered the conversation in a weird direction and was suddenly confiding that he used to be a musician. Oh? He played guitar. Is that so? He *almost* had a recording contract, a while back.

I nodded and thought, "Uh-huh. Is he hitting on me? It feels like a hitting-on-me kind of conversation now. I don't want him hitting on me. Wasn't I just politely discussing vacation time? Wasn't I just a whiny underling? I want to go back to being a whiny underling." The conversation felt just the tiniest bit wrong, like when you put one of your contacts in backward. To extricate myself from the awkwardness, I exclaimed, "My cheeseburger is ready!" and steered over to Jen and the other teachers.

There's something disconcerting not only in feeling like your boss's boss is hitting on you, but also in discovering that he wished he were somewhere else, doing something else. I didn't want to picture Chancellor Tom strumming a six-string and soulfully crooning into a microphone while having panties thrown at his head, or saying things like, "Yeah, the new track drops on Thursday, baby." I wanted to see him interacting with the students and tossing around ideas for curriculum development or something. I, idealistically, wanted my superiors to be enthusiastic about their jobs; enthusiastic, forthright and trustworthy and compassionate and jolly and grandfatherly. Yes, if they had to be men, I wanted my bosses to be jolly and grandfatherly. I wanted to work for Santa Claus. I trusted Santa Claus. Santa would never really wish he was a musician.

ℰℯℯℯ

A few weeks after the barbecue, Warren said to me, "I probably shouldn't tell you this, but..." I must admit that is my absolute *favorite* beginning to any conversation and said, "Yes, please go on." He went on, "Tom paid you a really big compliment." Uh-oh. I just nodded and said hesitantly, "Uh-huh," suddenly very sure that I did not want to hear what came next. Warren, oblivious to the strained tone in my "Uh-huh," continued, "Yeah, he was like 'You know, as big of a pain in my ass as Gretchen is, I absolutely love that girl.'"

Only Warren would consider that a compliment. As far as being a big pain in the ass, I could only speculate that it was a combination of (1) not being a welcome wagon at 10:30 p.m., (2) collecting a higher salary than the other teachers in the department, and (3) making presumed divalike demands.

I will explain.

While Warren had proudly informed me of my higher-than-expected salary, before I signed my contract and came out to Iraq, what he had neglected to tell me was that no one else in our department was making that much. Once I arrived in Suli he admitted this to me and said that the provost of the university and Chancellor Tom had both balked at the salary amount after visiting the Erbil campus. "We're paying her *more* to be up here? We should be paying her *less*!"

Warren had also warned me not to tell anyone how much I was making, but then felt free enough, himself, to run around cawing about it. He had managed to get me $10,000 more than the other instructors by presenting Erbil as somewhat of a hardship: we were more isolated (true), we didn't have the support or structure of the main university (true), and we essentially lived in our workspace (true). I didn't even receive a formal orientation, like the one given to all other faculty and staff in Suli; I was just sort of set afloat on my proverbial Erbil raft. It really *was* more of a hardship, but the provost and chancellor saw only manicured lawns, spacious villas, and a pristine neighborhood environment.

I finally decided to ask for a washing machine for the Erbil villas. It was absurd that we didn't at least have one, between Adam and me. It wasn't as much of a problem for Adam, since he went down to Suli every weekend and just used the washing machines there, but I needed to do laundry more than once a month, on our bank-transfer trips. When I made the request, Warren said, "Okay, but you have to ask for a dryer too."

But I did not need a dryer, I tried to explain to him. You could hang clothes on the stair railing and they were dry in twenty minutes. It was a dry heat. I just needed a washer. You could practically hear the banjo music blaring out of my villa as I hovered over the tub, scrubbing away like Granny Freaking Clampett, and I was nursing a perpetual backache from trying to thoroughly rinse the clothes. "If you don't request a dryer," Warren threatened, "you won't get a washer." Since Warren made occasional trips up to Erbil, he wanted the dryer for himself. He also wanted to make sure I was seen as the one whining about it. I surrendered the argument, and emailed the formal request for a washer and dryer, ultimately cementing my role as whiny pain in the ass.

Santa wouldn't have made me beg for a washing machine.

Chapter Fifteen

Serenity Later

That initial scary nighttime surprise-chancellor visit was just the first of many infringements on my desperately needed privacy. One Friday afternoon, back up in Erbil, Rana, the HR director, called me at 2:00 p.m. and simply said, "Do you have extra room in your villa?"

Although Warren was always ranting about Rana's apparent stupidity, I had to admit this was an ingenious way in which to phrase that question. "Do you have extra room?" Of course I had extra room. I had three extra rooms. I was caught off guard and so responded, "Um, yeah." She asked if she and another female coworker from the university could stay in my villa that night. I responded with a hesitant, "Sure."

This was not a social call, in the interest of spending time, being friendly, and getting to know the new Erbil girl (me). This was a request for a free crash pad for Rana and her friend Carey, the finance director who had shared my immigration experience with me. I liked Carey, and Rana had seemed nice enough when I had met her back in March, but I had had no further interaction with either of them since my arrival week at the school. There had

SSe

been no emails or phone calls to see how I was settling in or if I needed anything (like extra pencils or a washing machine). Rana seemed to ignore the "human" part of human resources. I would have loved to have visitors (hooray, new friends!) if I thought they were there to see me. This was not the case.

Scarlett had to deal with this in *Gone with the Wind*. Once the Civil War ended...

> Tara suddenly lost its isolation. And for months there-after a stream of scarecrows, bearded, ragged, footsore and always hungry, toiled up the red hill to Tara and came to rest on the shady front steps, wanting food and a night's lodging.

Dang freeloaders. When they arrived, Rana announced they were going to dinner with her brother and some friends, so they weren't expecting food, but Rana also did not invite me to join them. Mammy would have stood, sturdy arms crossed over her chest, shaking her head and clucking her disapproval at the poor guest etiquette.

When they returned from dinner and started getting ready for bed, Rana began complaining the pillows in Warren's room smelled.

"Are these sheets clean?" she demanded, her nose wrinkled in disdain. I was standing in the hallway, thinking about how she had called me a short three hours before arriving, and wondered if she had expected me to run around washing sheets and towels, and drying them in my new fancy dryer, for her arrival. I shrugged and admitted that I didn't know if they were clean. It was Warren's room.

Rana then set about opening other doors, searching for a more suitable sleeping situation for herself. She turned up her nose at the empty room with the single bed, as it did not come equipped with an air conditioner. In my opinion the only room suitable for her at this point would be one with one hundred mattresses piled up and a small pea in between the first and second mattress. Carey seemed fine with sleeping in Warren's bed, even with the prospect of smelly pillowcases.

Rana opened another door and said, "Why can't I just sleep in here?" I could almost hear Mammy saying, "Aw no you don't." I smiled tightly and answered, "That's my room." Imagine all those Confederate soldiers showing up at Tara, then stomping around the rooms, smelling the pillowcases and complaining, when they should have just been grateful they had a free place to stay.

I used to think I enjoyed nicknames that began with "Princess," but now I could see that you really had to earn a title like that. I could not believe how inconsiderate this girl was. She invited herself to stay at my house, didn't invite me out to dinner, complained about the quality of the bedding, and then expected to sleep in my room.

After they left the following morning, I called Warren and told him the entire story. "This was more of a hotel than a house!" I wailed. "Why do people just expect to come up here and stay in our villas? I have no privacy!" Privacy was so important to me, and I had thought I had communicated that to Warren during our many phone conversations and emails prior to my coming here. I missed my cozy one-bedroom apartment in Seattle, where it was just me and Herb. No smelly drivers, no "SURPRISE" chancellors, and no obnoxious, ungracious HR directors with an unfounded sense of entitlement.

That we lived where we taught was already kind of a challenge. There were random Kurds ringing my doorbell at indiscriminate hours of the day and evening—and on the weekends—showing up to inquire about English classes, and now staff and faculty, who viewed Erbil as an exciting weekend-getaway destination, expecting to come up and stay in our villas. I was losing my sanity. Warren claimed he understood and kept saying, "Gretch, that's *your* villa, it's YOUR villa." *How? How was it MY villa?*

I had finally put my foot down about the male drivers sleeping in my villa. There were about twenty different drivers who inter-changeably chauffeured people and supplies up to Erbil. I'd never met many of them, and they would just come in and make them-selves at home, preparing their dinners in my kitchen, helping themselves to my precious Diet Cokes. My cooperative veneer promptly shattered when one night I was sitting and watching TV, trying to ignore the fact that the hairy, hulking Ahmed had to stay overnight and was in the room downstairs, talking loudly on his cell phone. I was uncomfortable enough just knowing he was there, and the discomfort amplified every time I heard him bark into the phone. I was trying to immerse myself in an old episode of *Friends* when I saw that Ahmed had finished his phone call and was slowly and inexplicably making his way up the stairs.

GAH! The drivers know they're not allowed upstairs! FARK! I leapt from the couch out into the hallway and leaned over the balcony.

"Yes? What do you need?" Ahmed was carrying a plate with

some plums on it, and a can of soda, and held these items up as an explanation.

"No, thank you!" I could feel myself growing shrill, which was annoying. I hate shrill, but I was entering panic mode, with this essential stranger encroaching on my personal space.

Ahmed said, "For you!" and continued his slow climb up the stairs. GOD DAMMIT! (*Women are all whores…probably definitely single American women…*)

"NO!" I shouted, as he clearly wasn't getting the hint with my polite/stern voice, "PLEASE TAKE THAT TO THE KITCHEN, THANK YOU!" Ahmed looked irritated and said angrily, "It's for YOU!" His threatening tone was enough confirmation that I was justified in yelling, and I answered, "YES, THANK YOU VERY MUCH; PLEASE LEAVE IT *IN THE KITCHEN.*" He finally turned around and retreated to the main floor with the fruit plate and soda.

I had been double-locking my bedroom door at night and turned the key extra hard that night, just in case there was a triple-lock option. I did not feel safe, and not even the image of Joey wearing every piece of Chandler's clothing could perk me up. Jen later confided, "I can't believe you put up with that for as long as you did. I would have freaked."

After the disastrous Rana weekend, Warren said he would make it clear that no faculty or staff would be staying in "my" villa uninvited. Although he really seemed more bothered by the fact that Rana said his pillowcases smelled bad.

✏✏✏

Warren confided that Chancellor Tom had developed a casual theory about why Rana and I didn't get along. I thought it was just because she had poor manners and a wackadoo sense of entitlement, but Tom explained to Warren that Rana and I were both lionesses. We were both "strong, attractive women" and felt threatened by one another, had to prove our prowess, blah blah blah. I found it difficult to listen and roll my eyes at the same time and am not sure how the theory concluded, but I imagined it probably involved wrestling around in fur bikinis, a la Raquel Welch in *One Million Years B.C.*

Dear Santa,

Please consider the position of Chancellor at this University in Iraq. The climate might be a bit of an adjustment for you, but I would promise to help you with the Nice and Naughty lists, and I could probably find some people to help make the toys.

Sincerely,
Gretchen

Adam was technically living in Erbil with me, but only during the week. He went down to Suli every weekend, and yes, often-times people stayed in his villa too; he was just rarely there to deal with it. Adam had spent the prior semester working at the main university and enjoyed the Suli compound social life in the less-picturesque, but infinitely more private, moderately Soviet-looking concrete villas, with all the front-porch beer drinking and testosterone bonding and whatnot. We got along really well and had fun during the week, but Adam wasn't teaching any classes and was bored to tears. He was also pretty miserable, being so isolated up in Erbil, not to mention thousands of miles away from his fiancée. Not even the *Sex and the City* marathons could cheer him up, so Warren would send a driver to fetch him on the weekends.

I had to limit my Suli trips to the monthly bank runs. It was a three-hour drive through topsy-turvy mountains and wasn't something I wanted to do twice a week. Since we all make choices in our lives, and my choice was a sort of self-imposed isolation, I found things to love and keep me sane in Erbil.

1. **Facebook and Skype:** Technology helped connect me to my old life back home, and at least let me talk to, and look at, my supportive friends and family.

2. **Food:** The stores finally got Diet Coke, I became very friendly with Nutella, and there were peanut M&Ms and Snickers bars to remind me of the Western World.

3. **My new blender**, which I quickly fell madly in love with: It cost an incomprehensible $26, and was glass, with an apple-green base and rubber lid. It encouraged me to consume the requisite two to four servings of fruit per day in the form of smoothies, which *almost* counterbalanced the Nutella and candy bars.

I also did the unthinkable and purchased a bathroom scale.

There was a *60 Minutes* piece on *Vogue* editor Anna Wintour, where she claimed the scale at the *Vogue* offices was simply there for the purpose of weighing luggage and not making certain that all perpetually hungry employees felt daily body shame. Whether that was true, when I heard that I thought, *"Brilliant!"* and immediately ran out to get my scale.

I would never pay fees for overweight luggage again. NEVAH! (Here is where I visualized Me-As-Triumphant-Scarlett-O'Hara, or Me-As-Triumphant-Joan-of-Arc or She-Ra. I mean, how does She-Ra get around the overweight baggage fees? Her outfits are all made of metal.)

∾∾∾

There were other, unexpected joys in Erbil, the newfound Paris of Northern Iraq. One of them was Bakery & More, the Lebanese-run bakery Adam and I tried to walk to that one day. After being driven there by Chalak, I realized how far off we had been. Although it would have been worth the extra hour of walking.

Bakery & More offered croissants, cookies, cakes, and other fancy baked goods and had a refrigerated case with deli meats and cheeses on the first floor and a small restaurant on the second floor. The restaurant upstairs offered pizzas, sandwiches, and my Holy Grail of hangover cuisine: mozzarella sticks. *Naughty cheese.* This was officially one of my Happy Places. One of the men who worked there always gave me a big grin and a wave when I walked in, and then he would sneak me a couple of pieces of chocolate when no one else was looking.

Given the endless parade of sugar and fat, I really needed to find some way to work out. The Women's Fitness Center had been frightening, it was a million degrees outside (which killed the idea of just running around English Village), and my *Biggest Loser Workout* DVDs had lost their allure. Adam was still researching women's gyms, in hopeful anticipation of his fiancée coming to join him here. His fiancée would not have been okay with the bird-doody, broken-down equipment, velour-tracksuited aerobics gym, so he kept searching until he found the J&K, a mere five minutes' drive from the Village, very close to Ainkawa.

It was probably slightly sacrilegious for me to call the J&K Women's Fitness Center "Mecca," but I did anyway. You did have to pay to experience Mecca (about $15 per visit), but it was worth it. The entrance displayed a lush, finely manicured lawn and the lobby was a study in sprawling luxury. I mean, yes, it was still understated Trump, although with purple accents, rather than the usual gold leaf. There was an actual workout room, with actual, plugged-in cardio machines.

The workout room overlooked an Olympic-size swimming pool, where women wore bathing suits. Not the futuristic, confining burkinis, but regular tanks or even two-pieces. Men were not allowed inside J&K, so the women roamed about freely, wearing whatever they liked. One heavyset woman even liked running on the treadmill in her bikini. To each her own, and go sister, go.

Mecca, naturally, had a day spa. There was an honest-to-goodness nail salon, where I spent a deluxe hour getting a completely professional pedicure from a charming woman named Sangela. She was a godsend, and God sent her from Nepal. I have been to Nepal, and absolutely loved it, and therefore could not understand why she came here. I asked her why she left, and she said she could make more money here. I guess that shouldn't have been so hard to understand, since *I* could make more money here too. The Kurdish women who ran the salon were dismissive and abrupt with Sangela, which irritated me, and I wasn't certain but thought it might have been just because she was Nepalese. If no one was looking, I would slip her a little extra money before I paid the women at the counter.

It was weird to witness racism here, but I had seen and heard of Kurds talking about the Ethiopians and Bangladeshis like they were no better than animals. I felt like this was probably a backlash, because that is exactly how many Arabs and Turks (and some Europeans) viewed the Kurds. When will people learn to simply judge others by their shoes? It's so much more civilized. Crocs, you are low man on the totem pole.

So, aside from the possible racism of the Kurdish salon women, the J&K was another one of my Happy Places and a veritable bastion of serenity. Rumor around town was that the owner of the J&K had been granted $500,000 from the U.S. government in order to set up a women's refuge. I did consider the J&K to be a refuge, but probably not the kind the U.S. government had in mind.

Chapter Sixteen

Actual Assimilation

The next time I went down to the university in Suli I was careful to avoid Chancellor Tom's office. I only spent one day each month at the main university, and it usually consisted of floating between the teachers' office, the bank, the cafeteria, and Warren's office. I always looked forward to seeing Jen, and the other teachers, and some of the local Kurds who worked at the university, in particular the tea-and-coffee-boy Daroon.

Daroon was unwittingly instrumental in my assimilating into the Kurdish culture. Thus far, I had really only made an effort to incorporate things into my Iraq life that reminded me of home: Diet Coke, wine, Snickers bars, a day spa. That wasn't assimilating; it was procrastinating. Enter Daroon and His Magical Turkish Coffee.

Everyone adored Daroon. We would describe him as mellow in temperament and sweet in disposition. He always greeted you, arms extending with upraised palms, with a slight nod of the head, and a humble "Welcome."

Daroon called me "Flower," which was a much better nickname than "Gerts." Dara, one of the other teachers, had a six-year-old daughter whom Daroon called "Baby Flower," so Dara was subsequently "Mother Baby Flower." I later discovered that he called most of the female teachers "Flower," but that didn't make the nickname any less appealing. I would take compliments where I could get them. Whenever I was sitting in the teachers' room, Daroon would come in, look surprised to see me, and say, "Oh! Flower! Welcome, Flower."

Daroon, in addition to being a charming presence, made fantastic Turkish coffee. I tried to resist it at first, when Warren attempted to talk me into having a cup. I was finally learning to ignore Warren's suggestions. Baby steps. I explained to him that I hated coffee, and it didn't matter which country it came from. Warren refused my refusal. He had Daroon bring two Turkish coffees up to the office, in cute little china cups with saucers, which I eyed suspiciously after thanking Daroon for welcoming me. I squinted into the little cup, sniffed at it, and whined that I didn't want to drink it. Yes, *whined*. I really didn't want to drink it. Coffee was nasty. Warren rolled his eyes and said, "Just try it. You might like it, you might not. Just try it."

This was the Warren I liked. He wasn't calling anyone a skank; he wasn't wearing his Terminator sunglasses, gesturing wildly with a cigarette while making fart jokes; and he wasn't giving me the used-car-salesman hard sell about something I might not like. Of course, he also wasn't listening to me when I said I hated coffee.

I took a few sips. It wasn't bitter like normal coffee. It was strong but had a slight sweetness to it and was delicious. I loved it. I loved coffee! I was assimilating *and* being grown-up. I associated coffee drinking with grown-ups, and I never quite fit into that ideal. I was jealous of the grown-up coffee drinkers, always running around waving their Starbucks cups. When I found that I could get a chai latte in one of those cups I was thrilled. I could just fake being a grown-up.

Warren was pleased that I liked the Turkish coffee and patted himself on the back for suggesting it. It was such a welcome change to have him back like this. We just hung out in his office for an hour or so, talking, joking around, and drinking our Turkish coffee. I missed this Warren.

The Turkish coffees became a habit, and I drank them every time I went to Suli. I was a grown-up, Turkish-coffee-drinking flower who was *assimilating*. Warren should also be given credit for introducing me to za'atar, which, while not specific to Iraq, was very Middle Eastern and very awesome. It was kind of like a flatbread pizza with green herbs and sesame seeds and other spices, and we could get it at Bakery & More. Sometimes I would get crazy and eat za'atar and drink Turkish coffee at the same time.

Assimilating meant more than just consuming what the locals did. It also included dressing as the locals dressed. Contrary to my prior beliefs, burkas were not commonly worn in Kurdistan. I had yet to see one. I did see some hijabs/niqabs, which were the headscarves, and abayas, which were basically burkas minus the face-covering. The abaya looked similar to a nun's habit.

YOOX didn't sell nuns' habits, so I sometimes struggled with what to wear in Iraq. I wanted to be careful not to offend anyone, and remembered the Cultural Awareness pamphlet's "dress code" section. I had been trying to pay attention to what the local women were wearing.

After several months of close observation, I had reaffirmed my original conclusion: showing skin was bad, but covering your entire body with skintight clothing was perfectly fine. I was really surprised to see that so many women wore colorful tops with skinny jeans and high heels. Now, they may have been wearing those skinny jeans and heels with a hijab, but still. Also confusing to me was the seeming disparity between what was deemed sartorially acceptable and what was being sold in the clothing stores.

On another shopping excursion with Jen (we had to use my Maximall dollars), I was sitting in one of the comfy, loungy chairs set in the middle of the store, waiting for Jen to come out of the dressing room, and watching one of the friendly salesgirls arrange a rack of clothing. She looked at me, smiled, then selected a pair of Barbie-size denim hot pants from the rack. She hugged them to her chest, with the same dreamy, faraway look in her eyes that I get when talking about my love of cheese. I said, "Ahhh," aloud and laughed with her, but then found myself thinking "Can she even wear those? Where can she wear those?" Even with tights or leggings underneath, hot pants would still be pretty racy.

The only racy part of my Iraq ensembles these days were my shoes. Since my "commute" simply involved my walking down the stairs and into the classroom, there was no danger of my shoes being defiled by any of the dust, dirt, mud, or trash of the Kurdistan streets. There was an episode of *Sex and the City* where

Carrie went to Paris and accidentally stepped in dog poop in her Christian Louboutin pumps, and it made me cry a little.

My solution to the requirement of dressing nonoffensively was wearing Capri pants under just about everything. On one particular occasion I was wearing a loose safari/khaki sort of short-sleeved shirtdress with black Capri pants underneath (and Jean Paul Gaultier gladiators).

Dalzar had spent several minutes of class ranting about the fact that women in his office dressed like they were going to a nightclub. I was distractedly excited at the prospect of there being a nightclub in Erbil. I hadn't been dancing in ages. I gasped, "There are nightclubs in Erbil?!" to which he looked at me blankly and said, "No."

Deflated, I asked, "Then how do you know how women in nightclubs dress?" He simply answered, "TV." Dalzar then looked me up and down and declared, "Okay, you give Kurdish woman, uhhhhh, one million dinar? She not wear what you wear."

Renas stared at Dalzar, mouth slightly agape.

> **Me:** Okay...
> **Dalzar:** One million dinar, and Kurdish woman still not
> wear that.

One million dinar is around $100,000. It's a sizable sum to turn down.

> **Me:** Why not?
> **Dalzar:** Because it is not sexy for the man!

Cue uncontrollable laughter. It was the kind of doubled-over laughing where you can't really catch your breath, and there is wheezing and eye-watering, and you're seriously hoping you don't fart. This continued for about a minute, with me sobbing and laughing, while Dalzar and Renas just stared at me, perplexed. It was honestly one of the funniest things Dalzar had said in class, and he said a lot of funny stuff. I had to wave my hand back and forth, shaking my head, indicating I really couldn't explain my reaction to them.

I mentally filed the khaki shirtdress/black Capri pants ensemble into my "totally acceptable" outfit list. This assimilating thing was easy.

Chapter Seventeen

Inshallah

Renas and Dalzar were keeping me entertained, and I was trying to keep them engaged in the learning process. It was still making me crazy that Renas constantly spelled people "peaple." And Dalzar spelled "their" like "thier," although I had friends on Facebook who did this. There are a lot of Americans who can't spell.

Dalzar continued to bulldoze through conversations but was getting much better about listening, as I practically barked, "DALZAR! LISTEN!" at him frequently. He responded by pausing, nodding his head, smiling, and saying, "Yes!" with a flourish. Every time.

I instructed Dalzar do a couple of things that may have seemed unconventional in the teaching realm: quit smoking and watch *Oprah*.

Smoking was just a nasty habit. Watching *Oprah* was just good common sense (and would help Dalzar with his listening comprehension). After watching several episodes, Dalzar came to class one day and said, "I think…uhhhh…people like her very much— the black woman."

He had no idea. That was something else that perpetually

astonished me: how little the Kurds knew of the outside world. I had to keep reminding myself that they had been completely cut off from anything beyond the Iraqi borders throughout most of the 1970s, '80s, and '90s. I'm not sure when international television station broadcasts were permitted in Kurdistan, and that undoubtedly helped inform people about the outside world. But even in 2009 there were restrictions on which Kurds could even apply for passports. The students had never even heard of The Beatles.

Dalzar had a loud, sharp cough that often distracted from the lessons, so one day after a sharp-cough interruption, I just said, "Dalzar, when are you going to quit smoking?"

> **Dalzar:** *(with a curt nod of the head)* Yes!
> **Me:** Okay, how many cigarettes do you smoke a day?
> **Dalzar:** Yes, I am smoking, I know. Not good, I know.
> **Me:** How. Many. Cigarettes. Do you smoke in one day?
> **Dalzar:** How many?
> **Me:** Yes!
> **Dalzar:** Cigarettes?
> **Me:** Yes!
> **Dalzar:** *(thinking)* Hmmmm. I don't know. Twenty.

We discussed a reasonable plan for cutting down the number of cigarettes each day. I wanted him to cut down to ten the next day, then five, then two, then zero. But he actually looked very thoughtful and said, "Today? April 7? Twenty. April 24? Zero," with the flourishy head nod.

The next few times I saw him, I asked, "How many cigarettes

did you smoke today?" Each time the answer was "twelve," and I hadn't seen him smoking at all. During their break one night, Dalzar and Renas sat out on the deck, eating crunchy snacks, and Dalzar, looking very proud said, "Not cigarettes! THIS!" and shook the bag of crunchy snacks at me. So, if not English, they were at least learning healthy living habits.

After the crunchy-snack break, I was attempting to explain the concept of indirect speech, which involved detailed punctuation.

> Indirect: I told my dad to stop complaining about my shopping habits.
> Direct: "Dad, stop complaining about my shopping habits."

My dad had sent several disgruntled emails in response to the number of UPS deliveries he had been receiving of late (period). A pair of Dolce & Gabbana gladiator sandals may or may not have been the most recent catalyst (period). But I was still managing to pay down my debt (exclamation point)! And was making monthly donations to the ASPCA (exclamation point)! No judging (exclamation point)!

Many of the students here seemed to struggle with punctuation, as I had heard from other instructors and experienced with my own kids. (All the instructors called their students their "kids," regardless of their age. We adored them and felt responsible for them.) Dalzar was one of the worst punctuation offenders. There were run-on sentences, and then there were Dalzar's runaway sentences. There was almost no punctuation at all, and the thoughts just kept going and going. This was not surprising, since it was also how he spoke.

I took the indirect/direct speech lesson as an opportunity to stress the importance of punctuation, which required a virtual visit from Victor Borge, one of my dad's all-time favorites. (Dad, I'm not mingling with the locals, but I'm incorporating Victor Borge into my lessons!) I found a clip on YouTube, where Borge singsonged through a monologue, creating sounds to replace the punctuation marks. Like "Pfft" for a period, "Zzzwuit" for a question mark, etc. Renas and Dalzar loved it and would use some of the sounds in classroom conversation.

> **Renas:** Teacher (urrrt), have a nice weekend (ppppppt).
> **Me:** Thanks (zoink)! See you Sunday (zoink)!

I would always end the last class of the week by saying, "See you Sunday," to which Dalzar, or Renas, or both would answer, "Inshallah." Just like the Muslim airline pilots. "If God wills it."

My problem with inshallah was that everyone here would say it, as if they truly would have no control over any of the events themselves. "Hopefully you will do well on your exams!" "Yes, inshallah." "Well, inshallah, yes, but you are going to at least study, aren't you?"

❧❧❧

I was encountering some interesting individuals in Iraq. There were expats here who had lived in other Middle Eastern countries like Syria or the United Arab Emirates, but those countries were veritable vacation destinations in comparison to Saudi Arabia. There was no Middle Eastern country I found more daunting.

The university had sent someone from the ESL testing center up to Erbil for an appointment, and Adam and I took him to lunch. He was a middle-aged British man named Nigel, who had recently arrived in Iraq from Saudi Arabia. I was engaged with him in what I thought was a casual conversation about teaching English in foreign countries, and the conversation went a little like this:

> **Nigel:** I spent about two months teaching in Saudi but wasn't impressed with the school. The other teachers really had no social skills, and I had no interest in interacting with them.
>
> **Me:** *(American—it is important to note that I am American in this conversation)* Wow! Saudi Arabia! What was that like?
>
> **Nigel:** How d'you mean?
>
> **Me:** *(now curious American)* Well, I don't really know anything about it, just that women aren't allowed to drive there. And I'd heard that all women, even Westerners, have to be covered there, that it's really strict.

Although, this was information I had learned from Warren. The accuracy was suspect.

Nigel: *(nonchalant)* Nah, I saw a few girls without headscarves walking on the street.

Me: *(joking American)* Did you have them arrested?

Like "ha ha ha." Get it? Like they were being super naughty?
Try the veal! Tip your waiters! I'm here all week!

Nigel: *(now visibly angry)* You know, *you Americans*,
really…I hate talking to people like you about Islam.
You're all so…you really should get out and see more
of the world.

Me: *(now stunned and slightly uncomfortable American)*
Well…I've seen a fair bit…I mean, I ask questions if I
don't know things.

*Have you seen my "Where I've Been" map app on Facebook? I've
been places! I've gotten out and seen more of the world! Dammit!*

Nigel: *(self-righteous, condescending)* Yes, and then you go
and say something like "did you have them arrested."

Me: *(exhausted, exasperated American)* Um…I was kidding…I joke around a lot…I am not a very serious
person…

Adam had committed to staring intently at his lunch plate and
pretending to ignore the tense exchange that had bubbled up
beside him at the table. I kept silently inshallahing the conversation to end. There was a time and a place for seriousness, and it

was almost never when talking to me. I was so caught off guard with the sharp swerve the conversation had taken, I didn't know how to escape. I just sort of stopped talking and joined Adam in trying to pretend to eat my chicken kebab.

Oscar Wilde famously said, "Seriousness is the only refuge of the shallow." And he was British. I considered the irony of Nigel being British and coming from the home of Monty Python, yet not having much of a sense of humor; and then there were my students who came from Iraq, home of Saddam, and were both pretty hilarious. Inshallah, everyone else I come into contact with will be a little less uptight.

❧ ASTOUNDING ❧
ACCOMPLISHMENTS OF PART 2

Running total spent on overweight luggage:
$2,920. We're almost at the point where we
can laugh about it. Almost.

Debt eliminated: $8,882. Progress!

Countries traveled: 2—Austria and France. *Danke
schoen* and *merci*.

Pairs of shoes purchased: 3

Soul mates met: 0, but I'm seriously considering
calling up one of those female security officers at the Erbil airport.

Cultural tolerance level: 8—my assimilation
and the friendliness of the Kurdish people
bumped it up to 10, but the collective smell
of the men reduced it by two.

Part 3

The Honeymoon
is Over

Chapter Eighteen

Idle Threats

The washer/dryer argument was the first of many between Warren and me. As the months went on, it just seemed to get worse. We had never argued before, but that was the Old Warren. Turkish-coffee episode aside, New Warren was the person I saw emerging more and more frequently. Director, Boss-Man, and Fearless Leader, and we argued.

Some of the arguments were silly. For instance, based on one or two conversations he had with him, Warren was convinced Dalzar was the more advanced of my two students and would score higher on the TOEFL (Test of English as a Foreign Language) exam. After having taught both Dalzar and Renas for a couple of months, I felt justified in my assessment that Renas was actually the more fluent of the two. My disagreeing with Warren really seemed to annoy him, and the fact that he was ignoring my credibility as an instructor was annoying me.

The most taxing argument we had was regarding "my" villa, and how to deal with my alleged nonworking time. I pointed out that I shouldn't have to answer the door or answer questions on the weekends. I deserved weekends like any of the other instructors, but because the villa and the campus were one and the same, Kurds would show up on the weekends, ringing the doorbell or knocking on the door, asking questions and wanting to enroll in the courses. It infringed on my privacy, sure, but also on *my weekend.*

Sometimes they would show up when I was in my bikini, crouched out of sight on the second-floor balcony. The villa balconies had waist-high railings around them, and I would drape sheets and blankets all the way around mine to create a little private solarium for myself. It was the *weekend*; I wanted to lay *out.* Or, if not in my bikini, I might have been wearing shorts and a tank top around the villa. It was freaking hot (forty degrees Celsius!), and there was no air-conditioning in the hallways, foyer, bathrooms, or kitchen. I knew I couldn't answer the door in shorts and a tank top, but I also didn't think it was fair to expect me to wear long sleeves and pants all the time, you know, just in case.

During one of the villa/classroom arguments, Warren grew irritated and blurted out, "Well, Gretch, you know, if you've got such a problem with it, we can just bring you down to Suli to teach."

Warren knew I didn't like Suli, but he didn't know the reason was *he* was there, and when he was around, it always had to be The Warren Show. Drama seemed to follow him wherever he went, and it was exhausting. And since drama always followed him, it seemed to follow our entire department. There was an unspoken divide between CED and the rest of the university, and I could feel the separation whenever I went down there.

The CED staff didn't really mingle with the other instructors or staff, and I felt like a big part of that was because Warren considered everyone else to be outsiders. *We're the cool kids.* It was a little junior high. I felt like being in Erbil was the easiest way to disassociate myself from the dramatics and the clique-ishness and the general gossiping that is inevitable in any workplace. I wanted to be Switzerland and remain neutral.

He knew I preferred Erbil and he was threatening me. Since we were no longer coworkers, these were not simple disagreements. He pretty much had absolute power. It was just like Tara. When Jonas Wilkerson, that ugly, ruthless Yankee overseer, suddenly became a carpetbagger and didn't have to listen to Scarlett anymore, he threatened to buy Tara when it was auctioned off for taxes. The horror! "We'll bring you down to Suli" was the one weapon Warren could pull out of his petty arsenal to win the argument.

I would never have come here, knowing he would be my boss. He was not Santa. New Warren was one mustache short of a dictator, wielding his power with all the subtlety of a battering ram and casting out confidants if they dared to disobey him or forgot to show their undying gratitude.

Take Johnny and Chady. They were two Canadian Lebanese cousins from Warren's hometown whom he had hired to work at the university. After a year or so, Johnny applied for and got the position of director of general services; then, not too shortly after, Chady was made the director of procurement. The director positions were great promotions, but instead of being proud and happy for them, Warren behaved as if both had betrayed him, and before you knew it, they were among "the outsiders."

I didn't react to Warren's threat to banish me to Suli. I just sat, holding the phone away from my ear, waiting for him to finish his tantrum, and silently praying he wouldn't follow through with it.

e ᴐᴇ ᴐᴇ ᴐ

Although it was my preference, Erbil wasn't all sunshine and lollipops. In addition to the privacy issues, there were the bugs. Lots and lots of bugs. I hated the mosquitoes that would zip into the villa when the students left the doors open, which was all the time. Dalzar and Renas quickly learned the phrase "Were you born in a barn?" I hated the quick-slithering silverfish that wiggled across the walls and ceilings. I hated the little black something-or-others (which I just called "dirty flies") that had made themselves at home in the upstairs bathroom.

But I loved the spiders. Spiders ate the mosquitoes and bugs, and I just always appreciated them.

I was a huge fan of *Charlotte's Web*.

The spiders living in the villa had become my version of household pets. I'm not saying I had gone completely crazy, but I would talk to them. Mostly just friendly greetings like "Hello, there!" when one would surprise me in the hallway or "Don't forget to eat the mosquitoes!" or "Okay, but please just don't crawl into my bed" when I saw that one had made a little web in between the bed and the nightstand.

There were several different varieties of my villa spider pets: some were thick, and the color of the Saudi Arabian dust that blew into Iraq; some were plain brown, skinny, and spindly; and the one I almost stepped on, walking into the kitchen one day, was small, slim, and had faint stripes. I had no idea if any of these were poisonous. I jumped out of his way and then leaned down to scrutinize him. After a minute or so I whispered, "Don't get stepped on by other people."

I then slowly straightened up, thinking, *This must be one of those Oprah Aha! Moments. Ahaaaaaaaaaaaa. I am going to take my own advice.*

A few weeks after arriving in Iraq, I had started an online blog, which was basically just me recounting my initial impressions and then day-to-day stuff (Nutella, my blender, my scale, the usual) for my family and friends back in the States. The awkward conversation with Nigel made it into a post. I needed support from the people at home after that, and they confirmed that Nigel was humor-free and oblivious to irony.

It wasn't a private blog, so I suppose I shouldn't have been surprised when I received this comment:

> Well, I kinda agree with Nigel. In general most of American peoples are ignorant and shoot the darkness without knowing anything.

Ruh-roh. Someone's angry—angry and unable to properly use English slang.

For example, its really pissing me off, the way you write about the people where you live with…

Grammatical errors were a pet peeve of mine. At this point it was clear the person writing the tirade was not a native English speaker; however, that didn't make me any less anxious to correct the errors with my red pen.

…first thing you should be aware is that, you do not live in The Iraq..its called Kurdistan (you are offending people, or simply say Hawler "if you think your are an educated person').

Erbil was the Arabic name for the city. The Kurdish name was Hawler. This person was obviously unfamiliar with Miss Teen South Carolina 2007.

Secondly, you think you came from another planet or a paradise called USA to a such shitty place which you call it The Iraq.

Where is this person getting "shitty place" from? I had never said anything remotely close to that on the blog.

You should know this by now, when people lived in that place where you are know, your country never exist and when people were educated from the land you call it the Iraq, your people and country were never born and exist

I had a headache.

also if you think you are in a shitty or in such a dumb place,

Again, when did I say that? And who is teaching you English? I hate when people only know two or three phrases in a foreign language but go to great lengths to make sure they know how to swear properly.

why don't you go back to your country and get a shop assistant job, cause am sure the level of education you have is only enough to work in a news agent or a food store not in a university. —Arie

Why you gotta insult the news agents and food store people? What did they do to you?

Why was this person even reading my blog? I was used to comments like "More photos of the shoes please!" or "What did you make in the blender today? Love, Mom." Angry Arie was very clearly on a different page, of a different book, shelved in a different library far, far from mine. If I have to explain my writing to you, you are not my target audience. That is okay. It takes diff'rent strokes to rule the world, yes it does! Not everyone enjoys the same things, be they movies, or food, or hairstyles, or Disney characters, or tattoos, or sartorial ensembles; the list goes on. I can guarantee you, you will never see Mariah Carey in a loose-fitting fisherman's sweater and baggy cargo pants, and that is okay. It's just not her thing!

I publicly (via blog post) recommended that Arie stop reading my blog, as it was obviously not his cup of tea. I was perpetually baffled by people who would voluntarily spend time fuming over something (movie, book, music, etc.) that was not to their liking, when they easily could have shifted focus to something they enjoyed. Life is short, people. Use your energy wisely.

My mom freaked out a bit after reading that blog comment. She was like, "What if they come and find you???", and I had to agree that was a distinct possibility. I was living in the Erbil school building, and anyone interested in English classes, or stalking an unknowingly offensive teacher/blog writer, could easily find us. I hadn't even told my mom about the two additional attempted comments from angry Arie, which I blocked without publishing. One was more ranting about how I was probably "stupid and uneducated," and he hoped I wasn't being paid very much, and he and his friends would read my blog and laugh about the stupid things I said; blah, blah, angry, angry. The second comment called me a "Chicken Shit" for not publishing the previous comment. I wondered if "Chicken Shit" came up on Google Translator.

I was more annoyed than anything else. Late-breaking story: Internet trolls in The Iraq. The anonymity of the Internet had created a culture of spineless crybabies. While Arie was not, technically, anonymous, he was whining and complaining and name-calling from the safe comfort of the dark cave of cyberspace. Part of me wanted a face-to-face with this person, and I was secretly hoping that Arie would enroll in an English course. God knows his writing could use it.

I later calmed down, took a few deep breaths, and thought,

"Poor Arie is probably some high school kid who takes a lot of pride in his culture and community, and he was just lashing out at an imagined injustice." But he was also a brat. The best way to deal with foul-mouthed brats, who are not yours, is to ignore them. In the same way I ignored Warren's threat to make me move to Suli, I ignored Arie's last two comments. He gave up and didn't bother commenting again.

℮ ℮ ℮

My blog had not only attracted a disgruntled local, it had also attracted Australia Katherine.

One day while checking my email I received this, with the subject line "Heya":

> … happened upon your blog while googling "ladies gym Erbil" (to no avail!).. and thought i would drop you a line…
>
> Am also in English Village and (i think) quite close to you.
>
> In fact it was on my list of things to do to come and say g'day to you as we visited the university in Suli last week and Tom said there was a branch here. I work for a legal consultancy and we meant to ask you and Adam over for lunch.
>
> Apologies for rambling monologue.. too many cold and flu tabs.
>
> Would be good to catch up at some point!
>
> Katherine

I had a quick flash of irritation at the thought that Tom could have introduced us to Katherine months ago (she had been in Erbil two months longer than we had) but obviously hadn't thought to do so. Who cares about the Erbil kids? No one, wanh-wanh. I let the irritation pass and brightened to the thought that there was a new, sunny social spot on the English Village horizon.

Chapter Nineteen

Erbil is Da Bomb

As Dalzar was prone to talking and "uhhhhhhhh"-ing through nearly every lesson, listening comprehension continued to be a challenge for him. The English textbooks we used came with audio CDs to supplement the lessons.

> Listen to each conversation, then write the reason each person changed his/her mind.
>
> Marie: I remember that gorgeous Swede you were going to marry.
>
> Juliet: Oh, yes, Sven Svenson. He was some hunk.
>
> Marie: Whatever happened?
>
> Juliet: I guess my tastes changed. I married Luigi instead.

I turned off the recording and asked, "Why did Juliet change her mind?"

Renas and Dalzar: She tastes changed.

Me: Her tastes changed. Good.

Dalzar: Is apreecher?

Me: What?

Dalzar: Uhhhhh, yes, uhhhh apreecher is, uhhh, some persons give the advise?

Me: Appreciate? Preacher? What are you asking me?

Dalzar: Uhhhh, persons stand in front and tell many peoples things—apreech? adviser?

Me: Like, in church? "Preacher" would be the person telling people things. What made you think of that?

Dalzar: Yes. Uhhh, Martin King.

We had discussed Martin Luther King Jr. a few classes ago.

Me: Dalzar. We were just discussing the conversations and reasons for people changing their minds. What made you think of Martin Luther King?

Dalzar: *(smiling and nodding)* Yes.

I was shaking my head thinking, "No…" when Adam came in. "Uh, hey, I just got an email from Warren, and he said there's a suicide bomb threat for Erbil, and they're sending a driver, now, to pick us up and take us to Suli."

Me: What?

Adam: Yeah, I don't know. That's just what the email said.

Me: So we have to go to Suli?

Adam: Yeah.

Me: Like, now?

Adam: I guess.

Me: So, I have to stop teaching now.

Adam: Yeah. They're sending a car from Suli, so you'll probably want to pack some stuff.

Dalzar and Renas just sat, looking blankly back and forth between Adam and me. I didn't sense any kind of surprise, but maybe they just didn't understand what we had said. So I said to them, "I guess we have to go to Suli...so you guys can go...um...I am not sure when we'll be coming back? Soooo, I guess, just wait for an email from me...I'll probably see you on Sunday?"

I was vacillating between anxiety about a suicide bomber and annoyance at having to pack in a hurry. I think TV had desensitized me to actual danger. Thinking about the other expats and their evacuation protocol, I wanted to know what New Friend Katherine had to do. Did they have to evacuate as well?

I picked up my cell and dialed her number. There was no answer. I deduced she, and the rest of her company, were in a similar state of disarray and panic and were quickly planning an exit.

While sitting out on the deck of the villas with Adam and our hastily packed bags, waiting for the driver, my cell phone buzzed and I received a text message from Katherine: "Maximall is fantastic!"

What???

Katherine had been thrilled with my tales of the Iraqi Banana Republic and had clearly wasted no time in getting her shop on.

I texted back:

We're being evacuated due to suicide bomber, and you're shopping???

That text prompted a phone call.

> **Katherine:** What do you mean, "suicide bomber"?
> **Me:** Warren emailed Adam about an hour ago and said we were being evacuated to Suli due to a suicide bomb threat. Have you not heard anything about this?
> **Katherine:** No! I am going to call Brad; he's dialed into all the security issues in Erbil, and if anything like that is happening, he'll know about it. I'll ring you back.

When she called back, Katherine said that Dialed-In Brad had confirmed that yes, there was a suicide bomb threat in Erbil. There were three suspects, two of whom had been apprehended. The third was still at large, and was a female on foot.

One bomber? On foot? That was it? The trip to Suli was around three hours, and I had things to do this weekend. Katherine had bought a paddling pool for her backyard, and we were going to make drinks in the blender and everything, and there was a Progressive Dinner involving multiple villas and multiple meals… there were *things*! I did not want to miss the *things*!

I turned to Adam and said, "Ask Warren when we get to come back up here." Adam was already on the phone with Warren, and dutifully asked, "Gretchen wants to know when we'll be able to come back to Erbil." He was quiet while Warren was responding, and then said, "Uh-huh…uh-huh…okay, man, talk to you soon." Then he turned to me and informed me that Warren said we wouldn't be coming back until Sunday. I did not take this news well.

> **Me:** WHAT?! NO! I have PLANS! I don't WANNA GO TO SULI! I mean come on. The suicide bomber is on FOOT. Erbil is HUGE! English Village is so far away from the actual city. What are the chances she would come here? She would be walking forever.

Remember that day Adam and I walked to the restaurant? Yeah, that was an hour and a half of walking. A smart suicide bomber would want to explode in a densely populated area, not in a far-flung compound where the villas weren't even very close together. That would just be poor planning on her part.

> **Adam:** Warren says you don't have to come down.
> **Me:** *(excited)* Really?
> **Adam:** Yeah, but he says if you're not coming down, you need to send him an email right now, explaining what you're doing...
> **Me:** *(hurriedly)* Yes, yes, saying that I take full responsibility, blah blah.

I was halfway into the villa by that time, en route to my work computer to send the email. Hooray! Weekend fun, here I come! Stupid suicide bomber, trying to spoil my paddling-pool plans and blender-drinks plans and Progressive Dinner plans.

Chapter Twenty

The Real Housewives of Erbil

There was Western life for me in Erbil, thanks to Katherine: perky, energetic twentysomething Katherine, with her massive Rolodex of expats and neverending calendar of social extravaganzas.

Because Katherine worked for a legal consulting firm, she met all the Westerners who moved here, or at least the ones who needed legal assistance in setting up their various businesses or nonprofit organizations. She also put in the hours required to cultivate a very active social life, which was something I wasn't doing. Her schedule made me tired.

In one of her frequent emails she joked, "You've not been to the track? Lordy. You haven't LIVED!"

"The track" was the Erbil Speed Center, which was a mile down the road from our compound. It was composed of a sleek-but-smoky bar, a sleek-but-smoky restaurant, and an actual racetrack, neither sleek nor smoky, where you could drive go-karts.

Katherine invited me to the racetrack to "meet an astronaut." Astronaut Bill Shepherd was going to be at the racetrack and was being honored for something or other. Although I had never heard of Bill Shepherd, and wasn't particularly interested in the space program, I thought "Meh" and decided to go.

After a narrated video and speech from the guest of honor, Katherine and I were introduced to Astronaut Shepherd by his cohort Duke, a slight, thinning-gray-haired, weathered man in his sixties, wearing a polo shirt and khakis. The first thing out of Duke's mouth was, "See, Bill? I told ya we'd have girls for ya." I may have audibly groaned. I mean, really, dude? I was a teacher and Katherine was an attorney, but as far as Duke was concerned we were just a couple of hookers.

The astronaut was nice enough. He seemed fairly jet-lagged and bewildered at the surrealism of the racetrack bar in the middle of Northern Iraq. Duke, on the other hand, was neither nice, nor bewildered, and when he started a sentence with, "Listen, honey…" I had to tune him out. I chose, instead, to entertain myself by imagining Duke dressed in a pink ballerina tutu, licking one of those giant, round rainbow lollipops, and fluttering his false eyelashes at the other men in the bar.

You weren't allowed to bring pork products into Iraq, but there were more than enough servings of pig to go around.

Katherine was a force of resilience and diplomacy. She had built up a very high tolerance for bullshit and didn't mind going to the track for social interaction. "Carey and Scott are here from the university, and Sirwan is taking them to the track tonight. If you wanted to go say hi."

Carey was the director of finance, who had been my immigration partner back in March (and the one who didn't complain about unsuitable sleeping accommodations and smelly pillows).

Scott was a friend of hers from home who had recently been hired at the university. I totally appreciated that they had not asked to stay in my villa, but also thought it was odd that one of Warren's drivers (Sirwan) would be taking Carey and Scott to the race-track. Maybe it was a different Sirwan. I responded to Katherine and asked questions like "Where are they staying?" and "Who is Sirwan?" and "How does he know them?" and then pointed out that I was being pretty gossipy.

Katherine's response:

> This is not fun gossip at all!!
>
> Apparently he [Sirwan] went to college with them? Or something?
>
> Fun gossip is stuff like Sirwan pulling the moves on me and me getting confused and wailing to my coworker, "I don't un-derstaaaaaaand… is this what DATING is? It's crap!"! Can't I just tell him I'm Australian and we don't do this bollocks at home? Eeew… I think I might have kissed him when I was boozed but not so sure…"

Her gossip was definitely better. Katherine was ten years younger than I and had more energy for the hooking up and running around and drinking. I had done all that in my twenties, and while it was fun at the time, I was thoroughly relieved not to be doing it anymore, particularly here, where the world seemed to be shrinking at an alarming rate.

The Sirwan she was talking about was not Warren's driver, but the brother of Rana, Princess Smelly Pillowcase. According to the Erbil gossip, Sirwan was a bit of a man-whore and had been nicknamed Sleazewan by a number of people. I wondered if Rana had given Sirwan a copy of the Cultural Awareness pamphlet.

I didn't want to completely give up on a social life in Erbil, so when Katherine suggested I go with her and a few friends to Hawaiian Night at The Edge, I said okay. I let my curiosity about the social whirl of Erbil's gossip get the better of me. The Edge was a bar, which was in the middle of the concrete maze of the USAID compound in Ainkawa, and consisted of a shabby room with a bar, and an outdoor patio with swimming pool.

The USAID compound was exactly like the Iraq you would see on CNN, complete with gun-toting guards and high concrete walls garnished with curling barbed wire. After going through a security check, and having to leave our cell phones and cameras at the front checkpoint, we walked through the concrete maze of streets to the "bar," where we were greeted by a pretty Western girl in her twenties, handing out leis, dressed in a grass skirt and coconut bra. I was taken aback as it had been awhile since I had seen that much skin. I mean, I get it, it's *Hawaiian* Night, but seriously?

The girl's name was Corey, and she was well-known around the expat scene, in the notorious sense of "well-known." To me she seemed like a genuinely friendly, nice person. She exhibited none of the competitive cattiness that is prevalent in many social situations with females and would probably have no place in Chancellor Tom's lioness scenario. A couple of Katherine's friends referred to her as "Whorey," which I thought was kind of nasty and pretty catty. I just felt sorry for her.

I was talking to one of the ex-military/security guys later by the pool, and I asked about Corey. He said she had told him once that she felt like a nobody back in the United States, but here she felt really special, like she was really important. That was heartbreaking to me, but I guess if she felt special, then her life here was a sort of improvement. I still wanted to give her one of those "You're better than this!" pep talks, and a sweater to put on over the coconuts.

Later on in the night, after many mai tais, Katherine admitted to me, "Whorey hates me 'cause apparently she was sleeping with Sirwan and saw me and him out heaps." ("Foster's" is Australian for "beer." "Heaps" is Australian for "a lot.") It was just like college. Rana really should have her brother take a look at that pamphlet.

I made a halfhearted effort to be friendly and social at The Edge, but my favorite part of that night was discovering the pound cake on the buffet table.

At both the Speed Center and The Edge, I felt like I was part of an exotic traveling exhibit at a woman-zoo. The male-female ratio was probably close to twenty-to-one. The Western men there were a mishmash of entrepreneurs, consultants, and ex-military/security personnel (and astronauts), and the vibe was palpably predatory. It didn't even matter what you looked like; you were female. There were just so *many* of the men, leering or saying, "Well, helloooooooooo there," eyebrows waggling, and their inconsequential wedding rings flashing and clinking on their beer bottles.

It was almost worse than being in a woman-zoo; it was more like being a juicy cheeseburger in a room full of starving desert-island castaways. Everyone looked really hungry and really creepy.

It would not have surprised me one bit to run into Brandon, of the Royal Jordanian flight, spitting his chewing tobacco into a glass and screaming obscenities into his cell phone before turning to waggle his eyebrows at Katherine and ask if she wanted marry him in Lebanon, or Leinenkugel.

Erbil's expat social scene was something I could only handle in very small doses. Or really just one dose, like a tetanus shot. You only have to get boosters for those every ten years.

The social antidote to the creepy, lecher-ridden bars was the Katherine-helmed Progressive Dinner in English Village. This was a monthly occurrence and included all expats living in the English Village compound. The casual, emailed invitation would usually look something like this:

> Stop one: Dean's for drinks
> Stop two: Swedes for starters
> Stop three: Matt and Liz's for mains
> Stop four: TRC ranch for dessert

Like Warren loved giving nicknames to people, Katherine loved giving nicknames to her villa. She sometimes called it the TRC ranch (TRC was the name of the consulting firm she worked for), and at other times would refer to it as Club 319 (her villa number).

When I was first invited to Club 319, I was confused. Once

again, my subconscious was crying out for a dance club, and I exclaimed, "Oh my God, Erbil actually has a dance club?" I should have remembered, per Dalzar, that it did not.

English Village was home to so many Westerners I hadn't known were there: Dean, from England, who worked in insurance; Piers and Alan, also from England, who owned, and did the accounting, respectively, for TRC; Eric and Martha, an American couple who worked for a tomato-processing plant; Liz and Matt, who used to work for the U.S. State Department but were both now doing consulting work; and a whole mess of Swedes. It felt more United Nations than anything else. The Cultural Awareness pamphlet did not apply here.

Parties like the Progressive Dinners allowed us expats to temporarily forget that we were living in Iraq. The food was Western (courtesy of the deli counter at Bakery & More), the drinks were Western (Jacob's Creek Chardonnay), the dress code was Western (no Capri pants necessary), and the conversation was Western. We could just drink and laugh and discuss politics, religion, and sex freely. I hadn't changed that much, though: I was still uninterested in politics and really preferred to talk about my dress.

There were always hangovers following the Progressive Dinners. Always. And the best way to cure the hangover was a pool party at Katherine's villa. Katherine would fill up the new paddling pool she found at Naza Mall, one of the large local Targetesque stores, and invite a bunch of women over to sit on the cushy lawn chairs in her completely fenced-in backyard to enjoy the frothy drinks, made in the blender I dragged over in a duffel bag.

"Completely fenced-in yard" meant we could loll about in the sunshine in our whorish bikinis, slurping the frothy alcoholic drinks of the infidels, and complaining about our probably-deserved hangovers. This was the Real Housewives of Erbil: the cookie-cutter villas, the pristine, manicured lawns, the bright, hot sunny days, and the inane conversations about our kids.

Katherine's kid was her thirty-nine-year-old boss, Piers, who, while creatively entrepreneurial and dryly hilarious, was incapable of doing anything himself (he once sent her to his villa to get his "good shoes" because they had clients coming). My kids were Renas and Dalzar. There was also the incessant bitching about the gardeners and the housekeepers. Someone's gardener had left the hose on overnight and flooded her backyard; Katherine's housekeeper continued to wash her clothes, even after shrinking several cashmere sweaters and having Katherine beg her not to touch her laundry. Liz's housekeeper decided not to show up for a few days but still expected to be paid. Slurping our blender drinks, we unanimously agreed, "It is so hard to find good help," and then burst out laughing at ourselves.

꿈꿈꿈

I was down to one kid. Just one. Dalzar was still in the nest, but Renas had flown away to greener pastures. Can I mix animal metaphors? Renas would be attending the University of Texas–Austin. Hook 'em horns! And I had hopefully armed him with enough English to keep him from being wedgied, swirlied, or locked in someone's locker. That was really more of a high school thing, but I was feeling protective of my now-former student and was really hoping that everyone would be nice to him. If I were in Texas with him, I'd be packing his lunch and writing little notes of encouragement on his napkins. I was a little worried about an Iraqi Kurd going to Texas. I had seen an episode of *Primetime* that John Quiñones did on people's treatment of a Muslim woman at a convenience store somewhere in Texas, and it wasn't too encouraging. I just had to cross my fingers that Renas would have a positive experience there.

I modified the class (you know, the class of one) to suit Dalzar's learning needs. We would begin with essay writin', continue on to some book learnin', and then take a half-hour break where we would adjourn to the deck to have conversation practice, or as I preferred to call it, Chatty Time, with Adam. I thought it would be helpful for Dalzar to hear two native English speakers having conversations, in which he could also participate. Naturally, given Dalzar's mild ADD, we occasionally veered off topic. One day we were discussing the textbook's unit topic "Controversial Issues" and wound up discovering that Dalzar was a part-time beekeeper. Or had a beekeeping facility at his workplace. Or liked the letter "B," but I was pretty sure it was beekeeping-related. To my knowledge, beekeeping was not controversial in Iraq.

In June, we finished the semester, and class was over. Dalzar took Adam and me out to dinner as a thank you, which was sweet of him. It didn't help him pass his TOEFL exam, on which he received a score of 483 out of 550, but it was still a thoughtful gesture.

I was suddenly free, for the next six weeks, to traipse around The Rest of Europe and visit family back home in the United

States before returning to Iraq in August. I was looking forward to summer vacation but also looking forward to returning to Erbil. I loved teaching the students, and I had finally made friends and settled in. Erbil actually felt like home. Although the honeymoon was over, it looked like this marriage had some promise.

❧ ASTOUNDING ❧
ACCOMPLISHMENTS OF PART 3

Running total spent on overweight luggage: $2,920 (I do feel it is an accomplishment that this has not increased).

Debt eliminated: $14,063—SUPEHSTAH!

Countries traveled: 2—still just Austria and France from last time. I'm getting antsy.

Pairs of shoes purchased: 3—aren't you proud of me? Still only three at this point.

Soul mates met: 0

Cultural tolerance level: 9—it was pretty easy to focus on the positive when heading into a six-week vacation.

Part 4

··

Change is Good

··

Chapter Twenty-one

Happy Birthday! Kind of.

The first three weeks of my summer freedom were spent in Austria, Croatia, and Greece, and I didn't bother with a budget. I had never been granted the luxury of doing that before; I always had to pay attention to how much meals cost, how much transportation cost, how much shoes cost.

It was good that I was excited to go back to Erbil, though, because *not* returning was not an option; so said the credit card bills. When you allow yourself the luxury of indulging in the carefree, money-is-no-object vacation, you must continue to bring in those tax-free paychecks. Yes, I had eliminated much of the crushing debt, but not all, and my savings account was still empty. Plus, all my stuff was still in Erbil. I liked my stuff. But even more rewarding than having stuff was the sense of accomplishment that came from teaching my kids. I give you my Yahoo inbox:

JUNE 24—SUBJECT: Hi

Hello Mis. Gretchen, I reached Houston on Saturaday after-noon. I couldn't open my email since I left my home. I bought a laptop yesterday. We are 10 studnt in this scholarship but 4 of them not coming yet. We have an English language course in St.. Thomas University and our flats are in Rice University. The weather is hot with too much humidity, I don't like it. Until now I am waiting the TOEFL test, may be in these 10 will appear. I will inform you immediately. Thanks, Renas

JUNE 26—SUBJECT: Another Hi

Hello Mis. Gretchen, What is your class news? Are you still teaching? Or you in vacation? I have an English course here in Houston in St. Thomas University. It is some how boring we are 18 student in class. I really miss your class Mis. gretchen. In 6th or 7th I will move to Austin there is also another English course prepared by UT. Thanks, Renas

JULY 12—SUBJECT: TOEFL Score

Hi, Haw are you Ms Gretchen? I reaaly miss your class, thank you so much for your teaching. I got my score of TOEFL test of May 9, unfortunately it is 527. Any way, now I am in Austin, I reached there 3 days ago. Here also I have an english course at ESL and at end of the course we have an unofficial TOEFL test but the teachers said that this test is acceptable by UT (university of Texas). I hope this time I would be better. Whre are you now Ms Gretchen? In New Zealand or Brazil or or or…! I moved to Austin 3 days ago, and yesterday I went to San Antonio, it was a nice place. Now, I am living in a dormatory name Castilian. Regards, Renas

I received that last email on my birthday, and it was one of the best birthday gifts ever. One of my kids was using his English and successfully living in the United States.

e~e~e~

I landed at Dallas–Fort Worth on July 11 and practically French kissed the customs agent, I was so thrilled to be back in the United States. I didn't even mind the four-hour layover, where I sat at TGI Friday's, gorging on American milkshakes and American cheeseburgers, before finally flying to Portland to stay with my parents. I entered the house and made a beeline for Herb, who looked startled. I hadn't seen him in four months, and he had definitely put on weight. As I lifted up his fat body and pressed my face into his furry belly, I gave my mom a reproachful look. "He is fat, Mom!" Overindulgent grandparents, feeding him table scraps. Hmph. I could tell he was a little fussy and wanted to punish me for being gone so long, but he didn't try to jump out of my arms, and I hugged him tight and swayed back and forth singing, "Her-bie, Herrrrrrrrrr-bie."

Once in the comfort and quiet of my parents' living room, after everyone had gone to bed, I read through Renas's emails and got a little teary-eyed. I quickly responded with some encouragement, and thank-yous, apologized for the delayed response, and told him to keep in touch.

I basked in the sunshine of Renas's accomplishment and thought about how this experience was turning out to be pretty satisfying. I was as surprised as anyone, and I sat with my laptop thinking about how weird it was that I was really looking forward to going back to Iraq.

Then I saw Jill's email.

Warren had hired Jill as his deputy director, to eventually succeed him as director of CED when his contract was finished and he left Iraq (although knowing him, he'd leave before his contract was up). I had only met Jill once or twice, but my snap judgment upon meeting her was that I really liked her. She was a cheery, friendly, short-haired, blond Canadian, a few years older than I, who had spent time teaching English in Dubai and had the dubious distinction of having been Warren's baby-sitter when he was little.

Her email did not give me the same warm and fuzzy feeling that Renas's email had given me.

> JULY 12 - SUBJECT: Hi!
>
> Hey Gretchen,
>
> We have had an unexpected increase in enrollments for our summer conversation classes, and so we'll need you here in Suli for August and September. Please let me know when you will return to Erbil.
>
> Cheers, and see you soon!
>
> Jill

NOOOOOOOOOO! The blood drained from my face. This was not a good birthday present. I did not want to move to Suli! Erbil was my home away from home now! I decided I did not like Jill anymore. She wasn't the boss of me! Once we had gotten past his petty threatening, Warren had promised me I would be teaching in Erbil for the entire duration of my contract. Where was he? Oh yes, he was on his summer vacation. Stupid Warren, on his stupid vacation. He wasn't due back in Iraq until September and did not take time out of his stupid vacation to respond to my desperate emailed pleas for clemency.

I immediately began to freak out. Things were different in Suli. No one likes change. Never mind that I would be thrust into the belly of the university beast, with its dramatics and bureaucratic confusion and inappropriate-theory-concocting chancellor; there were no microwaves in the Suli villas. How would I cook? Okay, not cook, but how would I heat things up?

I really would be like poor, downtrodden Scarlett, forced to yank cold vegetables out of the ground and eat them raw. And even worse, the commute between home and school required coordinating with other teachers and drivers, not just walking down the stairs of the villa. My shoes! They were in danger! This was serious. There were also no Progressive Dinners, no Bakery & More, no J&K Women's Fitness Center & Spa, and no paddling-pool Real Housewives time at Katherine's villa.

Wow, I sounded spoiled.

Once again, I found myself sobbing into my metaphorical apron. "I can't think about that right now. If I do I'll go crazy. I'll think about that tomorrow." I'm pretty sure Scarlett would have been pissed if she had gotten that news on *her* birthday. I'm also pretty sure she would have marched straight to her closet, whipped open the doors, and proceeded to console herself by ripping open the myriad boxes from YOOX, Zappos, and Barneys that had been waiting for her. There is always solace to be found in Jimmy Choo gladiator sandals.

Chapter Twenty-two

Kicking and Screaming

My Portland-Dallas-London flight went smoothly. My two nights in London went smoothly. I accidentally bought a pair of Christian Louboutin suede fringe booties in London, but because they were on sale for half price, that purchase went smoothly. The London-Vienna flight went smoothly. Everything went smoothly until I had to check in at the Austrian Airlines counter for my Vienna-Erbil flight.

The counter may as well have been covered in prickly stucco, it so interrupted all the beautiful smoothness.

While I was home for summer, my friend Christine had gotten me the most awesome and practical birthday gift ever: the Balanzza. The Balanzza is a handheld luggage scale, which has been featured in such lauded publications as the Hammacher Schlemmer catalog and SkyMall. You attach the sturdy strap to the handle of your bag, then hold the scale in your hand and lift. Balanzza would tell you what your luggage weighed in both pounds and kilos. It was totally bilingual. Never again would there be a need to pay extra luggage fees! I had carefully weighed both of my suitcases, and both were at precisely twenty kilos (or forty-four American pounds). I was a packing genius.

The Austrian Airlines representative at the counter did not agree with my self-appointed label of packing genius and harshly informed me that my limit was twenty kilos. Total. Period.

Me: Twenty kilos total? Not per bag?

My insides went molten. *Not per bag*. This was for an international flight. Twenty kilos? *Total?* I attempted to explain to the counter representative that she must have been mistaken and that I was permitted *two* twenty-kilo bags, on the *same* airline, Austrian Airlines, flying the *same* route (just in reverse) from Erbil to Vienna, a mere month ago. Her very unsympathetic response was, "Well, you were lucky."

That was not the way I wanted to start my day, nor my return trip to The Iraq. Five hundred fifty euros later (around $800), both twenty-kilo bags were checked, and I defeatedly whimpered through the terminal toward my gate.

⌒⌒⌒

Back at the Erbil villa, I packed up two large suitcases for the two months I would be in Suli. Since I was no longer speaking to my hockey bags, I considered trying to shove the enormous microwave into a duffel bag, but that would have taken up shoe room. I was then whisked down to Suli, leaving a purportedly depressed Katherine in my wake. When I emailed her to wail about my unwanted relocation, she had immediately responded, "Is anything written down in your contract re: location? Am dismayed at this turn of events. Dismayed! Don't leave me!" I was certain her dismay and depression would only last until the next happy hour, or Progressive Dinner, so I wasn't too worried.

Once in Suli, I moved into the extra room in Jen's villa. Jen had taught classes through the summer and was leaving for her six-week vacation a few days after I arrived. We had a little time to catch up and gossip about all the stuff that happened with the university over the summer. She said it had been rough.

Jill had hired a handful of new teachers for short-term, three-month contracts. While Warren didn't have a knack for truthfulness, he was a quite gifted judge of character. Everyone Warren had hired for the regular term at the university all had some sort of personal connection to him (former coworkers, baby-sitters, etc.) and were all very solid, stable, easygoing-yet-hardworking, fun *and* funny people. I had to give him credit for that. I really liked the people in our department. Since Warren was back in Canada for his summer vacation, Jill had to do the last-minute summer contract hiring.

One of the people Jill hired was an older British woman named Virginia. Jen told me how Virginia would loudly and frequently proclaim how much she hated Americans, in addition to other random, unsettling outbursts. To put it in her preferred British vernacular, Virginia was barking mad. During one of her particularly bad episodes, she jumped out of the transport car and stood in the middle of a busy Suli street screaming, while everyone else in the car just sat in varied states of stunned paralysis. She was relieved of her teaching duties before I arrived, though, and I never saw her craziness up close.

I do not do well with Crazy. I am all about trying to rationalize things (international travel requires more than twenty kilos, total), and Crazy usually doesn't pay any attention to reason (no, it's twenty kilos total). Crazy screams and shouts and jumps out of cars, and all of that just takes far more energy than I have.

If Virginia was certifiable, Nina, another summer hire, was certifiable light. Jen warned me about Nina: she dominated conversations, made absurd comments, and frequently offended people. Dara and Kelly were two teachers in CED who were married and had brought their husbands and children to Suli with them. Nina informed them both that it was totally irresponsible to bring children there. She would proclaim to anyone who would listen that she was the only truly qualified instructor because she had completed a TOEFL teacher's course. She piped bizarre revelations into everyday conversation: "The only reason I went to Korea [to teach] was because I couldn't get laid in America." And during a very awkward car ride she growled to a twenty-seven-year-old Bobby, "You're just ripe enough for me." Dara confided that on one trip to Zara, Nina wore shorts that were so short you could actually see bum cheek. Where was the Cultural Awareness pamphlet? Did I take the last one?

Nina was thirty-nine, pale skinned, and very thin, with a wiry blast of red hair. She was smugly proud of her birdlike frame. She was obsessed with talking about weight, and would declare, "I'm thin and hot!" and would yammer on about how there were twenty-year-olds who weren't as thin or hot as she was. No one really knew how to respond to this.

She really didn't seem like a bad person, but she definitely had some sort of mental imbalance that resulted in her floating around in an alternate reality, where she was the Queen: the most beautiful, most fascinating, most intellectually gifted incarnation of human-unicorn there ever was. It was nice that some people were perfectly content in their delusions; I just couldn't find any common ground with them.

I felt bad for Nina but also suspected that she wasn't all there as far as mental capacity went. The best I could do was be polite and try to avoid engaging in conversation with her. Especially when she said things like, "I definitely want to have a baby. The world needs more Ninas! Don't you think?" I did not think. When Warren came back from his extended summer break and met the new hires, he said to me, "Oh my God, I feel like I need to shower after I talk to her. She is fucking weird."

Suli was going to be an exercise in avoidance tactics for me. In addition to a mentally wobbly coworker, Jen had also warned me that she had seen a scorpion crawl out of the drain in the shower.

 ᘓᕮᘓᕮ

The faculty and staff villas in Suli were about a twenty-minute drive from the university. We had three Kurdish drivers, Karzan, Karwan, and Sirwan, who each commandeered an SUV, to transport us around. Karzan and Karwan were half brothers who used to live in Baghdad and drive for Saddam Hussein's regime. "Saddam Hussein's regime" has a dark and sinister sound to it, but the brothers were these two diminutive, smiley, jokey nuggets. They were the Iraqi version of Chelsea Handler's sidekick, Chuy.

All three drivers were cheerful and funny, but Karzan was the one with *Rod Stewart's Greatest Hits* on CD. It was the little things that made life entertaining there, and one of those things was a morning commute through the crazy, dusty roads of Sulaimani, Iraq, singing along to "Hot Legs." It was almost too much when Karzan later got his hands on a Rihanna CD. We'd be speeding past old men on donkeys, belting out "Umb-e-r-ella, ella, ella, ey, ey, ey" in unison.

When his brother, Karwan, was driving, you had to keep your wits about you and prepare for crash position. Karwan had a lead foot and very little regard for weather conditions. On one rainy, slippery night he was barreling along at top speed, and several of us in the car were calling out for him to slow down. He grew indignant and said, "I drive for many, many years in Baghdad!" We responded, "That's nice, drive slower."

Karzan was probably the most entertaining conversationalist of all the drivers. He was the oldest, although probably still only in his thirties. One time, on the way from the university to the bank, Karzan asked, "You like chicken?" Steve was the only other person in the car, and neither of us was sure if Karzan meant the animal or the food. I asked, "Do you mean, to eat?" Karzan said, "NO no no, not eating, just animal," and then proceeded to tell us about the love of his life, Biss-Biss the chicken.

"Ahh, Biss-Biss. Biss-Biss BEAUTIFUL!" and he did this

thing where he touched all his fingertips together and held them up to his mouth. "BEAUTIFUL!" Steve and I were thoroughly amused by this. It was not common for Kurds, or other Middle Easterners for that matter, to keep pets (Section Five of the Cultural Awareness pamphlet). All the teachers had grown accustomed to the negative reactions of our students when we discussed keeping cats or dogs at home. ("But teacher, they are so *dirty*.") Karzan was one of the few exceptions. Karzan told us all about his "chicken-man" Biss-Biss. He did say "Rooster? Chicken-man?" asking us which was correct, but Steve and I preferred "chicken-man" so we let him continue to say that.

He waxed poetic about how he had had Biss-Biss for over two years, and how his family threw birthday celebrations in Biss-Biss's honor, and baked him cakes, and made him clothes to wear. Karzan told us how Biss-Biss had many girlfriends, and he was just so proud that I couldn't help laughing about it.

Once, when Karzan was driving Warren and me from Erbil to Suli, Warren started joking about taking me to Baghdad and selling me. "How much you think we could get for her?" he asked Karzan. I did not want to hear how much money Karzan and Warren thought I was worth. But before I could block the answer with a loud "I DON'T WANT TO TALK ABOUT THIS," Karzan had said, "Twenty thousand." I was mildly offended and blurted out, "Twenty thousand?!" at the same time Warren responded with a shocked, "REALLY?" He then said, very seriously, "Gretch, twenty thousand is a lot of money here." I was still offended. Karzan probably paid more for Biss-Biss.

Karzan used the word "beautiful" to describe nearly everything, not just his chicken-man. He would say "beautiful" with his hand held in front of his mouth, with all his fingertips pressed together. Rihanna's music? Beautiful. Random neighborhood children? Beautiful. The mountains of Kurdistan? Beautiful. The Black Moneeka? Beautiful. I'm sorry, the what?

The Black Moneeka was a car, specifically a large SUV. I did not understand the name. It was explained to me that "Moneeka" referred to Monica Lewinsky, because she was a "big girl" and the SUV was a "big car." So whenever we would pass a large, shiny black SUV, the drivers would say, "Ahhhh, Black Moneeka." I was mortified that Monica Lewinsky was infamous enough to have made such a lasting impression on the Iraqi people for this length of time. An ancillary thought snuck in: "Maybe her handbag line would sell well here."

Since moving to the Middle East I had become hyperaware of how Western females were represented to the Middle Eastern community. We were, largely, assumed to be hos, and it was exasperating to be unfairly labeled. If the most action I'm getting is a couple of strategically placed squeezes from security at the Erbil airport, I do not deserve the "ho" label.

It didn't help that while the television censors here removed any and all kissing scenes, they would leave in the "morning after" scenes with the naked couple in bed (covers pulled all the way up, mind you), which popped up all too frequently in most romantic comedies. It made me very aware that the common depiction of American women, via both movies and popular television programs (*Grey's Anatomy*, *ER*, *Brothers & Sisters*, and others) is that we all slept with men on the first date, if not within the first ten minutes of meeting. While that was not a big deal to a Western man, it just reinforced "whore!" to the men in the Middle East. File under: Other Stuff That Makes Me Kick and Scream.

Chapter Twenty-three

The New Students

I finally had more than two students, and some of them were even female. Yay! I really, really wanted to get to know some of the Kurdish women, for a more well-rounded perspective on the culture. I was given two conversation classes of Level 2s, the same as Renas and Dalzar. I had seven students in my 3:00 p.m. class and twelve in my 6:00 p.m. class. On the first day, I spent a few minutes familiarizing myself with their names. This took a bit of work. "Dalzar" and "Renas" had been phonetic, and easy, and there were only two of them. Now I was faced with an avalanche of "Pshtewan" and "Kazhwast" and other names that begged the use of a sneeze guard.

I went around the room with my attendance sheet, and mentally pigeonholed my first class: AbdulKareem (the old one), Sarkawt (the smiley one), Peshang (the shy one), Awat (the cute one), Hawkar (the confused one), Solin (the young one), and Avin (the pretty one). Surface labels are awful, but they help me remember people before I get to know them. I have no idea how sanctimonious, politically correct people do it.

The classes were two and a half hours long, and the students got a fifteen-minute break in the middle to go outside and walk around, get snacks, and speak Kurdish. I refused to allow them to speak anything other than English once they set foot inside the classroom. On the second or third day of class, the cute one stayed behind and hung around my desk. By this time I was starting to see him more as the flirty-jokey-one-who-had-been-giving-me-the-eye, and I was wary of him. I narrowed my eyes.

He said, "Teacher, can I ask you personal question?"

I had been assured by my coworkers that the students would never ask anything about your marital status or dating situation, because it was not acceptable conversation in their culture.

> **Me:** *(hesitantly)* Sure.
> **Awat:** Are you married?

Yep, that was pretty personal.

> **Me:** No.
> **Awat:** How old are you?

We have confirmed that Awat understood the meaning of the word "personal." I tried not to roll my eyes.

> **Me:** Thirty-nine.

He nodded his head, grinning, and looked thoughtful for a moment. He then said: "Teacher, you are very good teacher. We think you very good. Everyone respect you." It was like the entire class had unknowingly designated Awat as class spokesman. That was really nice to hear, a mere three days into the class, but I thought it might have been more flirty sucking-up than a legitimate compliment. That would get him nowhere, but I still accepted it. And I was now frequenting the tearoom for my daily dose of "Hello, Flower" from Daroon.

There was at least one student in the second class who would not have agreed with Awat's assessment and just stopped showing up after four classes. I can't say I was sorry to see Behaz go. He was "the scary one" who referred to Saddam Hussein as "King Hussein."

◠◡◠

There were several occasions in class when I just wanted to give my students a big hug but could not (Cultural Awareness pamphlet #3: Personal behavior—no hugging). Once was when Saman divulged that he had spent nine years in one of Saddam Hussein's prisons. Saman was short, with graying hair, probably in his fifties, and was the most mild-mannered, respectful, sweet man in the class. It was absolutely heartbreaking for me to hear him say that. It also gave me an Oprah aha! moment when I figured out that must be the reason he and Behaz disliked each other.

I also wanted to hug Kazhwast and Rozhan, two sisters, who told the class how they had walked across the mountains, with their family, from Iraq into Iran in the middle of the night when they were little, in order to escape the rebel rebellions. As usual, I had to have Wikipedia explain this to me:

Thousands of civilians were killed during the anti-insurgent campaigns stretching from the spring of 1987 through the fall of 1988. The attacks were part of a long-standing campaign that destroyed almost every Kurdish village in areas of northern Iraq where pro-Iranian insurgents were based and displaced at least a million of the country's estimated 3.5 million Kurdish population. Independent sources estimate 100,000 to more than 150,000 deaths and as many as 100,000 widows and an even greater number of orphans. Amnesty International collected the names of more than 17,000 people who had "disappeared" during 1988. The campaign has been characterized as genocidal in nature. It is also characterized as gendercidal, because "battle-age" men were the primary targets, according to Human Rights Watch/Middle East. According to the Iraqi prosecutors, as many as 180,000 people were killed.

The students would tell these stories in such a matter-of-fact way, and no one else seemed surprised to hear them. They were just commonplace for the Kurds. Most of my students had grown up without fathers, and nearly every student had had at least one family member killed in an automobile accident. This was something I was not surprised to hear, judging from how people drove in Kurdistan, but that didn't make it any less tragic.

For all the hardship and difficulty these people have had to endure, they, collectively, had a fantastic sense of humor. This made teaching easy for me, since I had a challenging time being serious at all. I could not keep a straight face when we were working on the "Eating Well" unit and the students were learning phrases to describe their food likes and dislikes.

One of the phrases was "I'm not a _____ lover" (I'm not a coffee lover, I'm not a vegetable lover, etc.), and I overheard one of my male students loudly declaring, "I'm not a selfish lover" to his conversation partner. He meant "shellfish." I cackled out loud, had tears streaming down my face, and had to apologetically say, "No, no, it's nothing, keep practicing."

Another time, we were studying the present perfect tense, and I asked the students to come up with their own present perfect sentences. Peshang said, "My mother *was calling* me to help her in the kitchen." I asked, "Did you then go into the kitchen to help her?" and he said, "No." When I asked, "Why not?" Peshang answered exasperatedly, "Because I have a sister!"

I was the only one laughing at that. The students just looked at me quizzically.

e∽e∽e

After the first week Awat stayed behind after class and asked if it would be okay if he sat and talked with me between classes. He said, "You can ask me anything! I will tell you everything! But only if is not too much bother for you." Awat was really funny. I would often catch him snickering to himself when I was struggling to explain something to Hawkar, whose perpetual confused expression caused me to pull my hair out. Awat was also sharp and very eager to learn English. I thought this could be a golden opportunity to get the inside scoop on Kurdish men. I was comfortable enough with him, in spite of his flirty eye contact, and knew that he probably really would tell me things that I would otherwise never hear.

Adam had told me that many of his male students talked about frequenting Turkish prostitutes, and Warren claimed that most of the Kurdish men he knew were not exactly bastions of Muslim integrity. I was expecting to hear similar salacious and intriguing things from Awat. I was kind of disappointed.

Over the next few weeks Awat would stay behind, after the rest of the class had gone, and we would spend the next half hour talking. Instead of telling me about the local whorehouses, he told me a story about how he used to have this good friend, but one day the friend was on his cell phone, arranging to meet a prostitute. The friend was married, and when Awat overheard the phone conversation, he ended the friendship. He made a motion like he was dusting off his hands, which was a Kurdish way of indicating they were finished with either someone or something. He said that friend was not a good man, and he didn't want to be friends with someone like that.

We talked more about how friends could disappoint us, and people who were untrustworthy and he said, "Teacher, we have a saying in Kurdish: Never trust a woman!"

Me: Um, that is a terrible saying. Why is that a saying?
Awat: BELIEVE me, this is true!

He used "believe me!" where I would have said "seriously." But I thought his emphatic "believe mes" were far more amusing, so I never corrected him.

Me: Please explain this to me. That is really an awful thing to say. *I* am a woman!

He said, dismissively, "Yes, but you are different," and then proceeded to tell me a story about another friend who had a girlfriend who then left him for a man with more money. Well, that wasn't unique to Iraq.

> **Awat:** Women only want money!
> **Me:** Hmmm. Okay, well, would you ever marry an ugly woman?

He stopped and seemed surprised at the question, and I could tell he wanted to answer no. He looked thoughtful for a moment, dark eyebrows furrowed, and then said, "I see. I think..." and then he explained another saying to me, which involved using markers and the whiteboard, where he drew a picture of a candle, and then what looked like a lantern. The basic gist of that saying, or what I could gather from it, was something like "It is better to have a simple candle with a flame than a fancy, showy lantern." "Lantern" was definitely the wrong word, but something like that. Plus the saying was Kurdish, so the exact words didn't matter. It was kind of a sweet sentiment, but I was still troubled by the whole "never trust a woman" thing, so I continued on with that conversation.

> **Me:** Okay, so your problem is you think women only care about how much money a man has, right?
> **Awat:** It is true!

Me: Well, do you know any women who have their own
   jobs?

Awat: Ahhhh…no.

Me: Okay. How do you think women here get money?
   They either get it from their fathers or from the men
   they marry.

He looked like he was considering this as a legitimate excuse,
and I was just pleased to have made him try to view it from a different perspective.

There were, in fact, many women who worked in Kurdistan.
When I went to Warka Bank, I would see at least six or seven
women working there. For the sake of my argument, though, I
was relieved that Awat didn't know any of those women.

The Muslim culture is so slanted in favor of men that I couldn't
help but be on the side of the women. Jill, our deputy director,
was living in Dubai when she met her now-husband, Morris. Jill
was a forty-year-old Canadian, and Morris was a slightly older
Brit. The mandates for the United Arab Emirates stated that if
Jill and Morris wanted to get married in Dubai, Jill would have
had to get permission from her father. I vacillated back and forth
between hysterical laughter and despairing sobs with that one.

Chapter Twenty-four

Awat's Happening

The following week I was having the students silently read through and then complete an in-class assignment. As my eyes traveled around the room, gauging who was finished with the assignment and who needed more time, I caught Awat staring at me. His steady gaze was unsettling and a sly smile played around his lips. I quickly looked to the next student, then back at the papers on my desk. This was happening more and more frequently. I would be explaining something to the class, and as I searched their eyes for comprehension and understanding, when my eyes met Awat's, I saw something slightly more amorous than comprehension and understanding. I was alternately flattered and annoyed by it. Who did this kid think he was? *I'm tryin' to teach here, quit giving me the sexy eyes!*

During our post-class chat, I asked Awat how many girlfriends he had, because I was still confident in my original assessment of him: *playah*. With a laugh he admitted, "Three!" and told me how he had three different SIM cards for his cell phone, to keep the girlfriends separate. I found this to be mildly entertaining, although, being female, I was still offended on behalf of girlfriends everywhere.

He said, "Yes, three girlfriends..." and here he looked me over, slowly, from head to toe, then continued, "but none of them are sexy." I missed about half a second before quickly recovering and (pretending I hadn't noticed the once-over) asked, "Why are you with them, if you don't think they're sexy?"

He thought for a second and said, "For..." then seemed to be searching for the right word. I cautiously finished his sentence for him: "Practice?" He said, "Yes!" then paused, looked worried and quickly added, "But not in the bed!" That had been precisely what I was thinking, but I wasn't prepared for him to just come out and say it. Yikes! He really would tell me anything.

This admission led to Awat telling me that he would only kiss a girl after he had married her. This surprised me. It was how Muslims were supposed to behave, but from all the other stories I had heard, it was not typical of men in Kurdistan.

He continued, "One girlfriend, I very love her. She do anything for me. I tell her my favorite color is red, she wear red clothing. One night, very late, she call me. She say, 'Can you get car for tomorrow?' She want to drive up to Korak Mountain. I know she want to go there to do bad things, so I tell her no."

So, they just talked on the phone, the relationships weren't physical, and none of the three girlfriends were sexy.

The following week, Awat told me he ended things with all three girlfriends. Ruh? He explained that he did a "test" over the weekend. He bought a new SIM card for his cell phone and called each girlfriend, pretending to be a friend of his. (He said he covered the phone with a T-shirt to disguise his voice.) He claimed to be Awat's friend who was "richer than Awat," and then asked each girl if they would leave Awat and be his girlfriend instead. They all said, "Yes." Oh my God. What? WHAT?! I didn't know why I was so shocked and surprised by everything, but really? All three of them? That was profoundly discouraging, and not only because these girls were so gullible, but also because it completely confirmed Awat's saying "never trust a woman." Believe me!

How did not one of them recognize Awat's voice? I really couldn't believe it. I also couldn't believe that a small part of me was thinking, "Sooooo, you're saying you're single now?"

❧ ❧ ❧

Since these were conversation classes, when some of the students would come into the classroom early, I would *conversate* with them (and teach them not to say "conversate" since it wasn't a real word). One day I was talking with Bawan about some of his extended family, who were living in England. He said, "My fiancée live in England," and I said, "Oh, congratulations! You're getting married?" to which he replied happily, "Yes! She is my cousin!"

According to the Internet (and the Internet is always sort of right), approximately 42 percent of marriages in Middle Eastern countries involve first cousins. There had been some recent studies (conducted by a genetics researcher at the University of Washington, not just Wikipedia this time) that said cousins marrying each other wasn't as risky (as far as reproduction went) as was originally thought. I thought they needed to do more studies on this. If first cousins were repeatedly marrying and reproducing in the same family, that had to exaggerate risks of birth defects or other genetic messiness. Plus, reproductive risk or not, yuck.

The more I delved into this issue as it related to Kurdistan, the more I began to understand the culture, or at least pretend to understand it. My brilliant, totally unscientific "in a nutshell" breakdown, based on my brilliant, totally unscientific, haphazard Google research, was that families there were so closely tied, through both birth and marriage, that they had developed a fundamental wariness of outsiders. Why would you marry a complete stranger when you have several perfectly good cousins to choose from? Keep the money and the secrets in the family.

In one of our earlier conversations Awat said that he would "probably" end up marrying one of his cousins. He said it so casually, like it was just an inevitability. After several weeks, the subject came up again. Awat was complaining about Kurdistan and saying that he wanted to move to Europe. I said, "Well, don't you have to live here? Aren't you marrying your cousin?" and he shrugged and looked pointedly at me and said, "Maybe not."

Day after day, Awat and I would sit and talk, about relationships, about family, about travel, and even about religion. I asked if he thought I was going to go to hell because I wasn't Muslim. He looked at the floor, shaking his head, and answered, "I hope not." He would stay until I kicked him out, right before my second class was to start. Several students from my second class were usually waiting outside the classroom-trailer for me to let them in, and Awat would nod to them, and they would nod back.

I discussed this new, odd friendship situation with Jen, who had spent a great deal of time with her Kurdish students and seemed to have a fair grasp on the culture. Her opinion was, "He is definitely pursuing you." She went on to explain that everything he had been doing—the early flattering, the after-class chats, the personal topics of conversation—were actions of a Kurdish male courting a female. I felt like a subject on Animal Planet. This should not have surprised me, because the "relationships" he had with his girlfriends seemed to consist entirely of phone calls and texting. Jen went on to point out that those students in my second class, who saw Awat leaving the classroom long after his class had ended, were probably fully aware that he was pursuing me but thought that I was too naïve to realize it. *I do believe they are correct.*

One day, after class, Hawkar and Peshang had hung back with Awat and were chatting with me and discussing the meaning of names. "Teacher, what your name mean?" I explained that, as far as I knew, "Gretchen" meant "little pearl" or something like that. Peshang said, "My name mean 'Leader.'" "Means," I corrected him. Hawkar joined in with, "Yes, my name 'Helper.'" I then looked at Awat, who smiled at me when he said, "Awat means 'Hope.'"

⁂

When we returned home to the villas, after class, Ellen and I would usually exercise by walking and running for forty-five minutes around the compound. Ellen was a new teacher I had instantly bonded with. She was an easy-breezy California girl in her late twenties who peppered her sentences frequently with "like" and "ohhhhh, I don't knowwww." Some people assumed she was a ditz, but they were wrong. She could tilt her head and smile and singsongily whip a razor-sharp observation out of nowhere. She came to Iraq directly from two years of teaching English in Istanbul, Turkey, and was very much over Muslim men and the Muslim culture in general. She was the perfect person to discourage my burgeoning crush on Awat.

I told her all about our daily conversations, and what Jen had said, and then listed all the reasons why it was an impossible and ridiculous situation, other than the obvious fact that he was one of my students:

- He was twenty-four (fifteen-year age issue).
- He was Kurdish (cultural issue).
- He was Muslim (religious issue).
- He was not allowed to drive (freedom issue).
- He did not work; he just spent hours playing PlayStation (that was just annoying).

Dear Mary Kay Letourneau,

You seemed to be able to make things work, and I was wondering if you had any advice…

And if those five reasons weren't enough, Awat also lived with his mother. This was not uncommon for unmarried men and women in Iraq, but he told me that he and his mother shared a bedroom. I seriously hoped that was not common.

A few years back, one of Awat's older brothers was killed in a car accident. His oldest brother and older sister were both married, so Awat was the only one left in the house (although the house was a duplex, and the oldest brother and his wife lived right next door).

The car accident explained why Awat's mother would not let him drive, and I could kind of understand her clinging need to have him close by. *Kind* of. She wasn't really subscribing to inshallah if she thought she could control whether Awat crashed his car. He told me he used to try to sleep in other rooms in the house, but his mom would find him and make him sleep in her room. They were so close, Awat explained, that when they would go to friends' or relatives' homes for dinner, everyone knew that Awat and his mother would share a plate. There are red flags, and then there are *red flags*, and I was suffering from temporary color blindness.

I noticed in conversations with Kurds that they were always very quick to point out that their culture was superior to Western culture where family was concerned. When the weather was nice, most Kurdish families would spend their weekends having family picnics in parks or in the mountains. They were always doing family stuff. They would say things like, "We are very close to our families. We do not move away from our parents after university." I moved in with my parents for two months right before moving here, so I felt like I had some street cred. But when I had told some students I was going to Paris during Nawroz (the Kurdish New Year), they looked confused and said, "But your family is not in Paris." All family, all the time. At one point, I asked Awat, "Doesn't that make it really easy to get sick of your relatives?" He only hesitated a second before admitting, "Yes."

Spending every weekend with your family, living with your family, sleeping in the same room with your mom when you were a twenty-four-year-old man, and then marrying your cousins.

I could not entertain the idea of a crush on him. Absolutely not.

e∽e∽e∽

The day I decided I had to find out Awat's astrological sign, to see if we were horoscopically (probably not a word) compatible, should have been an indicator that my common sense was broken. It was not one of my most sensible moments. Determining astrological compatibility was of primary importance, if I was interested in someone: *When is his birthday? What is his sign?* I didn't make all my decisions based on my horoscopes; just most of the romantic ones.

Water signs were compatible: Cancer, Pisces, Scorpio. It was an easy process of elimination. I foolishly ignored the process once and dated a Gemini. Things did not go smoothly. I took all the horoscope stuff with the grains of salt around a margarita glass, but would still feel like the universe was green-lighting my crush if the guy I liked was a Pisces or a Scorpio.

I went around the room asking everyone their birthdays. It wasn't a complete waste of valuable English-teaching time; it did require them to recite a month and a date, which most of them needed practice with anyway. Awat was, unfortunately, a Pisces. What happens when you mix a green light with a red flag? I don't know, but it's probably going to end up the color of shit.

Chapter Twenty-five

Virginity Soap

Six months had passed since I began my contract and moved to Iraq. I had finally stopped marveling at the spelling discrepancies in the street signs, I had finally stopped staring at wandering women in abayas, I had finally stopped gaping at pickup trucks carrying fifteen people and a donkey in the flatbed, and I had finally stopped noticing the locals noticing me.

I had finally, also, understood that I wasn't *really* living in Iraq. Kurdistan was a completely different place. So different and so separate from the rest of Iraq, in fact, that Awat made an emphatic statement that put it into perspective for me: "I HATE Iraq. I HATE it! When Iraq football [soccer] team play? I hope they FAIL!" That was serious. Kurdistan versus Iraq.

It was like the Yankees–Red Sox rivalry.

The next "match" was Kurdistan versus Canada, when Warren had to observe my class for a performance review. Warren took a seat in the back of the room, but I knew his personality, and this wouldn't merely be an observation. He couldn't help himself. His ego was driven to be the center of attention at all times, and it was killing him to try to stay quiet while I attempted to teach a lesson. To his credit he did try, but my students were entertained by his gregarious personality, and the men wanted to discuss soccer with him, so I waited politely for several minutes while Warren and Awat good-naturedly argued about Real Madrid and Manchester United, blah blah blah, how was I going to be evaluated on this? I finally held my hand up and shouted, "Enough!" then smiled and reminded Warren he was supposed to be evaluating, and I was supposed to be teaching.

Warren later asked if I wanted to discuss the evaluation casually at the villas and I said, "No." Whether or not he realized it, I really took my teaching seriously and expected a professional evaluation, to be discussed in his office at the school. I didn't want him to just snort through a bunch of jokes about it over beers on the front porch.

He obliged, and the following week I had a meeting with Warren in his office to discuss my performance. He took a sip of his Turkish coffee as I sat across from him expectantly. He began with, "Okay, I don't want you to get a huge head about this..." Great. Nice, professional start to a performance review. I smiled wanly as he continued, "but you're one of the best, if not *the* best English teacher we have at this school." Wow. That wasn't what I had been expecting. I didn't want him to think my ego had exploded, so I cautiously said, "Thank you," while thinking that after all his supreme bullshitting, I couldn't truly enjoy that praise anyway. Who knew if he was telling the truth? What

I could enjoy was how I was simultaneously annoyed and entertained by his visible struggle to compliment me. This wouldn't
have been the case with Old Warren, but New Warren had been
feeling the rift between us as much as I had. He was nothing if not
observant, and since he had returned from his summer break, I
had been carefully avoiding him.

eↄeↄeↄ

Much to my surprise I was having a great time living in Suli. I
had the privacy I desperately craved in the way-off-campus
villas, loved my students, had adjusted to the new schedule, and
was really enjoying the social life with the other teachers. We
drank together, had game night with board games together, had
Saturday brunches (sometimes with smuggled bacon) together,
and commiserated together. There was much to commiserate
about during the Islamic holy month of Ramadan.

According to Wikipedia:

> It is the Islamic month of fasting, in which participating
> Muslims refrain from eating, drinking, smoking, and indulging in
> anything that is in excess or ill-natured, from dawn until sunset.
> Fasting is meant to teach the Muslim patience, modesty, and
> spirituality. Ramadan is a time for Muslims to fast for the sake
> of God and to offer more prayer than usual. During Ramadan,
> Muslims ask forgiveness for past sins, pray for guidance and help
> in refraining from everyday evils, and try to purify themselves
> through self-restraint and good deeds.

There was a virtual meltdown at the villas when people discovered there was no alcohol being sold anywhere. "Oh my God! We should have stocked up!" Ellen practically screamed, brandishing a nearly empty bottle of vodka. I was more concerned with where I was going to eat during the day. No restaurants were open before sundown, including my favorite falafel cart, which was two blocks from the university and had been my main source of lunch since I moved down to Suli.

Classes had to be moved up by two hours, so that students could all get home in time to break the fast and eat dinner. It also meant that they would be dehydrated and hungry during class. The instructors all had to be sensitive to this, and therefore could not eat or drink in front of the students.

I could not make it through a two-and-a-half-hour class without having water ("I've seen her dehydrate, sir. It's pretty gross."), so when the students would leave for the fifteen-minute break, I would duck my head under my desk and drink from my water bottle. There were a few days when Awat and Peshang would stay in the classroom, so I had to ask, "Do you mind if I drink some water?" They were overly gracious and would gush, "No problem! No problem!"

Awat later said to me that he had told his mother all about me and how I would ask permission to drink water. Awat's mother had said, "She is very polite. She is better than some of the Muslims at the market." Apparently, there were quite a few Muslims who didn't take Ramadan very seriously and would openly eat and drink during daylight hours, which was beyond offensive to the Muslims who were observing the fast. I was just pleased his mother approved of me.

I was in with the mom.

✐✐✐

Teaching in Suli was giving me an entirely new perspective, not to mention a window into the hypocrisy of the culture. The Cultural Awareness pamphlet had explained that there was no homosexuality in Islam and that it was a "cultural" thing to see men holding hands with other men. Except many of the men I saw holding hands with other men appeared to be gay. My gaydar is pretty strong, and there's a marked difference between holding hands and lovingly caressing hands, or lower backs, or thighs. I was kind of glad the gay men had managed to create a loophole that rendered their behavior acceptable, but there didn't seem to be any loopholes for the women.

One afternoon I was browsing the beauty aisle of a random, run-down store, and came across something called Virginity Soap. There was only one bar (virginity was in high demand in these Muslim countries), and I grabbed it and shrieked with glee, at the same time thinking, "Ucchhh, this is pretty bad."

An apple-cheeked, pubescent blond smiled at me from the front of the package, which was written both in English and Arabic. Additional print indicated it was "Made in Thailand" and "Manufactured and Distributed by Young & Sweet Skin Care—Paris, France." This was a wildly diverse, multicultural bar of soap if ever I had seen one. "Touch Me! Please" was etched in gold print above the words "Virginity Soap." Also on the front of the box were the phrases "With Rose Extracts," which was nice, "NEW," which was also good, and "Skin Whitening," which was deeply troubling. I know that many Asian countries were very big on skin-whitening beauty products, but most of those were to be used on the face. These were the directions on the side of the box: "Wash it over your sensitive area. Rinse well. Please apply gently everyday." (This was before I had heard that anal bleaching was sweeping the nation back home. Possibly just the porn nation, but the fact that I was even aware of it made my stomach churn a little.)

The instructions on the back of the Virginity Soap box:

> Touch Me! Please Virginity Soap enriched with herbal extracts for cleansing the most sensitive area of women without leaving any residue, maintains the proper natural moisture of the skin. Protect irritations and bacterial infections that cause inflammation, itching, burning sensation and unpleasant ordor. It also tightens the varginal muscel.

Spell-check didn't even know where to start with that.

There was Virginity Soap for women, but no comparable product necessary for men. Ellen, Jen, and I would have furtive and somewhat reluctant conversations, where we admitted that we were starting to feel a little racist. *Virginity Soap is bullshit! What is* wrong *with these people?* We had also discovered that many of the restaurants in the Kurdistan region of Iraq had designated men-only sections. Women, with their loose varginal muscles and screaming children, could eat in the other section.

I was particularly disenchanted with what Shaima, one of my students, told me. Shaima was extremely bright and eager to learn

English to become a journalist/translator. Despite that she was an extremely intelligent and capable human being, she couldn't go out to buy a birthday gift for her husband. She and her husband had just moved to town and didn't know anyone. Since she was a woman, it was not suitable for her to venture out on her own, even to run a simple errand, and she didn't want to have to go with her husband because it would have ruined the surprise. Lame culture, ruining fun birthdays!

The regional rules, however unwritten, were proving to be the metaphorical restrictive ankle straps for the Iraqi women, invisibly tethering them to the confines of their homes.

Travel to other cultures is supposed to expand our minds and tolerance. Living in other cultures doesn't have quite the same effect. Sometimes, becoming culturally aware means learning unpleasant things about said culture. It's not all folk dancing and beautiful, handmade textiles.

Chapter Twenty-six

Common Sense, Totally Broken

We were halfway through the course when my students asked if I would be teaching them again next term. I explained, apologetically, that I would be going back up to Erbil to teach there. (Part of me was wistful at leaving my new Suli friends, the students, and Awat. The other part of me was all, "Hooray! Progressive Dinners! My microwave!")

I was extremely flattered when my students all seemed upset by this news. Avin said to me, "I told my family all about you, how you are such a good teacher, and so beautiful, and I want to be just like you." The ugly teenager inside my brain cried, "Beautiful? Really? You think I'm beautiful?" The moderately less vain grown-up inside my head smacked the ugly teenager and yelled, "There is a more important message here!"

Avin was twenty-one years old and close to graduating university with a degree in psychology. Her English was very good, and she spoke with an awesome level of confidence in class. In the first week, we had been discussing the local culture and how it was not acceptable for women to be out and about after the sun set. Men could run around freely and have dinner with their friends or just hang out on the street. Unless they were accompanied by a male family member, women could not. They were assumed to be whores.

I asked the class what they thought of that unwritten rule. Not surprisingly, the women didn't like it, and Avin went so far as to cross her arms and shake her head violently and say, "I HATE it! I HATE THAT RULE!" She was as emphatic with her hatred for the cultural restriction as Awat was with his hatred of Iraq's soccer team. The men in class were mostly in their early twenties and said they didn't like the rule, but they also really didn't seem particularly concerned with it. Like "Well, whatever, I really just wish I were playing video games right now."

There were plenty of people in Iraq who would claim that the women were perfectly happy and content to stay at home. "They prefer it!" And I was sure there *were* some women who had no desire to go out in public, regardless of the time of day. But there were also plenty of girls and women like Avin.

For the first time it dawned on me that some of the female students might view me as a role model. Wow. I was like a grown-up, less-annoying version of Hannah Montana.

Must remember to use newfound power only for good and not for selling records and mediocre, bubblegum-poppy feature films.

❧❧❧

Awat brought the subject up of my leaving when we were having our after-class chat. He said, "I will miss you … if only—you know 'if only'—it mean 'wish'? There is song by West Life…" And then he began reciting the lyrics to some song by some British band called West Life:

> If only you could see the tears
> In the world you left behind
> If only you could heal my heart
> Just one more time
> Even when I close my eyes
> There's an image of your face
> And once again I come to realize
> You're a loss I can't replace

Oh my God. I was completely agape, and said, "Wow, that's, um, romantic." Even though I was secretly entertaining a crush on him, I had to remain outwardly professional. He was still my student.

I wasn't even sure if he realized what he was saying or how it sounded to me. I quickly changed the subject and avoided eye contact. I noticed that he was wearing a new watch, a nice leather-banded, large-faced watch, and I complimented him on it. I asked if I could try it on, and once it was on my wrist he said, "You keep it!" I exclaimed, "Noooooooo, no no no." He asked, "Why?! I want you have it. I like it for you." I pointed out that I already had a watch, and I really liked his watch on *him*.

What was happening?

While I was trying to ignore my growing feelings for one of my students, I discovered that Nina was fully embracing her feelings for one of hers. In one of the car rides from school she had non-chalantly asked, "So, if one of my students wanted to invite me to their house, would it be okay for me to go?" Teachers were often invited to get-togethers at the park with their students, or for group coffee meetings, or even one-on-one meetings between same-sex student and teacher.

I asked, "Is the student a female?"

Nina said, "No…"

I offered, "If it's in a group situation, it's fine, but if it's just one of your male students, inviting just you to his house, I would say no." I would absolutely not have gone anywhere with Awat alone. I couldn't be trusted with myself.

The next night, Ellen, who was Nina's roommate, said Nina had been dropped off at the house in a red BMW by a Kurdish man. We deduced she had not listened to our advice when the red BMW continued to appear at the compound. I couldn't really begrudge her wanting to have some sort of social life. She hadn't bonded with anyone from the university, and she was probably pretty lonely. But life is likely to be lonely when you say a lot of weird stuff and frequently offend people.

‧‧‧

We had one week of vacation coming up. Eid al-Fitr was the finale to Ramadan, when the month of fasting would be finished and the Muslim families could all celebrate with dinners and parties. We would not have class that week. After that we only had one week left and then the semester would be over. Awat said, "I think I will cry when this class ends. I don't want to say good-bye." I didn't want to say good-bye to him either.

Conversely, all of the teachers were really looking forward to saying good-bye to Nina. Everyone who had been hired on the three-month temporary contracts (Nina, Bobby, Ellen, and Kelly) had interviewed with Warren, and Bobby, Ellen, and Kelly were offered the official one-year contract. Nina was not, although she was unaware of this. It was somewhat awkward to work with her, as Bobby, Ellen, and Kelly couldn't discuss their renewed contracts, per Warren. He claimed he was worried that if Nina knew her contract wasn't being renewed, she would leave during the vacation and not come back. This would leave Warren with a class of students for which we would have to find a substitute. Nina was constantly bringing up the topic and would say things like, "I sure wish they would let us know if our contracts were being renewed."

So, in addition to feeling uncomfortable around her due to vast personality differences, we had the added pressure of having to be dishonest. Once Nina was gone, the general atmosphere would be positive and easy again, and we wouldn't have to think of how to carry on awkward conversations about her hotness or her wild theories. I was sure there were people, somewhere, who were Nina-kind-of-people, and I wanted her to find them. But they weren't here.

···

Chapter Twenty-seven

The Straw That Broke the Donkey's Back

···

I went to Stockholm, Sweden, for the Eid break and was certain the trip would give me a little perspective. I simply could not be romantically interested in one of my students. It was ridiculous. He was a Kurdish Muslim who was fifteen years younger than me and slept in the same bedroom as his mother. I'd just been in a little surreal bubble for too long and needed to get out of town, get out of the country, get out of my head a little.

Stockholm seemed like the ideal place to go, not only because I was one-quarter Swedish and wanted to get back to my roots, but also because there was a new airline, Viking Air, that flew nonstop to Stockholm from both Suli and Erbil. That flight could also be extended to continue on to London's Gatwick airport. That was going to be a possible option for when I next flew back home to the United States.

The luggage allowance of thirty kilos alone was enough of an incentive for me to fly with them. Stupid Austrian Airlines and their measly twenty kilos. I'd show them. My new favorite airline, Viking Air, would give me ample luggage allowance and perspective.

In hindsight, I maybe should have gone with someone on the trip, though, so I didn't end up alone with my own thoughts. Even though I was supposed to be clearing my head, I was still thinking about Awat. Without the distraction of someone else's chatter, I checked into my hotel room and thought, "Oh, I wish he were here with me; he would love this. It has PlayStation." Seriously. I had a vivid dream about him during the trip, where there was passionate kissing and a movie theater. The movie theater wasn't significant; it was just all I could remember other than the kissing.

When I arrived back in Suli, I found this in my work email inbox:

From: Awat

To: gretchen

Subject: hi teacher how are you, i wish nice trip for you, enjoy your time and g0ing

What? (Later he explained he had trouble sending this message, and when I showed him the above he said, "No, I sent another," which I hadn't received.)

The universe was giving me a sign. The sign was that we needed to work on Awat's writing skills, but I ignored that. The *real* sign was that he had *emailed* me on the *same day* that I had the *dream* about him. That was something, wasn't it? Anyone? Horoscope? Bueller?

So, I returned from Stockholm, without the perspective I was looking for, but with two beautiful new sweaters, a ruffled Lanvin top from a fantastic high-end consignment shop, $100 worth of fashion magazines, and no overweight luggage charges.

e~e~e~

My first bright, sunny day back at school, I was walking to class and saw Awat strolling toward the classroom cabin. Oh God, he was really gorgeous. Tall, dark, and handsome, just like in all the romance novels. Jen had even admitted there was just something different about him. She said, "He almost seems like royalty or something." He was wearing a blue button-down shirt that I hadn't seen before, with chest hair teasingly peeking out of the top, and aviator sunglasses, and...ohhhhh, this was not good.

He grinned widely when he saw me, and we joined up and walked the rest of the way to the classroom together. Without looking at me, his head bowed, he said softly, "I missed you."

Dammit, where was that perspective? What was wrong with me? I responded in appropriate teacherlike fashion with, "Oh, that is so sweet, thank you!" and said nothing about how I was thinking about him while I was away and wished that he could have come with me, and that I had had a kissing dream about him, and other completely inappropriate thoughts I had had over the break.

After class he told me he had to go up to Erbil the following Monday. I said, "I will be in Erbil then! You should stop by the villas and say hi!" He seemed excited about this and agreed, "Yes! I will visit you! And I will bring my fat friend!" I understood that

244 I Have Iraq in My Shoe

since it was a long trip, he would want to bring a friend along for
the ride. I assumed they would take a taxi, since Awat said his "fat
friend" was also not allowed to drive. Class would be completely
finished by then.

We would be outside of the university environment for the
first time.

♋♋♋

My head was spinning with the delirium of seeing Awat again; at
the same time I was trying to process the horror that had happened in Suli while I was gone. The night I arrived back, I walked
into the kitchen where Jen was having a late-night snack. I asked
her how the week had gone here, and Jen said, "Well, not great.
Nina was attacked."

>**Me:** WHAT?! Attacked? What do you mean attacked?
> Not raped?
>**Jen:** Yeah, she was raped.

Oh God. The red BMW guy.

>**Me:** What happened? Where was she?

Jen proceeded to explain that Nina had been out walking, after
dark, by herself, outside of the compound, and two Kurdish men
in a truck grabbed her. I exploded. "WHAT? Ellen told her, specifically, *not* to walk outside of the compound by herself! WHAT

WAS SHE DOING?" I was outraged because she knew better, or she should have known better.

Ellen and I had gone running one afternoon, on the trail that wound around out behind the compound into an open expanse of land that led up toward the mountains. It was broad daylight, in the middle of the day, and it was just the two of us. Two Kurdish men on a small motorbike drove up the trail and started following us. They ended up driving back and forth, past us several times, and calling out "Choni!" while slowing the bike down.

The driver of the motorbike looked drunk. Initially we just ignored them, but when they continued to circle us, I finally lost my patience and barked "GET THE FUCK OUT OF HERE!" There was a time and a place for cultural sensitivity, but it certainly wasn't when the "culture" was harassing you. I didn't feel threatened, but I could tell Ellen did. The Kurds were both small, and at least one was drunk. I was pretty sure we could have taken them. I know fake kung fu.

They eventually drove off, but Ellen was very shaken up by that experience and said, "Nina comes running back here by herself a lot. I'll have to tell her not to do that anymore."

So my reaction to hearing that Nina had been attacked was a mixture of horror at the attack and helpless outrage at her general lack of common sense. I felt guilty for being angry, but at the same time where was her *brain*?

- She had been walking by herself, after dark—not advised.
- She had smiled and waved at two random Kurdish men in a truck—nooooo.

- She had accepted a ride from the two random Kurdish men in the truck. NO NO NO—STRANGER DANGER!

Jen said that since it happened, Nina had been telling everyone about the attack, including all the new faculty and staff who had only arrived a week ago. She was also still trying to get her contract renewed to stay in Iraq. Warren had two university employees approach him, on unrelated, separate occasions, and suggest that he offer her a new contract. He was stunned and asked, "Did Nina ask you to talk to me about this?" and both said yes.

At the same time that she was attempting to secure another contract to stay in the country where she was brutally attacked, she was also worrying about the repercussions of the rape. She confided to Jen that she was worried that Iraq practiced sharia law. In extreme fundamentalist Islamic societies, if a woman is raped, she runs a high risk of being charged with "zina" (extramarital fornication), and she can be punished by public whipping or even stoning to death. This was luckily not a common practice in Kurdistan.

The university had offered to fly one of her relatives, or close friends from home, out to meet her in Dubai to escort her back to the United States. Dubai? Why didn't they offer to fly them all the way here? For some reason Nina ended up asking Ellen if she would fly with her to Dubai. Although they were roommates, Nina barely knew Ellen. They had different schedules and were like ships passing in the night. Ellen thought that was odd and asked if anyone from home was coming to meet her and Nina said, "No," and then admitted that her parents didn't want to come, and her sister didn't believe her story.

If her own sister didn't believe her, I wondered if she *had* made up the story? Who would make something like that up? Warren was convinced she was lying and said Chancellor Tom and the provost were also skeptical.

She had just said so many things that were beyond bizarre that it was incredibly difficult to take her word for anything, although it felt very wrong to even have an inkling of disbelief about her story. I was always the first to stand up and yell and scream about injustices to women, and yet here I was, questioning what had happened. *If it had been anyone else.*

There was no positive side to any of this; either Nina was making the story up, and two innocent men would likely be imprisoned, if not put to death; or she was telling the truth, and it really did happen, but she had an incredibly negligent, calloused family and no one to really turn to. It was a lose-lose situation.

She would only be in Suli a few more days, and I kept thinking, "I should say something. What should I say?" I couldn't overcome my unease with her and felt like I was a horrible person because I wasn't offering her any support. *Shit, shit, shit, say something to her! Why can't I be a better person?*

Nina had wisely gone to Buddha Jen for support, and Jen was helping her get through the fallout. She had to suffer through what could only have been a completely humiliating doctor's exam, with the questionable Dr. Aso. Dr. Aso was the university's doctor, who had once responded to a female instructor's horrible case of food poisoning by saying, "This is good for you. You will lose weight and be thin." I had heard people say that Dr. Aso was just a veterinarian, rather than an MD, which made me wonder

(A) why he was considered the university's doctor, and (B) well, we really didn't need a B, did we?

I truly believed that leaving Iraq would be the best thing for Nina.

Nina avoided those last few days of class and had someone fill in for her. She also, understandably, decided not to attend Student Appreciation Night, which was the end-of-semester send-off for the students who completed their course.

The party was held at a local restaurant called Castello, which was known for its pizza. We had finally expanded beyond Assos and the hummus and chicken kebab dinner. All the teachers were driven to the restaurant in the shuttle bus, and we had about a half hour to mill around and take photos before the students showed up. Things around the school had been weird and tense since Nina's attack, and I think we were all kind of relieved to have the student get-together as a distraction.

The second Awat walked through the door I forgot about everything else. He was the first of my students to arrive, and he looked gorgeous. The previous day, he had been mulling over wardrobe options. "I have black suit, and gray suit, and blue suit..." and I said, "Oh, I love blue!" He replied, "Then I will wear the blue suit!" The Kurds were very big on suits, but being in a still-developing country the suits were made with cheap fabrics and interesting cuts.

They reminded me of the *Saturday Night Live* sketch from the late '70s with Steve Martin and Dan Aykroyd's "Two Wild and Crazy Guys" with the tight, flared pants and the scary plaids. Awat's suit was neither wild nor craaaazay. It was a deep Russian blue, and he was grinning ear-to-ear; he looked amazing.

My other students showed up, and as the evening went on, we had a great time eating together, laughing, and telling stories. I was really going to miss them. I was still being the appropriate teacher, and not behaving any differently toward Awat than I did toward any of my other students, except that he sat next to me at dinner, and at one point asked if he could eat off my plate. Like he did with his mother. Ucchhhh.

My male and female students had grown very comfortable around one another and seemed more like a family than just a class, which made me so proud. After finishing dinner, we were milling around when I noticed an empty room just off the main area. I peeked in and saw two comfortable-looking couches, with several cushy chairs, all surrounding a large, low coffee table. I decided that room was there just for my kids, so I brought them all in and we sat down and pretended we were the VIPs of the party.

Toward the end of the party, Pshtewan, one of my students who was raised in a very traditional, conservative household, took a moment to solemnly say to me, "Teacher. You were a very, very good teacher, and I want to say 'thank you.' I was surprised." Then it was my turn to be surprised, for surprising him. How low were his expectations?

Student Appreciation Night was turning into Gretchen Appreciation Night, when Gulan, one of my non-headscarved girls in that same second class, grabbed both of my hands and gushed, "Teacher, thank you SO much." Gulan was the "glossy one." She was the most Westernized-looking female in the class and wore fashionable outfits and a lot of makeup and always had her hair looking just so. She continued, "You teach me so much more than just English." I promise I did try to teach them to use past tense verbs, like "taught," but sometimes in real-life situations they would occasionally forget. I wasn't entirely sure what else I had taught her, but she seemed really enthusiastic about it, and that made me happy.

Then it was Peshang's turn. He had been the bane of my teaching existence on more than one occasion. Peshang was twenty-one years old and could be a little intense and angry sometimes. He would grow borderline enraged in class if he said something that I couldn't understand. I would say "Again, please?" to get him to repeat it, in a hopefully more understandable way, but Peshang would just repeat the exact sentence that hadn't made sense to me the first time, only louder and angrier. There was one day where he was just an unbearable little shit, and I was operating on a very short, PMS-induced fuse. I ended the class early, and then went home to vent about the day. I told Ellen that I had just voted Peshang "most likely to become a terrorist." I was really pissed.

One day I asked him to stay after class after a particularly fussy-baby outburst. With one eyebrow arched I looked him straight in the eyes and asked, "Do you *want* to learn English?" His eyes bugged open wide and he seemed completely shocked that I would ask that. "YES!" was his emphatic response. "I study every day! My family know I want to learn English very much!" So I said to him, "Because sometimes I get the feeling that you don't really want to be here, and don't really want to learn English. I want to *teach* you English, but you have to want to *learn*."

At the end of the student appreciation party, I was shaking his hand and wishing him well and he looked at me, in a very earnest, intense way, and said, "Teacher, I want to apologize. For every-thing. Thank you very much." It was an unexpected, truly rewarding moment. Terrorists are seldom remorseful, so I take back what I said.

This was really why I was here. I was strangely making a differ-ence. Yes, I was making money, and paying off my debt, and taking vacations and buying shoes, but I was also positively affecting the lives of people who had been through some serious struggles.

Awat was one of the last students to leave, and was standing with two of my other students from his class. I was shaking hands, and saying, "Good luck!" and Awat said, although laughing a little, "I think I will cry!" I rolled my eyes, "Oh you will not. And you're coming up to Erbil on Monday, so I will see you then."

He nodded his head, and said, "I think I will bring you shifta!" Shifta was a traditional Kurdish dish, which was kind of like small lamb burgers. "My mom will make it!" he declared.

I stopped and looked at him with my brows furrowed and said, "No. I want you to make it."

His eyes popped out of his head and he cried, "WHAT?!"

I repeated, "You can bring shifta on Monday, but I want *you* to make it."

He started laughing and said, "No, no. I will help my mom—she will make it." I was enjoying this, and really liked the idea of making him cook, since it was such a "woman" job in his culture.

"Your mom can help *you*, but I want you to make it," I said.

He thought about this for a few seconds, then his expression changed. He looked very confident and exclaimed, "Okay! I will take pictures for proof!" I laughed and thought he was probably going to have his mom make it anyway.

I said my final good-byes to the remaining students, told Awat I would see him on Monday, and went back to the villas with the other teachers.

The next day I was checking my work email and had this in my inbox:

> From: Awat
> To: gretchen
> hi, best teacher in the world, last night i coud not sleep. i miss you very much

Oh, holy shit. My heart pounded. Jen and Ellen were shocked and then worried. "Gretchen, no! He's Muslim! No!"

I started thinking about Monday. He was officially no longer my student. The more time I spent with him, the more I was convinced that it wasn't just a simple crush. I thought about him constantly. I hadn't felt like this about anyone in a very, very long time, if ever. I felt connected to him on a much deeper level. He truly could be my soul mate. He could be the Ashley to my Scarlett! Or, wait, Rhett was actually The One, wasn't he? I couldn't really use a *Gone With the Wind* analogy in this situation.

This was getting complicated.

~~~

The night before Nina left, a large group of us was sitting out on Johnny and Chady's front porch, having some beers and talking.

Nina came out of her villa with a large red suitcase and rolled it over to where we were sitting. Everyone immediately stiffened.

Nina chirped, "Hey there!" and we all responded with a hesitant "Hey…." Attempting to diffuse the tension and make small talk, I asked if there was anything in her suitcase. She said, "No, not yet," and I took that opportunity to steer far away from the elephant on the porch and voice my complaint about the poor use of suitcase props in the beginning of the Debra Messing movie *The Wedding Date*. Debra Messing's character was going on an overseas trip, and her bags were very clearly empty, and that irked me, although, in hindsight, it was a brilliant way to avoid overweight luggage fees.

Nina responded to my nonsensical tirade by saying, "Oh, people say I look like Debra Messing." That was not the direction I wanted the conversation to take. While everyone else remained silent, possibly marveling at how Nina looked absolutely nothing like Debra Messing, Jen, ever the diplomat, said, "Yeah, I can see that; you've got the red hair." Nina quipped, "Yeah, I also get Julia Roberts a lot, but I'm much hotter than her!"

Nothing was more bizarre than this. Nothing. No one said a word. I mean, because what do you say to the girl who had recently been attacked, in the strange foreign country where you were all living, and who was now leaving, but not before telling everyone how she was hotter than several beautiful, internationally famous celebrities? This was why people were uncomfortable around her. I was at a loss. *Shit, shit, shit, say something. Make it better.*

After an awkward silence I blurted out, "God, I know. People are constantly telling me I look like Angelina Jolie, and it's *so* annoying."

Everyone looked at me and burst out laughing. I looked nothing like Angelina Jolie, and no one was constantly telling me that I did, but I was still not sure whether to be offended by the sheer force of all the laughing. Nina, on the other hand, did not laugh. She just stood there with her big, red, empty suitcase, and a puzzled look on her face. Part of me felt like hugging her, and another part of me couldn't wait for her to leave.

e⁓e⁓e⁓

The university administration waited three weeks before addressing Nina's attack with the faculty and staff, and even then, they didn't really address it.

An actual town hall meeting was held, under the guise of discussing general expat safety. By this time I had gone back up to Erbil and was not able to be present for the meeting, but Ellen and Jen gave me the CliffsNotes version.

Chancellor Tom referred to the attack as "the incident," but he didn't really say anything beyond the fact that there had been one. Based on "the incident," most of the new faculty and staff were anxious and wanted to know whether it was safe for them to walk around the city. Ellen and Jen said these questions were answered by the female dean of students, who Chancellor Tom was now (allegedly) secretly dating and who dressed like Joey from *Friends* when he was wearing all of Chandler's clothing.

She took the recent trend of layering to a new level and was always covered, neck to toe, with sweaters and multiple scarves. There may have even been some opera gloves as well. She did not mess around with the dress code. Jen and Ellen said that during the meeting, while she was supposed to be addressing the general security questions from the new faculty and staff, she went from tense to psychotically shaking, and finally began shrieking a tirade about how the Western female staff was currently dressing. The town hall meeting devolved into a disastrous verbal kerfuffle.

Nina's attack had unintentionally thrust us into a new war zone, and the enemy was tank tops. The administration was more concerned with discussing how the female staff members were dressing at the villas than addressing legitimate safety concerns.

We were told from Day One that we could dress however we wanted at the villas, as they were completely blocked off from the city, and we could feel like we were at home there. The Cultural Awareness pamphlet specifically noted "Dress Code—University building, local markets, and shopping malls." It did not include the villas. We dressed as we would have at home: shorts and tank tops in hundred-plus-degree heat. The overdressed dean of students was threatening everyone's right to comfort by suggesting that, even when inside the villas, we should cover up.

Upon hearing about the tank-top tirade, I wanted to stand up and yell, "Hey, LADY, this is UNACCEPTABLE! UNACCEPTABLE!* You can't cover up this sexy! The sexy is on the inside!" You also can't just come in here and start swinging

---

*When faced with adversity, or perhaps an obstinate authority figure, or simply someone who is not helping you achieve your objectives, my friend Card's dad says, "You need to say to her, 'Hey, LADY, this is UNACCEPTABLE!'" Card's dad is of the generation where all women worked in the steno pool, and men in management positions said, "Have your girl call my girl," and things of that nature. On many occasions, I now find myself saying "Hey, LADY," but just inside my head.

your judgmental accusation lariat around. I heard Mammy's dis-approving voice inside my head: *"You can't show your bosom 'fore 3 o'clock, Miss Scarlett!"*

The oppression is now coming from inside the building.

Strife seemed to be swirling around the university, and another jarring event occurred not long after "the incident." Someone scrawled an anonymous, threatening note and taped it to the overdressed dean of students' office door one afternoon. The resulting murmured gossip that spread like a water-main break throughout the school was that it was a death threat from a disgruntled student. Chancellor Tom exploded. In an email-read-round-the-world he managed, in one fell swoop of the "Send" button, to offend every instructor at the university by suggesting we were indirectly responsible for the death threat. We weren't effectively "controlling" our students, or teaching them proper respect or some crap. Then he venomously spat out an order that we were no longer to refer to our students as "our kids," as if that somehow encouraged violent, anarchic behavior. I wasn't the only one who did this, we all thought of them as such, and it was more a term of endearment than anything else, but Chancellor Tom was not having it: "This is not a family." (Well, if it was a family, we know who would play the rageaholic stepfather.) Rather than assuaging the university's potential collective worry and anxiety with calm, rational guidance, his rant just drove a sharper wedge between the administration and the instructors. The Tom Pappas email was an awesome spectacle of written temper tantrum. He may as well have ended it with, "You threaten my girlfriend, you meet me at the bike racks at 3:00 p.m.!" The irony of all this was that his, again alleged, girlfriend, the one who had shrieked the loudest protests at the town hall meeting, was married. My guess was that the judgmental lariat swinging was designed to deflect any judgment that may have been heading her way.

The proverbial fan had been hit twice at the university, the drama had escalated to outrageous soap opera levels, and I was relieved to get back to the relative calm of Erbil.

๑ **ASTOUNDING** ๑
ACCOMPLISHMENTS OF PART 4

Running total spent on overweight luggage: $3,720. It is astounding that in spite of my careful planning and dedicated use of the Balanzza, this number continues to increase.

Debt eliminated: $33,453—shazam! I'm feeling terribly impressed with myself at this point.

Countries traveled: 5—Austria, France, Croatia, Greece, and England.

Pairs of shoes purchased: 10. I would like to remind everyone that this is a running total. I would also like to point out that two of these were gifts for my sisters. Never mind that Ellie decided to sell hers on eBay for a horrifyingly low amount. It's the thought that counts. But really, Ellie, Stella McCartney slingbacks for $27? Someone was a happy bidder that day. No, no, it's the thought that counts.

Soul mates met: 1—I think.

Cultural tolerance level: 7. I am not a fan of fasting, whether for religious reasons (Ramadan) or otherwise, and a brutal attack by locals on a Western female did not help this rating; however, learning more about the culture via my fantastic students pushed the needle on this one higher than it would have been. In contrast to my above-average cultural tolerance level, my university administration tolerance level was at an all-time low.

Part 5

Love! Exciting and New!

Chapter Twenty-eight

Afternoon Delight

I was triumphantly returning to Erbil, where no one would tell me I couldn't wear a tank top in my kitchen. For this semester Steve would be joining me as my coworker/villa neighbor instead of Adam. (Adam's fiancée had secured a job with the university and joined him in Suli, so he was happy and I was happy for him.) Steve was the one-who-was-not-Brandon, from the Royal Jordanian flight, Joe's brother Same-Same. He was a little needier than Adam, and a little aimless at times, but for my first weekend back, he was still down in Suli, so I had Erbil all to myself.

Adam was being replaced by Steve, and Chalak (our Man-About-Town) was also being replaced. He had been fired, basically for excessive sitting-on-the-porch-swing-and-smoking, rather than working, and also for talking about Warren behind his back.

Chalak's replacement was a cousin of Rana, the HR director. I desperately wanted to know how to say "nepotism" in Kurdish. Apparently he needed a job, and even though he didn't speak English, they hired him to be our driver. All I knew about him was that his name was Dadyar and he was married with five children.

On Dadyar's first day he brought our new Ethiopian cleaning woman, Vana, to the villas around 10:30 a.m. I was rejoining the Progressive Dinners and had volunteered to be "appetizers" on the circuit that night, so I needed Vana to clean the deck and the downstairs area of my villa. No one had been in Villa #69, the boy villa, for a couple of months, so it didn't need to be cleaned. Nevertheless, Dadyar took Vana over to Villa #69. I was in Villa #70, enjoying my lunch and getting a bit of sun in my makeshift solarium on the balcony.

At 2:00 p.m., I looked down at the deck area and saw that it still hadn't been cleaned. That was strange. I went downstairs, walked over to Villa #69, and tried to open the front door. It was locked. I rang the doorbell. There was no answer. I called Dadyar's cell phone.

> **Dadyar:** Hello.
> **Me:** Where are you?
> **Dadyar:** Home.
> **Me:** You went home?
> **Dadyar:** Yes, home.
> **Me:** Uh…okay, but the deck still hasn't been cleaned.
> **Dadyar:** You at villa?
> **Me:** Yes.
> **Dadyar:** Okay, I coming now.

I was curious to see where Dadyar would be coming from, as I didn't really believe that he had gone home, so I peered out the window like Gladys Kravitz and watched. Less than a minute later

I saw both Dadyar and Vana emerging from Villa #69. They had been inside the villa for over three hours.

What the hell was that? It was Dadyar's first day of work. What was going on? I marched down to the deck, all sassy boss-lady with hands on hips, and demanded, "Where were you? Were you in that villa this whole time? Why was that door locked?"

Dadyar was either not terribly bright or an excellent actor, as he looked genuinely perplexed. This could have been because he didn't understand what I was saying. I usually spoke more clearly and slowly with the Kurds, but I was irritated and the sentences were rattling out of my mouth like machine-gun fire. Vana, on the other hand, spoke a little more English than Dadyar and looked like she knew exactly what I was saying and what I meant. Her face said, "Uh-oh, busted."

I really didn't have time to serve Moral Judge & Jury Judy Duty, and I still needed the deck and downstairs cleaned. I turned to Vana and calmly said, "I need you to clean the deck, and the downstairs in this villa," and pointed to my villa. Vana asked, "Now?" and I said, "Yes please, now." She replied, "Okay, I go finish five minute other villa," so I said, "Fine." Dadyar and Vana both walked back to Villa #69, and I turned to go back inside Villa #70 to call Warren.

It was the weekend, and it was hot outside, so the CED staff in Suli was partying on Ellen's villa roof. Warren was drunk when I called him, and therefore did not sympathize with my ranting. He saw that it was me calling, on his cell, and answered the phone "GERTS! YOU BIG WHORE!" If I hadn't been so frustrated, and looking for resolution to the current problem, I would have hung up on him. As it was, I just ignored the slight (or what he probably considered a hilarious greeting) and told him what had happened so far.

Warren: Huh. So, you think she was takin' a ride on the old baloney pony?

Me: Um…okay, gross, but probably. They were in there for THREE HOURS!

Warren: Did she do any cleaning?

Me: You're missing the point, THREE HOURS!

Warren: *(kind of more sober)* Okay, Gretch, here's what I want you to do. Can you go over there, and just see if she cleaned anything?

Me: Yes. And I will keep you on the phone while I do that. You do get, though, that I don't care so much about the cleaning at this point? Does it really matter if she cleaned anything over there? The door was locked and they didn't answer it even when I rang the doorbell. It's his FIRST DAY OF WORK.

Warren: Yeah, that's weird. Just see if she cleaned at all.

Still holding the phone, I went to the front door of Villa #69 and tried to open it. They had locked it again.

Me: *(outraged)* THEY LOCKED IT AGAIN!

I rang the doorbell, and this time Dadyar answered. I yelled, "WHY IS THIS DOOR LOCKED? THIS DOOR SHOULD

NOT BE LOCKED!" He gave me the same dopey, perplexed look as I walked in the villa, still holding the phone up to my ear.

> **Warren:** Did she clean anything?
> **Me:** It doesn't look like it.

Upon seeing me, Vana had quickly grabbed her mop and was dragging it dramatically back and forth in the upstairs hallway. I marched up the stairs and asked, "What have you cleaned today?"

> **Warren:** Does it look clean?

Vana directed me to the upstairs bathroom and said, "I clean here," and then led me down the hall to the living room and said, "I clean here."

> **Me:** *(to Warren)* So she's showing me the upstairs bath-
> room and the living room, which I'm pretty sure were
> already clean since no one has been living here recently.
> **Warren:** So…do you think she was cleaning, or do you
> think she was gettin' poked?
> **Me:** Erm..gross, but the second one.

Warren was clearly less concerned with the seriousness of the situation and was really more enjoying the opportunity to trot out all of his vulgar euphemisms for sex. I marched back down the stairs, out the door, and back to Villa #70, leaving Dadyar and Vana in a state of semi-bewilderment in Villa #69.

Warren: Okay, Gretch, here's what I want you to do. I want you to send me an email, telling me just what you've told me and seen today. Is it okay if we handle this on Sunday?

Me: Sure, that's fine.

I sat down and hammered out the email, certain that my detailed documentation would lead to the swift dismissal of the inappropriate Dadyar, and while I did this Vana finally cleaned the deck, and then the downstairs part of my villa. I paid very close attention to the time she started cleaning the bathroom and the time she finished, to have a general comparison for her "work" over in Villa #69. Maybe it *did* take her three hours to clean two rooms.

It only took her twenty minutes to finish the bathroom in my villa. I also peeked out the window while she was cleaning the deck, only to see Vana bending over one of the tables, scrubbing away, while Dadyar stood behind her, holding a rag and gazing lovingly at her backside.

Warren's "handling" of the situation on Sunday consisted of telling me that he couldn't really fire Dadyar after only one day of work. I, conversely, thought that would be the ideal time to fire him, but Warren spun the situation by yammering on about Dadyar being Rana's cousin, and how he needed to be careful about how everything was worded, blah blah blah, nepotism and bureaucratic bullshit. The administration probably had their hands full down in Suli, distributing newly revised copies of the Cultural Awareness pamphlet, with complimentary bars of

Virginity Soap, and trying to make sure all the female staff members were wearing oversized sweaters.

So, Dadyar was our new driver/assistant/man-about-town. He didn't speak English, seemed to be dishonest, and may or may not have been having a torrid affair with Vana, our pert Ethiopian cleaning lady.

Chapter Twenty-nine

Shifta

After a very fun Progressive Dinner, where I got to catch up with Katherine and my other Erbil friends, and eat appetizers on the newly cleaned deck, I went inside and sat on the living room couch with my laptop and checked my email. There was one from Awat:

> Hi, the bes teacher i have ever had, i want viste you tomorro if you dont mind, with terrefic shfta. how about 11am? i am waitting for your answer

Our class had been a conversation class. We hadn't worked on writing at all. You would think that the infantile appearance of the emails would be a turn-off, but you'd be wrong.

I responded:

> Hi! You are always welcome to visit, especially if you are bringing food. 11 a.m. sounds fine—I will be here, probably unpacking.
>
> See you and your fat friend tomorrow!

I was looking forward to seeing him and was also really curious to see how fat his fat friend actually was.

He reconfirmed:

> ok. see you tomorro, good-bye

Maybe we should work a little on the writing when he comes up.

❧❧❧

Awat made the shifta, all by himself, and brought photos for proof. He showed up at my door, 11:00 a.m. on the dot, wearing the blue shirt I loved, and swooning ensued. His "fat" friend, Hawre, was not actually fat; he just had a little bit of a belly. He spoke absolutely no English but did speak Friendly Smile and seemed to be really sweet.

Since the shifta had traveled three hours, it needed to be warmed up, so Awat lit the stove and found a frying pan. Watching him stride around my kitchen, looking like he knew exactly what he was doing, was too much. He was all smiles and casual confidence. This was terrible.

To make things worse, the food he had cooked was delicious. I had invited Steve out onto the deck to be social and to enjoy the food with us. Every half hour or so Hawre would say something to Awat in Kurdish, and Awat would just dismiss him with a wave of the hand and say to me, "He want to go home. I say no. I am the boss."

We talked about food. The shifta was amazing, and I was so thrilled to be eating something that wasn't hummus or chicken kebabs.

I asked Awat what he brought for dessert (and was only half kidding). He bemoaned the fact that he hadn't thought of dessert, and said we should have had fruit. Awat mentioned that he loved peaches, and Steve snarked, "Ahhhh, *peaches*. Do you love peaches? I love peaches. Peaches, isn't that what you call girls'… you know," and here he held out his hands in front of his chest to indicate breasts.

Oh, for crying out loud, Steve.

Steve looked from Awat to me, shrugging uncomfortably, and said, "What? We can talk about that, can't we?" Awat shook his head and said, "Only if is okay with Miss Gretchen." I said, "No, we don't need to talk about those kinds of peaches right now, Steve," and rolled my eyes. I was ready for Steve to go back to his villa. I had just asked him over to be nice.

Awat and Hawre stayed for three hours before I finally made them leave. Poor Hawre was supposed to meet friends at his house, and he had been so patient with Awat all day. I felt sorry for him.

The day had been far more formal than our private classroom talks, and I wasn't sure what to make of that. The departure was equally formal, since there were four of us standing there, saying things like "thank you" and "have a safe trip home."

Awat spotted my cell phone on the counter and exclaimed, "You have a phone?!" He couldn't have really been that surprised—everyone in Iraq had a cell phone. I said, "Yes."

And he asked if he could have the phone number. For a split second I thought, "I should say no," but instead said, "Okay," and let him plug the numbers into his phone. I had one additional brief moment of misgiving about that, but then thought, "How can I keep in touch with my soul mate if he doesn't have my phone number?"

At 5:30 p.m. my cell phone rang. I had been looking through the photos on the CD Awat made for me. Some were of him cooking (for proof), and the rest were from the Student Appreciation Dinner. Awat's name popped up on the small screen of my phone, and my stomach jumped a little. It was a cocktail of excitement, remorse, and massive twinges of guilt.

> **Me:** Hi!
> **Awat:** I calling to assure…

Awkward pause.

> **Me:** Are you calling to let me know you got home okay?
> **Awat:** Yes, I arrive home…my mother and brother's
>   wife and sister send their greetings.

The connection was kind of bad, and that combined with the language barrier made the conversation kind of stilted. It was completely different when we were face-to-face, and I realized how much of our communication had been nonverbal.

> **Me:** Thank you! Tell them I said hello! I sent you an email.

I wrapped up the conversation because the line was cutting in and out, and I felt nervous. After he had left, I had sent him an email and attached a few photos I had taken while he was being all sexy and cooking in my kitchen. You could really never have too many sexy-man-cooking photos:

> I am so excited to have REAL FOOD to eat!!! Thank you so much for making shifta, and coming over for a visit. It was good to see you.
>
> My favorite photo is "Awat preparing," because you're smiling. You should smile in all your photos—you have a beautiful smile.
>
> Good luck with your new class, and I'll talk to you soon.
>
> Gretchen

The tone of the email was more casual than I felt. His response came a few hours later and must have been sent right when he had gotten home.

> i am so sorry i do not imidatily replay your email because my enternet conection did not working, i am in the coffe Internet now…thank you for everything, especially for photos. be sure i will smilling in photos, sure i will visit you again

WHEN?

He had gone to an Internet coffee shop specifically to email me. This was crazy. Even though we were no longer student/ teacher, we were still twenty-four-year-old/thirty-nine-year-old, Kurdish/American, and Muslim/not.

Assimilating is a good thing, but I had inadvertently surpassed normal assimilation. I had reached the point where I thought it a completely feasible and logical idea to date, and maybe someday marry, my Muslim student. I began Googling things like "marrying a Muslim" and "Kurdish weddings" and, of course, had to reinvestigate "oral sex and the Koran."

I had completely lost my mind.

Islam is not known for its open-mindedness, or support of women, so I had to find out just how challenging things would be—you know, when I married my sexy, young Muslim Kurd.

Wikipedia was unable to assist me with this, so here are a few things I discovered from various forums and message boards:

- "At first, the man will be charming and considerate. He knows, about a woman he is pursuing, that 'once she is in the cave, I can eat her.' The man will change and become his true self after marrying."
- "If the man is unhappy, it is all your fault, and if he divorces you, the children are his. Arab men have very hot blood, so easily hit women, and the Koran says that is OK."
- "On the wedding night the man places his hand on his new wife's forehead and orders out all the evil."
- "No alcohol could be served at the reception."

None of these things were good, because I was sure the "once she is in the cave, I can eat her" idea did not have anything to do with oral sex. And I absolutely could not imagine a wedding reception without wine.

There were also so many horror stories about Western women who had fallen in love with, and married, Muslim men. The infamous *Not without My Daughter* story was frequently mentioned as a cautionary tale.

Chapter Thirty

Crazy Pills

My social life was certainly looking up, but things with work were going from bad to worse. The first minor annoyance was that I had to "go Security" again, this time with Steve and Dadyar. Dadyar drove us to the same small building where Chalak had taken Adam and me so many months ago. I wondered why they had to ask me the same questions all over again. Somewhere in the undoubtedly overflowing filing cabinet of Erbil's Security Department, there are now two documents detailing my single status, my parents' retirement, my irrelevant American work history, and, if the recording secretary had a sense of humor, possibly the fact that I enjoy long walks on the beach.

Nothing made sense in Erbil now. We had a new Man-About-Town who spoke even less English than our last driver, and we also had Andy. Andy was sent up to Erbil in October to "coordinate" things, facilitate structural changes to the villa (they were turning the main floor of Villa #69 into a testing center), and to generally handle any issues that arose.

At first Andy seemed like a great "go-to" guy. He was constantly asking, "Anything I can do for you guys? Just let me know." He was a large, pale man with thin blond hair and a very small head, whose daily uniform was loose-fitting cargo pants, cargo shirts, and work boots. Andy lived in Villa #69 with Steve, and Steve said Andy spent most of his spare time on the Internet, Skyping with his wife who was a Filipino nurse, living back home in her country. We weren't sure of Andy's medical acumen, but he kept the refrigerator stocked with various prescription pills.

Andy always seemed to be in the middle of doing something, or going somewhere, or going somewhere to get something for the other thing he was working on. I received an inordinate number of either phone calls or texts from him on a daily basis, usually just asking me to reconfirm something I had confirmed for him the day before. "Yes, Steve and I have class tomorrow, and again, no, we don't need any additional supplies, but thanks."

As the weeks went by, we noticed that Andy needed an awful lot of reassurance in regards to his projects, and also needed to confirm and reconfirm, and then reconfirm yet again, anything Steve and I had talked to him about.

Andy's progression of crazy was slow but steady. Steve and I grew increasingly uncomfortable with every interaction we had with him. The university had arranged for him to teach an off-site class for some company, and when Andy would leave in the mornings, Steve and I would get together and compare notes on the level of craziness we had last experienced.

Steve had the winner. He had planned to go to Oktoberfest at the German restaurant a few weeks back when some friends came up from Suli; however, Andy had given him painkillers for a sore back. The painkillers were actually Xanax, and Steve had taken two, rendering him completely comatose. While the rest of us were sitting at the outdoor picnic tables, drinking real German beer out of steins, eating sauerkraut and bratwurst, and waving our steins around to the imported oompah band (or, as I drunkenly referred to it, the Oompa-Loompa band), Steve was at home, stoned on the couch.

Andy had been told, by Warren apparently, to give interested Kurds who stopped by inquiring about classes a spiel about the classes, as well as a tour of the classrooms. These, of course, happened to be in my villa. Andy would call and text, asking me to unlock the door in order for him to conduct his tour. I would typically oblige.

One night, around 7:30 p.m., Andy called with the usual request. It was dark outside, I had PMS and was cranky, and had gotten into my pajamas for the evening. We had never had a visitor show up this late before. I was so fed up with the lack of privacy, and the possibility of a potential student seeing me in my jammies, that I told Andy no. "It is too late for someone to just be showing up for a tour," I said.

Andy became aggressive on the phone and growled, "Well, you'd better be the one to tell Warren then!" I responded, "Okay, I'll send him an email." God, it was ridiculous how terrified some of these people were of the Wrath of Warren. Honestly.

I sent Warren this email:

Hey,

I know you want Andy to show potential students the facilities—this is fine. But I do not want people wandering through here at all hours of the night.

Andy just called, and had 2 students he wanted to show the classrooms to.

I said "No"—it's 7:30 p.m. He wanted me to let you know (I think he's worried about getting in trouble). He was a little fussy about it, and was like "well, what's the problem…are you scared?" My reasons shouldn't be in question. It's supposed to be my home.

"It's YOUR villa, Gretch. YOUR villa."

I think tours are fine between 9:00 a.m. and 6:00 p.m., and I am happy to leave the doors unlocked to allow access downstairs. But, again, I am also living here, and need to have some boundaries. Sheesh.

Questions? Comments?

Gretchen

Andy took it upon himself to send Warren an email of his own, and copied me:

Warren,

As per our conversation, I had told you that once in a while potential students/clients have expressed interest in enrolling in the CED program in Erbil.

In villa 69 Steve and I always let the students inside so they can sign their name, give us their email, and phone number. We then tell them a little bit about CED and how we are very professional and growing.

He crapped on about how detailed and diligent he was in his recruiting and talked about how he showed prospective students the "students supplies, computer lab, fresh painted walls, a beautiful deck, umbrellas, tea and coffee room, projectors" and then continued on about the problems he was having with my reluctance to cooperate with him, despite the fact that he and Steve were there "for protection." The email was very long, very annoying, and very full of brown-nosing, and if Andy really thought I would consider a self-medicated loon "protective," he needed another Xanax. He signed the email:

Regards,

Andrew David Hall, CED Coordinator-Erbil

Working overtime 9–4 Sunday to Thursday—Text me if you need me.

Oh, for crying out loud. That last part was actually part of his standard email signature; the "working overtime 9–4 Sunday" part. I was so over Andy and his psychotic brown-nosing. In my PMS-addled state, I just wanted to fire flaming tampon missiles at his window.

I responded, only to Warren:

Jesus. Does he make this big of a deal about everything?

Warren responded:

> Saying Jesus makes baby Jesus cry… :(

Warren was fresh off vacation, much more relaxed. We hadn't seen much of each other since my performance review, and things felt distantly calm between us. We worked out a compromise with the villa tours, and Andy apologized for going ballistic on me. I mentioned my concerns about Andy, and his self-medicating, to Warren, and he said he'd "keep an eye on it."

Chapter Thirty-one

He's Just Not That into You

I probably should have been self-medicating. The Awat situation was skewing my sense of reality. I had emailed him on the Sunday he would be starting his new English class. He was a little apprehensive about having a new teacher, and I wanted to see how his first day of class had gone. I did not receive a response. Hmmm, that was odd. Monday passed, then Tuesday, then Wednesday, then Thursday, and no email from him.

I emailed Ellen:

> I haven't heard from him since I sent him an email on Sunday. I just asked how his new class was going, who his teacher was, etc....haven't heard back. Although someone called me yesterday (while I was teaching), and the number was suspiciously close to the one he gave me, and I know he has 3 SIM cards. I have the feeling he didn't want me to know it was him calling, which also makes me think maybe he never received my Sunday email. Hmmmm. Such games.

It might have been him calling, but it also might not.

Ellen responded that she hadn't seen him on campus that week, and maybe he was out of town. I responded:

> Part of me just wants to let the whole Awat thing go, but I totally miss him! He just made me laugh, and I really loved spending time with him:(And he cooked for me!!! I swear to God, I ate shifta all last week. And it was awesome. I even gave like half of it to Steve, and still had enough to get me through the week.

Ellen was supposed to be the voice of reason, given her disdain for Muslim boyfriends, but she was in the throes of her own romance with Johnny, the Lebanese Canadian director of general services, and was definitely in a state of "Love can conquer all" because she said, "A man that cooks is a keeper! I say keep it going."

I had read *He's Just Not That into You*, cover to cover. Several times. It was one of my favorite books. If you emailed the object of your affection on a Sunday, and he didn't respond for a week, and you knew he didn't have a job and was probably just playing PlayStation in his living room… He's Just Not That Into You.

When Awat finally did send a casual email, saying he had been "busy," I didn't bother responding. I was too old for this crap. I was not one of his typical clueless giggling "girlfriends" who would wear his favorite color every day and beg him to go do bad things on the mountain. I was a grown-up! I had standards! I had a surprising lack of red clothing! What I had mistakenly thought was a special connection quickly dissolved into a typical disappointment in a matter of minutes. You should always, always listen to your gut. Your gut, and lame, careless emails. "Busy." Busy with what, Alpha Protocol? Chaotic Shadow Warriors?

All that next week I berated myself for being stupid. How totally embarrassing that I actually thought this might be a real relationship. He was twenty-four! He was Kurdish! Ridiculous. I felt completely humiliated but also relieved that I hadn't told anyone but Ellen, Jen, and Katherine about it. My shame increases in direct proportion to the number of people who are privy to my pathetic grasps at romance.

By the end of the week, Erbil had wrapped itself around me in a forgiving hug, and I was feeling back to my normal self again. I had my microwave and my blender and the J&K gym and spa, and my old Erbil life. Thank God for "out of sight, out of mind."

Then on Friday I was checking my email and saw Awat's name pop up in my inbox, with the subject line "complain." God, that was so typical. He didn't email me for a week, and then just wanted to complain about how he didn't like his new English teacher or whatever.

hi ms.gretchen how are you? why you silent? why donot send me email :(? anyway i am fine, i wish you be fine too,

It was unbelievable how unconcerned I was with poor punctuation and creative spelling when it came to him. My stomach flipped. Stupid involuntary nervous system response.

I thought about the situation for the rest of the afternoon and finally arrived at a conclusion. My common sense had fixed itself and was no longer broken. Absolutely not. I was too old to be playing ridiculous pretend relationship games with someone who was completely inappropriate in the first place. I needed to cut this off, with a proverbial sharp Ginsu knife. This relationship was the aluminum can that needed to be sawed in half.

What could I say to him to clearly break off all communication? In Dating Land, what was the quickest, surest way to get rid of a guy? Tell him you love him. Rita Rudner famously said, "Sometimes they leave skidmarks." My common sense might have still been a little bit broken, because I decided I would tell Awat I was in love with him, and he would be so freaked out that he would not respond, and I could go back to being a happy spinster. Ninety-nine percent of me wanted that to happen, and the foolish 1 percent secretly hoped he would respond with a declaration of undying love. (The percentage was probably closer to 80/20, but the foolish part of the percentage was really the minority.)

> Awat,
>
> I'm sorry. This is more complicated than I was prepared for. I think I might be a little bit in love with you, which is not good, and I thought it would probably be best if we didn't keep in touch anymore.
>
> I will trust you not to repeat this to anyone, and I truly wish you the best of luck with everything! You are a very special man, and I will miss you.
>
> Gretchen

I did not receive a response for five days. With each day that passed I thought with relief, "Okay, good, that was the right thing to do." On the fifth day I received this:

> it is ok, do not be sorry, i respect your opinion, i wish in my heart i did not make any mistakes, thank you for every thing, good bye

Ouch. I flashed back to that romantic West Life song he had recited to me and how he had made such a big deal out of not wanting to say good-bye. This "good-bye" stung.

I went to great lengths to overanalyze and read too much into the email, aside from the lack of adequate spacing and proper use of capital letters:

- He respected my opinion—that was a good thing.
- He wished in his heart that he did not make any mistakes—was that a good thing or a bad thing?
- Did he mean that he made a mistake and gave me the wrong impression? Or did he mean that he hoped he hadn't done anything to make me cut off the communication?

See why this was hard? But if he had *really* liked me, he would have fought a little harder to keep up the communication. If someone cares for you enough, they will ignore all reasonable suggestions and recommendations and just make it happen. But nothing was happening, and I found myself swimming in more humiliating rejection.

290 I Have Iraq in My Shoe

⟞⟋⟋⟋⟋⟋⟍

To make things worse, I had given my phone number to Ashton, one of the Australian security guys, at the Progressive Dinner, and he had been calling repeatedly, despite that I never answered his calls. He was a perfectly nice, attractive, funny guy, who was unhappily married. He insisted on walking me back to my villa after the late-late after-party of one Progressive Dinner.

In typical drunken fashion, I thought I could solve his marital problems by counseling him while we walked. I had seen photos of his wife, and she was a stunning Russian woman whom Ashton had gotten pregnant, then married and settled down with in Australia. Yes, yes, oh, poor you. Stuck with a beautiful wife and healthy baby waiting for you at home. But he continued to lament his self-imposed station in life, and I continued to drunkenly discharge advice, explaining that if he was so unhappy, he could get a divorce but still support the child, blah blah blah. Just call me Oprah.

I was able to keep him at arm's length at the door, thanked him for the gallant walk home, and when he insisted I give him my phone number, I said, "No." He persisted. Finally I was like, "Oh, okay, fine." It was easier to just give him the number than continue arguing with him.

So, instead of receiving calls from Awat, I was receiving calls from Married Ashton, and when I refused to answer any of them, he would send texts:

Gretchen. You keep ignoring my calls…so I'm texting! Any plans for later tonight? Cheers, Ashton

He must not have had PlayStation. Maybe if he hadn't been married—distraction is always the best way to cope with the crushing disappointment of rejection. TV would help. TV always helped.

TV did not help this time, because the universe decided that, on one of only five English language channels for me to choose from, it would be comical to repeatedly show the movie *Prime*, where a forty-something Uma Thurman hooks up with a hot, twentysomething guy. When I tried the other four channels, my options were *Monster Garage*, a couple of nondescript '90s movies where it's dark and gray and there are a lot of explosions, or *Flirting with Forty*. Fortysomething Heather Locklear goes to Hawaii and hooks up with hot, twentysomething guy. Who was in charge of Middle East programming?

My iPod was the only safe place for entertainment. I could pick and choose my episodes of *30 Rock*, and decided to skip the one titled "Cougars." *30 Rock* and *Family Guy* were my empathetic, consoling, hilariously distracting best friends, and I watched them over and over and over, laughing until I cried, then crying until I laughed again.

It was lonely times in The Iraq.

Chapter Thirty-two

Blockheads and Kissing Cousins

Marilyn Monroe sang, "When love goes wrong, nothing goes right..." Love went wrong, and so did my new class. It was wrong to compare one class to another much in the same way that it was wrong to compare one of your offspring to another. Or in my case, to compare one pair of shoes to another. But we did it anyway. My new class was, plainly put, not very bright. If my new class were a child, I would say they would most definitely be repeating kindergarten. If they were a pair of shoes, they would be Crocs. I am sorry Crocs lovers, but you're wearing gardening clogs outside of the designated garden area, and it's an affront to all the other shoes.

In an effort to generate positive buzz about the Erbil CED program, Warren and Jill arranged a pro bono contract with the Ministry of Planning. I had a class of nine students in Level 2 (English novice speakers), and Steve had eleven in Level 3 (intermediate English). One of the most noticeable differences between my first semester and this one in the Erbil villa was the number of students and, subsequently, the concentration of body odor.

The villa seemed large when there was just one person in it; however, introduce twenty native Kurds, only five of whom were women, and the villa became an oppressive Crock-Pot of unpleasant smells. Basically, my entire villa smelled like body odor Sundays through Wednesdays. When any of the Suli staff would say, "Oh, you're so lucky! That setup in Erbil is sweet!", I would ask them how their trailer/classrooms smelled at the end of each class, then say, "Okay, multiply that times ten, and imagine it being released in your home." Lucky and sweet, no.

The problem with the ministry class was not that they weren't bright, but rather that Warren wanted to cram as many students into one class as possible, regardless of language aptitude. A couple of my Level 2 students really should have been learning the alphabet, but Level 2 they were, and Level 2 we would have to plod through.

At the beginning of one class, I explained we would be "choosing hotels." "What is choosing?" I asked, rhetorically. "Selecting, picking, etc. If you have four hotels, how do you *choose* at which one to stay?" One hour into class, I read aloud from the textbook, "How important are these factors for you in choosing a hotel?" The jovial, portly, gray-mustached Rabar says, "Teacher, 'choosing' is what?" Sigh.

I was especially concerned with the potential of Ahmed. His knowledge of English was extremely basic, and he struggled with every lesson. The textbook we used had a variety of activities, one of which was "pair work." Pair work was done in each unit, and at the beginning of the course, I paired off every student with a partner. It was unfortunate that Ahmed's partner was Rabar, because they were "the confused one" and "the even more confused one." Both men were truly very sweet and respectful, and seemed to want to learn, but the course material was just so far beyond their comprehension that it would have been impossible to teach them and the other seven students at the same pace.

For the pair work in every unit, I would always say, "Okay, get together with your partner and…" whatever the instructions were in the book: get together and practice introducing each other, get together and discuss your food preferences, etc.

One day, in our fifth or sixth week of class, we came to the Pair Work section of unit 4. I said, "Okay, get together with your partner and practice the conversation model." Ahmed raised his hand and said, "Teacher. I do not know what is 'partner.'" We had been working with partners for the past three weeks. This was not a new word. I thought he was kidding, so I laughed. He looked confused. Then I looked confused and asked, "Really?" Everyone else in the class looked confused, and looked at him like *they* thought he was kidding. He said, "Partner. I not understand." I was flabbergasted. I could not believe that he was saying he didn't understand what "partner" meant, since we had been doing the pair work every week, and every time my instruction would be, "Get together with your *partner*." But I wanted him to understand it, so I decided to make it very clear. I started with Dastan in the back corner of the room:

> **Me:** Dastan, who is your partner?
> **Dastan:** My partner is Solin.

Me: Solin, who is your partner?

Solin: My partner Dastan.

Me: Aryan, who is your partner?

Aryan: My partner is Azheen.

Me: Azheen, who is your partner?

Azheen: My partner is Aryan.

I literally went around the room to every student and asked them this question. I saved Rabar and Ahmed for the end.

Me: Rabar, who is your partner?

Rabar: My partner is Ahmed.

Me: (*triumphantly*) Ahmed, who is your partner?

Ahmed looked at me from under confused eyebrows, and paused, then said, "You?"

Everyone burst out laughing, including me, although mine was that laughter that is close to crying with frustration.

My frustration erupted more frequently with the ministry class. I couldn't figure out why, but they just seemed less sharp than all three of my previous classes. Perhaps it wasn't a matter of intelligence, but interest in the class? The ministry students were taking the class free of charge, at the insistence of their boss, many of them studying at a level that was too advanced for them. My other students had enrolled voluntarily, and had been so much more motivated. I missed my Suli classes. I missed Awat.

"...The clock won't strike, the match won't light, when love goes wrong, nothing goes right."

Not only was the new class not smart, but they were also not honest. They were cheating. The day after the first exam, I graded the tests and passed them back to the students, so we could review the correct answers and they could see which answers they had gotten wrong.

Two of the students, Seraj and Hidayat, each surreptitiously changed one of the answers, then approached me and claimed I had made a mistake when correcting their tests. Since there were only nine students in the course, I remembered every error that each student had made. I remembered that Seraj had incorrectly identified a verb, and I remembered that Hidayat had left an answer blank. It was obvious to me that Seraj had added "ed" to the verb to make it correct, and Hidayat had filled in the answer that had initially been blank.

I could not believe that grown men would try to cheat on a language exam. I spoke with each one separately, looked each one in the eye, and said, "Did you just change this answer?"

One of the lessons we studied in Level 2 was about body language, and there was a study that showed 70 percent of communication was nonverbal. In their nonverbal way, they were admitting to cheating. Both of them shifted uncomfortably, paused, and said, "No…" while smiling nervously. So, in my nonverbal way, I told them I was not changing the grade on their exams. I narrowed my eyes and said, "Yes, you did." They both accepted this and went back to their seats.

I felt like I was teaching eight-year-olds. In class they would whisper answers to one another. If I called on Rabar to answer a question, Hawall would bend his head close to Rabar's desk and mutter something under his breath. I was practically yelling, "Cheating will not help you understand English any better! Hawall, what will Rabar do if he is talking to a native English speaker and doesn't understand what that person has asked him? You won't always be standing next to him to whisper the appropriate response."

In addition to this, during the classroom break, someone went into my refrigerator and drank an entire bottle of my mango juice. I didn't see this happen; I just saw the evidence of the empty container later. Dalzar and Renas never ate my food.

God, what was wrong with everything? Erbil wasn't the same anymore. Cheating and lying and eating my food were the new standard: Dadyar and his cleaner-girlfriend, Married Ashton, my new students.

What the hell?

⌁⌁⌁

In addition to his Level 3s, Steve was teaching a beginner-level conversation class, and Dadyar was permitted to join the class with his wife, Tavan. The class was in the evening, so there was, disappointingly, no chance for an awkward-but-inevitably-scandalous soap-opera-esque run-in with Vana, the pert Ethiopian cleaning lady. Roughly three weeks into the course, Steve sent me a borderline frantic email:

OMG OMG OMG! *[Sometimes Steve could be a little like your best girlfriend.]*

We were studying a unit called "Family relations" in class tonight, and we were talking about everyone's family tree. For practice I would say "Dadyar, what is Tavan?" and Dadyar would answer "She is my wife." When I asked Tavan a similar question "Tavan, what is Dadyar?" she answered "Dadyar is my husband," paused, then continued "Oh, and my cousin!"

When love goes wrong, nothing, nothing goes riiiiiiiiiiiiiiiiiiiiiight.

Chapter Thirty-three

Georgie Catstanza

I was as discouraged with New Erbil as I was with New Warren. No one likes change. *Bring back Classic Erbil and Classic Warren, please.* Katherine had called an end to the Progressive Dinners because they had gotten to be too much work, and all sorts of people were showing up without contributing food or drink. Several of the really fun English Village expats had packed it up and moved back to their respective countries, and the village was starting to feel more like a ghost town than a Happy Place.

The ghost-town ambiance was enhanced by the periodic dust storms that swept through the region and blanketed everything with almond-toned grit. They were sort of exciting to observe, from the safety of my living room, and I sat with my face pressed against the window watching the dust whip and swirl through the empty streets. Someone had said the dust blew in from the Saudi Arabian desert, which made it sound very romantic, but there were so many people spouting off random, unsubstantiated theories about Iraq that I decided to remain content in my ignorance of the actual facts, rather than make myself rabidly crazy trying to get a straight, confirmed answer.

For example, the population of the cities in Iraq seemed to be nothing more than general guesses. After a Google search I found that Erbil's population ranged from an unlikely 170,000 to 3.3 million within the short span of seven years. After my second visit to the master statisticians at Security, I was confident they were probably counting me as two people. Who knew what the real number was?

In spite of my despair at the diminished luster of my former home-away-from-home, life still had to go on, and Steve and I settled into a comfortable routine, not unlike an old, sexless married couple. After class we would make lunch, and then bring it out to one of the deck tables to eat while we enjoyed the sun and took in the lazy neighborhood vibe.

We had also befriended a sassy little kitty cat who seemed kind of stray, but kind of not. He was mostly white with gray and brown patches, and had the sweetest little face. He would run right up to us and try to rub against our legs. At first I was wary of touching him (Number 5 in the Cultural Awareness pamphlet— don't touch stray animals), and Crazy Andy would start bellowing about scabies, but I gave him a close once-over, and he seemed surprisingly healthy and clean for a stray, and I had seen him groom himself on numerous occasions. It is not smart to touch stray animals anywhere, but I just couldn't help myself—I loved him! I named him George, like the Bugs Bunny cartoon where the giant Abominable Snowman wants to hug Bugs and squeeze him and keep him and call him George. I wanted to hug, squeeze, and keep this little kitty cat, but I knew that I could really only get away with the "call him George" part. I kind of felt like I was cheating on Herb, but it was fun when Georgie became part of our daily routine. He magically appeared around 11:00 a.m. every day, when the students started showing up.

Georgie was a social kitty and preferred to be around people. I suppose he also preferred to be around the turkey I was leaving in the heavy glass ashtray I had designated as his food dish.

If Georgie was out roaming the neighborhood, and I saw him in the distance, I would call "Georgie!" and clap my hands, and his ears would perk up and he would come bounding down the street and through our front yard. He was the sweetest, cuddliest kitty, and would just crawl into my lap and then fall asleep. Before we could stop him, Georgie would run right into the villa if the sliding glass door was open, and after a while I just got used to him coming into the classroom while I was preparing for class. He would jump into my lap and make himself comfortable while I sat at the computer. In one of his increasingly rare Old Warren moments, while visiting Erbil, he had given Georgie the clever last name of Catstanza.

Georgie was the one shining spot in the rapidly downward-spiraling world of Erbil. There would be occasional days when he wouldn't show up and I would worry about him—was he getting anything to eat? Were other people in the compound feeding him and giving him water? Katherine confirmed that she had seen him in her neck of the compound, five blocks away, being fed by one of her neighbors. I was only jealous for a second, and then felt relieved that he was being cared for by other people too.

Several families with children had moved into some of the villas on our street in the compound, and we would see the kids riding their bikes back and forth. One day we were sitting outside and George had joined us hoping for some table scraps. One of the little boys parked his bike in front of our deck and cautiously approached George.

The boy's name was Barzan, and he was Kurdish and had recently moved back from the United States—specifically Texas, although he couldn't remember the name of the city. It was weird how the Kurds chose Texas—Renas had gone there too. Maybe the similar climate was part of the appeal. Or maybe it was the barbecue.

Barzan was eight years old and spoke English very well, so Steve and I chatted with him while he played with George. I was curious about the Kurdish families who had moved away from Iraq in the '90s and asked him what his father did in the United States, specifically Texas. Barzan told us his dad had worked at a pizza place.

I was certain this was probably one of those typical immigrant tragedies, where a brilliant surgeon or professor was forced to take on a menial job in the new country, so I asked Barzan what his dad did now that they were back in Kurdistan. "Nothing," he responded, "he just hangs out with his friends." That kind of blew my romanticized ideas.

Barzan said he really missed Texas and wasn't happy to be back in Iraq. This was a refrain I kept hearing from Kurds who had been displaced to various Western countries (the United States, United Kingdom, Sweden, Germany, the Netherlands, and others), then had to come back. They hated having to return to Kurdistan. They found it disorganized, dirty, unsophisticated, and generally backward.

I kept hoping that the relocated Kurds would explain the

concept of hygiene to their countrymen and women, as my villa was still reeking of body odor on a daily basis. Unit 5 in our textbook was titled "Personal Care and Appearance" and focused on personal hygiene products, how to ask for them, and where to find them. Excellent! A natural segue into the odor issue. One of the exercises was a survey about ways to improve appearance:

> Would you try…?
> Diet, exercise, massage, creams & lotions, hair removal…
> etc.

The students were required to mark "definitely," "maybe," "probably not," or "absolutely not" for each option.

I went through the list and had the students raise their hands for each category they would try. We came to "deodorant," and Rabar raised his hand and asked, "Teacher, what deodorant?" Finally, a teachable moment. So I said, "Deodorant, you use it under your arms…for when you sweat…to smell good!" and I pantomimed the under-the-arm swiping. Rabar's brow remained furrowed, and he just shook his head and shrugged. I knew they had deodorant in Kurdistan; I had seen it on the shelves at the store. Whether anyone was *buying* it was a completely different issue. My villa would never smell pretty.

ᕫᕬᕫ

I couldn't even ask Crazy Andy for some Xanax to help me cope with my increasing depression. Warren finally fired him.

Although that, in and of itself, was cause for celebration. He hadn't been fired because of any of the complaints Steve and I had about him, but instead because he went behind Warren's back and complained to Jill about an assignment. He had circumvented Fearless Leader, and Fearless Leader was pissed.

Warren loved to use the word "insubordination," and this situation was the perfect opportunity. Warren was so furious about Andy having gone behind his back that he drove the three hours up to Erbil that same day in order to confront him—veins popping out of his temples. He made me sit in on the conversation so there would be a "witness."

What I "witnessed" was a testosterone-fueled pissing contest, which is not my preferred entertainment milieu. No costumes, no fun music, no snacks. There was an uncomfortable exchange between the two of them involving Warren saying "insubordination" a bunch of times, sometimes followed by "gross incompetence," and Andy looking vacant or bewildered and claiming not to understand what was happening. Warren had had a conversation with Andy two weeks prior to this, basically warning him to get his act together, since there had been multiple examples of Andy's inability to follow specific instructions. I think he must have increased his meds. I started to feel like I might need backup when the tension escalated.

> **Andy:** I've been doing this for thirteen years…what've you been doing? Selling cars…
> **Warren:** Running a business, Andy, that's what I'm doing with CED, running a business.

Andy: I'm not going to be anyone's bitch.

Warren: I'm not sure what you mean by that…

Andy: I mean, I'm not going to be CED's bitch, and just not question anything.

Before the situation could devolve into fisticuffs, Warren reminded Andy that he had already been given at least two verbal warnings: one just five days ago, and one two weeks ago. Andy whined, "I thought that was just a couple of guys having some beers." And Warren said, "It should have been."

I should have been happier about Andy's departure, but it was a hollow victory. I couldn't seem to pull myself out of the funk. And I tried hard. I tried self-medicating with Nutella; I tried retail therapy with a pair of brown leather Marni platform pumps at YOOX. I even made a trip down to Suli for some good girlfriend time, where Ellen's resounding war cry of "There will be CARBS" made everyone gleeful. She wasn't getting along with Johnny and had, instead, become romantically involved with her oven, and was baking up a storm of cookies and cakes.

But the cookies, cakes, and Nutella were just making my pants tighter, and I wouldn't get to enjoy the shoes until I went home for Christmas break. I was also worried that Georgie Catstanza had become too dependent on me for food. I was going to be leaving for three weeks and was imagining him shivering and emaciated, meowling at the sliding glass doors. I did what I thought was the noble thing, and gradually cut down on the days I gave him turkey and tuna, so he would stop expecting it and be able to forage elsewhere, while Steve and I were gone for break. That depressed me even more. I needed help. I needed Psychic Sahar.

Chapter Thirty-four

Psychic Sahar

I had planned to fly home for Christmas, and to maximize my frequent-flier points, I once again flew through London.

London was where I was to have my portentous psychic reading with Psychic Sahar.

Katherine had discovered Psychic Sahar via Google and planned to have a reading done when she was on holiday in London in November. Upon her return, I was tingling with excitement and dying to know what Sahar had said. What lay ahead for our Miss Katherine? I practically shrieked, "HOW WAS SAHAR?" into Katherine's ear on the phone. She responded "Oh, right, I didn't go. I decided to get my teeth whitened instead."

This was the opposite of what I had wanted to hear. I was profoundly disappointed in Katherine's lack of commitment to foreseeing the future. Tooth whitening? How are whiter teeth going to help you fulfill your destiny? Unless your future is in toothpaste commercials; I really shouldn't judge. I wanted confirmation of Sahar's psychic skills, and as Katherine had not tested her credibility, I would have to blindly trust that she could help me with my dilemma. And as it turned out, Katherine's tooth whitening didn't even happen because the dentist she visited informed her she would be unable to drink coffee or red wine or any dark liquids for at least one week after the treatment. That was pretty much all Katherine had planned on doing for the rest of her trip in London: drinking coffee, red wine, and other dark liquids. So it was a fail on all counts. No guidance from Sahar, and no bright, Chiclet teeth.

It was up to me to look into my own future. My biggest question was, "Did I make a mistake with Awat?" Maybe, despite all basic logic, reason, and common sense, he was the one for me.

Two and a half months had passed since Awat's "good-bye" email, and I had spent much of that time wallowing. After spending three hours a day, four days a week seeing him, talking to him, and laughing with him, the ending was abrupt and I missed him.

I could no longer make simple decisions by myself. I needed some guidance. Sahar, help!

Psychic Sahar's website gave several options for a reading. I chose a full life reading:

A Full Life Reading is a comprehensive, or "wholistic," one-hour, long-term psychic reading covering all aspects of your life including career, relationships, health, and finance. It's a bird's-eye view of your life, if you like. It can help you better understand your life's purpose and how to realize it by reflecting back at you where you are at now, where you are meant to be; offering guidance on how to "get there."

I needed to "get there." If you had questions about people, she required you to bring in photos of those people. I printed a photo of Awat and tucked it into the purse I would bring to London.

e~e~e

It was Christmastime on Oxford Street. There were lights and wreaths and miles of garland lining the street, which was choked with black cabs and red double-decker buses. I hadn't allowed enough time to squeeze and push through the throngs of harried shoppers, bustling along, swinging armloads of shopping bags, to get to Sahar's office flat on time. I was ten minutes late, huffing and puffing, sweating and apologizing, when I walked through the door. It was not the serene, psychic-ready state I had been hoping to present, but Sahar was very gracious and welcomed me into her cozy living room. Sahar was probably in her fifties and about my height, with thick, black hair and a low, calm, slightly accented voice. We both sat down at a small, round table next to her living room window.

I had done a couple of tarot-card readings before and was always careful not to volunteer any information about myself. I assumed, if they were legitimate, they would just know what they needed to know.

Sahar began by asking, "Why are you here?"

Not a good start. *Wasn't she supposed to know that?* She's supposed to be psychic. I told her I was there because I had questions about love and my career. (Mostly love, but I felt ridiculous having that be the sole reason for my $200 visit.)

She nodded and asked, "Have you brought pictures?" I pulled out the photo of Awat and handed it to her. She didn't look at it right away but started asking me other questions.

Sahar: What do you do for a living?

Seriously, isn't she supposed to know things like this?

Me: Well, I'm currently teaching English...in Northern Iraq.

Her eyes popped open wide.

Sahar: Really! How interesting.

Why did she not know this already? And shouldn't she at least be hiding her obvious shock?

Me: Yeah, it is definitely interesting.

She had begun shuffling some tarot cards on the table while still chitchatting.

Sahar: What made you decide to do that?
Me: Oh, an old friend talked me into it...

How much more information was I going to feed her?

Sahar: I am from Iran, originally, so I know that must be
  quite a change for you.
Me: Uh-huh.

She finally stopped shuffling the cards, then picked up Awat's
photo and concentrated on it. She asked me to close my eyes
and try to empty my mind. I had never been able to do that.
Thoughts were always spastically ricocheting through, especially
when I was trying to quiet them, making sure there was never
any stillness. And if it wasn't thoughts, it was a song, *"Wiiiide
opeeeen spaaaceeees…"*

Sahar said, "If you are unable to empty your mind, just
think of a mantra, over and over, 'What's my future, what's my
future…,' okay?"

I said, "Okay," and was grateful I wouldn't mess up the reading
with the nonstop yammering in my head.

We sat in silence for a good couple of minutes, which pass
by very slowly when the only thing you're permitted to think is,
"What's my future, what's my future…" She finally said, "Okay,
you can open your eyes." And then she looked at me with her
head sort of cocked to one side and said, "You are a very, *very*
interesting person." Clearly, she had the gift.

She began telling me things she saw ahead for me, but I was
impatient to get to the Awat issue. She finally pointed to his photo
and said, "You have a very special connection with him, but it is
not romantic. It is almost as if you want to take care of him, to
teach him things."

She was really good.

"I'm not saying this because of the age difference, but it's as if you want to mother him."

Ew, no.

"This is not the man for you. He is very special, yes, but you need someone who has had more life experience; someone who is more spiritually...you see what I'm saying?"

I actually did. She was making sense.

She continued, "You have a very old soul, with a lot of life experience in your consciousness, and although you connect with people, and you're busy, busy, I'm also getting that you're very popular, but there is a sense of loneliness. There is a theme within your consciousness, which is lonely. You haven't found anyone on your mental, spiritual, intellectual experience, so he could be younger or older, but no one is on that wavelength, because you're a very old soul; you need someone who has depth."

She asked me what I did to unwind, to have me-time, and I explained, "Well, I actually do a lot of me-time stuff. I write...," and here she said, "Perfect, we'll come back to that, because I know you said you were a teacher, but for me you are a writer, you write, you are published, la la la la la, everything. The first thing I saw when you sat down, there was a book over your head."

I had not said one word about writing. I didn't mention my copywriting, I didn't mention my blog writing, and I didn't mention the book I had begun to write about the Iraq experience.

Holy crap.

She would say "la la la la la" either as conversation filler or when she could sense I wasn't really fully understanding what she was talking about. Like when she said I was a time traveler, and my eyebrows involuntarily raised a bit. She went through the rest of the hour telling me intriguing things and making suggestions on how I could clarify issues in my life, but I was still fully hung-up on the love question.

If not now, when? *When will this happen for me?* Tish Durkin met her great, glove-fitting love in Iraq. Why couldn't mine be there too?

Sahar went back to Awat's photo and said, "This is not your guy. I don't mean that he's shallow, but when you play a piano, you want to be able to play all the keys. With this man, you would just be playing one octave. I don't think you have met your match yet in this lifetime."

She paused and said, "Here, help yourself," and handed me a box of tissues. She said she saw me being "completely settled" in life (career, love) in the next eight years.

Eight years? God, that was so far away.

I believed Sahar and was completely on board and had no doubt she was right when she said I would meet The One in the next few years.

"You have nothing to worry about; I don't see any conflict as far as religion or culture. He will be very grounded, a very old soul connection; you've missed each other through several lifetimes…"

I was sobbing uncontrollably at this point. She was right; there had been a sense of loneliness, for quite some time. Before I met Awat I had doubted I would ever meet anyone I was both attracted to and felt a strong connection with. I had probably piled all my expectations onto that thin thread of a connection, without stepping back to ask myself if it was really all I was imagining it to be.

"There will be a beautiful man for a partner, you will want for nothing."

Could you maybe give me a little more information, though? A hint, like what color hair does he have? Or, what city does he live in? An email address?

I had arrived at Sahar's out of breath and apologizing and was leaving the same way: out of breath from crying and apologizing for using an entire box of her tissues. I later discovered I had been PMSing, which excused some of the crying. Not all of it, just some.

I exited Sahar's flat in the dimming light of the late afternoon and turned south onto Edgware Road to walk back to my hotel, breathing and moving slowly, trying to absorb everything I had just been told. By the time I reached Oxford Street, my emotions had wrung themselves out, and I was able to laugh at the fact that Edgware Road was almost entirely composed of Middle Eastern businesses and restaurants, including one called Slemani (yet another spelling of Sulaimani). Now that was cosmic humor at its best.

Chapter Thirty-five

The Joys of Travel

For Christmas, I gave British Airways $150 in luggage fees. Now *I* am Santa. How was it possible that, after all my research and planning and weighing and packing and weighing and repacking *and my Balanzza*, I had to pay overweight luggage fees on my way back to Iraq yet again? How, I ask you!

Remember when I was all excited about Viking Air, the far more reasonable alternative to Austrian Airlines with their outrageous $1,400 round-trip flight and stupid incongruous twenty-kilo maximum allowance? The sticklers at the London-Gatwick Viking Air counter made certain I did not travel unscathed.

> **Stickler:** Right, now, we'll need to weigh your hand luggage.
> **Me:** What?
> **Stickler:** Your hand luggage, your carry-on bag, we need to weigh it.
> **Me:** *(reluctantly placing my purse on the scale)* Okay...
> **Stickler:** Right, that's eight kilos. You're only allowed five...oh, but I see you've your laptop in there. Well,

just take the laptop out and carry it by hand when boarding the flight.

Me: Okay, and then I have this carry-on...

And I try to give Stickler my small Tumi duffel that most certainly does fit into the overhead compartment:

Stickler: You're only allowed one piece of hand luggage.
Me: I thought I could have one purse and one piece of hand luggage.
Stickler: Yes, but that bag is too big to be a purse, so it is your hand luggage.

Stickler was telling me that the purse I was carrying, the one that was slung over my shoulder in purselike fashion, was "too big to be a purse." I wanted to tell her that her teeth were too big to be teeth, but there they were, sticking out of her gums, barely being covered by her lips. I was fuming, as not only was I struggling with the mild language barrier of the American "carry-on luggage" versus the British airline parlance of "hand luggage," but Stickler was now dictating what constituted "purse" versus "hand luggage." If I had my druthers, and a decent Internet connection, I would have directed her to the online website where I purchased my "hand luggage," and she would find it listed under "purses."*

---

*Okay, that's not actually true. It is listed under "handbags," but "handbag" is really just another name for "purse." Who is this woman to tell me that my purse is not actually a purse, but a carry-on bag??? The number of question marks used when writing about these things is directly related to the number of veins popping out of my neck at the time of confrontation.

So I had to check both my overweight suitcase AND my small Tumi duffel, which should have been my carry-on bag, or hand luggage. All in all, my extra baggage weight totaled ten kilos (twenty-two American pounds). I was instructed to go over to the now-all-too-familiar counter, where I would pay the airline extortionists. I should have at least received some sort of frequent-overpacker punch card. *One more punch and you'll receive a Balanzza luggage scale! What? You already have one? Then how…never mind.* The nice British man, who was not employed by a particular airline and therefore was not a legitimate candidate to bear the brunt of my rage, checked his computer screen, then my slip of paper, and ruefully informed me that each extra kilo costs 10 pounds sterling. So, I had to pay 100 pounds ($150) because my purse was apparently not really a purse. *Chloé doesn't make hand luggage!* I wanted to scream at Stickler and her mouthful of piano keys, while I was simultaneously screaming at myself: *Oh my God, when will I learn to travel light?*

Probably never. This just continued to happen, and yet I persisted in packing heavy bottles of "special" mouthwash (Crest), which I could not get in Iraq, and heavy bags of "special" trail mix (Trader Joe's Sweet, Savory & Tart Mix), which I also could not get in Iraq. Not to mention the shoes I had been partial to lately were of the platform variety, and the platforms weighed roughly three times what normal shoes weighed. Heavy shoes. BLAAT! Gatwick didn't have an Xpress Spa.

On the flight into Erbil I had the aisle seat. The middle seat remained unoccupied, and a Kurdish man sat at the window. As usual, I was polite but not friendly to the other men. Friendliness was too often mistaken for wink-wink, wakka-wakka, and I preferred to be thought of as slightly bitchy as opposed to the hooker alternative. The flights were mostly men, with the occasional hijabed wife and screaming child thrown in for good measure. I had been polite to my seatmate, had reminded the flight attendant that neither of us had received dinner rolls like everyone else, and had helped him pass his garbage to the flight attendant after the meal.

My shiny, new *Elle UK* magazine was resting in the vacant middle seat as I stifled cackling laughter while watching an episode of *30 Rock* on my iPod. I was interrupted by a finger poke from the seatmate and looked over in his direction. He was looking at me expectantly and motioning to my *Elle* magazine, which had a heavy-lidded Kate Hudson gazing at us from under pastel-hued eyeshadow. I finally understood that seatmate was asking if he could look at the *Elle* magazine.

There was little to no chance that this guy was at all interested in celebrating "25 Years of British *Elle*!" Or "Fashion Graffiti!" Or seeing how Domenico Dolce and Stefano Gabbana create sartorial magic in their Milanese studio.

I immediately soured; our prior pleasant airplane olive branch was thrown out the emergency exit. He wanted to perv on my magazine. I shot him a disgusted look, spat "No," and shook my head violently before grabbing the *Elle* and tucking it safely into my purse under the seat in front of me.

I was being unfair. My American male coworkers had also asked me if they could have the fashion magazines when I was finished. I had laughed and called them perverts. My tolerance did not extend to the Middle Eastern men. I just knew they had been raised differently.

Women were all whores. Never trust a woman.

∽∾∽

A week before leaving Iraq to go back to the United States for Christmas, I had planned out my return and prepared (or rather, tried to prepare) Dadyar for my airport pickup. I was to be arriving at an awkward time, just after midnight, in the early hours of December 31. This would have been confusing to the average bear, which meant I needed to take extra pains to explain it to Dadyar.

I printed off a page calendar of the month of December and drew a circle in the space between December 30 and December 31. I held the page up in front of Dadyar and said, "I am arriving *after midnight* on December 30, so technically *very, very, very early* on December 31." I also printed out my flight details, which listed the flight number and flight arrival time, as 00:20, December 31. Dadyar glanced at the papers and, with a dismissive wave of his hand, said, "You call me, I come." I said, "Yes, but it's important to me that you understand *when* to come," and I went over the calendar and the flight details again. I did not feel confident about his comprehensive skills.

∽∾∽

As scheduled, the flight landed in Erbil just after midnight, in the early hours of December 31. It was dark and rainy. I was tired and cranky. And hungry. And desperate to get away from my pervy seatmate. The second the seat belt sign went off, I placed my first call to Dadyar, who had said, "You call, I come." Remember how he said that? With the dismissive waving away of my printed out instructions and details?

There was no answer. I redialed his number. Twelve times. Twelve calls, during which I disembarked the plane, took the shuttle bus to the terminal, and stood in line waiting to clear customs. Dadyar finally called back while I was waiting with my luggage, and in a panicked voice said, "HELLO?" I said, "I am at the airport." He said, "I am coming!"

It could have been worse. He might not have called back. I might have had to attempt to take a taxi home, without any cash handy. He showed up a half hour later and was apologizing profusely and saying, "I think you coming tomorrow!" I said, "You didn't answer your phone. Were you sleeping?" He told me that no, he hadn't been sleeping, but had instead been hanging out in Ainkawa with his friends.

When he dropped me off, I wearily told him that I needed to go to the store in the morning to get food, as I didn't have anything to eat in the house. I said, "Please be here at nine o'clock." He sort of shook his head and said, "Ohhhhh, no nine. Half past?" I was already annoyed at his incompetence, and wanted to get to the store early, so I repeated, "No, please be here at nine. I really need to get to the store."

Nine in the morning and no Dadyar. I stood at the window,

watching the rain pelt the empty street and thinking, "Seriously?" I finally had to call him at 9:20 and say, "Where are you?" to which he gave his standard "I am coming." He showed up at 9:30, just like he had wanted to.

I climbed in the car and asked, "Why weren't you here at nine?" and he said, "Ohhhhh, not get bed 4:00 a.m., very tired." So I had to ask why he had gotten to sleep so late, and rather than even trying to lie about it, he told me that after he dropped me off, he went back to Ainkawa to hang out with his friends. *Me Tarzan, man. Do what I want.*

I was only happy after Dadyar had dropped me off at the villa, then driven away. I was fully stocked with food and wine. Never mind that my TV and Internet weren't working, as seemed to be the case each time I returned from a prolonged absence. I would call the IT department later. I could start my new year off just fine, as long as I had cheese and wine. And accidental rhymes.

⌘ ASTOUNDING ⌘
ACCOMPLISHMENTS OF PART 5

Total spent on overweight luggage: $3,870. I mean, for crying out loud.

Debt eliminated: $33,453—the silver lining!

Countries traveled: 7—Austria, France, Croatia, Greece, England, Sweden, Jordan.

Pairs of shoes purchased: 13. This sounds like too many, but it's not. You're not the bosses of me.

Soul mates met: 0. Curses. Foiled again. Back to square one.

Cultural tolerance level: 1. This place is on my last effing nerve.

Part 6

Clarity

Chapter Thirty-six

OMG!

Soon after Christmas break, we had another week off. The various Islamic holidays and school breaks had been a selling point when Warren pitched this position to me and had been one of the few things he told me that did not require embellishment. I had decided that I needed to explore a little bit more of the Middle East. Aside from a brief trip to Jordan in November, all my other vacations had been to European countries in my attempt to balance living in Iraq with my idea of Western normalcy. Since women are hassled less in Middle Eastern countries if traveling with a man, I thought it would be both smart and hilarious to travel with my friend Josh. Josh was one of my favorite people in the universe, and he loved a good adventure as much as I did.

We would be Fancy-Shoe-Wearin' Female and Outrageous Gay Male, the American Superhero Duo, on a Middle Eastern Extravaganza in the Sultanate of Oman.

A *sultanate*. So exotic. I wanted to take Flying Carpet Airlines to the sultanate but had to take the flight out of Erbil on the more traditional, less exotic Gulf Air.

I was also totally enchanted with their unit of currency, the

Omani rial. When researching the exchange rates online, I discovered that the abbreviation was OMR. This was just so close to the overused texting/cyber slang of "OMG," and I also discovered that things in Oman were fairly pricey, so that led to the natural decision to call the currency the "Oh My Gods." As in, "How many Oh My Gods is that silver dagger?"

My Gulf Air flight required a stopover in Bahrain before continuing on to Dubai. I had booked business class, because it was really only a few hundred dollars more than economy. In the recession days, back in my old life in Seattle, I would have gasped at the idea of spending over "a few hundred dollars" on a plane ticket, much less an airline upgrade, but I was fancy now.

⁓⁓⁓

I met Josh at a Costa Coffee shop in the Dubai airport. After some excited squealing and fierce hugging, I released him so he could go secure the rental car. Then we were off on our Middle East adventure. The travel information Josh had stated that women should cover their hair when driving in and around Oman, so as soon as we crossed the Emirates-Oman border, I wrapped my head up in a pashmina scarf.

The first gas station we stopped at was called an "oasis," which we both found hilarious. It was a far cry from the clichéd Middle Eastern mirage "oasis" of a shimmering pool of water, flanked by waving palm trees. This oasis had a food mart. Josh pointed out that I was garnering some unwanted attention from all the Arab men who were at the gas station. I couldn't get away from the damned zoo, even with my "sexy" hair covered. Josh dubbed the men "Stare Bears." Ellen and Jen were going to love that.

⁓

Josh was an American travel writer for MSN in Sydney, Australia, and had done all of the legwork and planning for this trip. He secured two nights (free of charge) at an über-deluxe seaside resort at Zighy Bay on the Musandam Peninsula of Oman. It was ridiculously posh, right on the Gulf of Oman with a staggering backdrop of mountains and a beautiful expanse of unspoiled ocean. We enjoyed a beachfront pool villa, complete with two resort bicycles and a personal butler. We didn't actually use the butler for anything, but we rode the bikes around the sandy paths and up to the spa villa, where we had massages and spent time in the steam room.

Part of the deal of being granted opulent, luxurious free digs was having to schmooze with hotel management for at least one of the two nights.

The woman (we'll call her Kersten) we had dinner with was Australian and had only been with the resort for a few months. She was in her forties, single, slightly paunchy, with long, stringy blond hair and a round moon-shaped face. She showed up twenty minutes late to meet us and then proceeded to dominate the conversation by one-upping anything Josh or I said.

She went on and on about her frequent trips into Dubai, where the men would "literally stop on the street" to talk to her. "I mean literally, stop their cars—the light would turn green, and they'd be there, stopped, to talk to me." I didn't doubt that the men stopped to talk to her, as she was blond and Western, and most Arab men thought all Western women were whores. It wasn't necessarily a compliment if they stopped to talk to you. She also made a point of telling us that she knew "loads of sheikhs. I'm friends with heaps of them."

Josh and I were both curious as to what a sheikh actually *was*. I mean, you hear the word, and can visualize what they look like, but are they royalty? What makes a sheikh? Kersten explained that it was sort of a combination between royalty and a political post. The sheikhs presided over various regions and had a lot of money and power. They sounded to me like the modern-day equivalent of dukes and lords from Middle Ages Europe. Anyway, Kersten was friends with heaps of them. She was also overly flirtatious with the married Muslim chef Ali. She crowed about getting private cooking lessons from him, and then mentioned the annoyance of having to meet his wife, upon the wife's request. I said, "Oh, wow, you hadn't met his wife? And you were getting private cooking lessons from him?" I was no fan of conservative Islam, but I was pretty sure that wasn't exactly culturally sensitive of her. But what did I know? She knew loads of sheikhs.

Painful as the meal was, it was free. And tasty. Josh was thrilled to death with all the typical Middle Eastern mezze like hummus, tabouleh, and baba ghanoush. Ali could definitely cook. I really hoped that was all he was doing at the resort, but I didn't want to be Moral Judge & Jury Judy on my vacation.

❧❧❧

After paragliding off a cliff down to the beach at the resort on our last day, we had to pack up, wrap up my hair, and head back out on the road. We were going to Muscat, the capital of the sultanate! We enjoyed the passing scenery of many sandy outposts, a few farms (complete with Omani scarecrow dressed in a caftan and headscarf), and we passed through several small towns.

Josh had done his best with the arrangements; however, some of the details had been left to Mona, the Sydney-based representative for Oman's Ministry of Tourism. Mona (a wildly coincidental anagram of Oman) had been somewhat remiss in her communications with Josh, or with the ministry, and when we arrived at our allegedly reserved hotel in Muscat, we were told that there was no reservation for us. This was after a very long day of driving across the sultanate (I just don't even want to use the word "country" when "sultanate" is available), and we were exhausted and bordering on cranky. When I removed the pashmina from around my head and neck, an odd feeling of liberation washed over me. I hadn't realized I was feeling so constricted, but the second I took off the scarf I felt more relaxed.

We were supposed to have a free room at the Intercontinental, and were also supposed to have a message from the tour company, which would supposedly be picking us up the following morning for our desert extravaganza and fort and palace visits. But we had no room and no message. Josh finagled and wrangled things with the manager of the Intercontinental and finally secured a room for us. The manager agreed to contact the Ministry of Tourism the next day for payment. This just left the matter of our tour. We decided to go to the room, get a good night's sleep, and have a nice breakfast before trying to contact the tour company about our plans.

❧

When we got down to the lobby in the morning, we found a stuffed sausage of a man, sporting a sharp goatee and Ray-Ban sunglasses. He was dressed in the traditional Omani garb of a long "dish-dash" (essentially a floor-length caftan), matching cap, and Prada sandals. I wasn't sure if the Prada sandals were standard Omani issue. He made a point of dramatically looking at his watch before pushing himself up from the couch and introducing himself as Kamil. He was behaving as if we were late, although we explained to him that we hadn't received a message that he would be coming at all. He seemed surprised by this.

We checked out of the Intercontinental and loaded our bags into the SUV of the tour company and proceeded with the requisite small talk. Kamil informed us that he had lived in the United States, specifically Jackson Heights (in New York) and Connecticut. He said, "United States not for me." I asked if he had been anywhere other than New England, and he gave me a blank look. So I rephrased it to, "Have you been anywhere outside of Jackson Heights and Connecticut?" He said, "No," but then continued to expound on why the United States was not for him, with its crowded cities and unfriendly people. I got the distinct impression it would be a waste of breath to discuss the vastness of the United States and the fact that there were so many different types of regions and cities, etc.

One of the big tourist attractions in Muscat was the Sultan Qaboos Grand Mosque. That would be our first stop of the day. Kamil surveyed my outfit, which I had thought was culture-appropriate: scarf covering my hair, long drawstring pants, flip-flops, and a top I had bought in Iraq that was empire-waisted and dropped below my hips. He pointed out that my wrists were showing. My wrists? It was a three-quarter-sleeve top, and I didn't know that my wrists had to be covered, so I dug in my bag and pulled out a long-sleeved cardigan. *You can't cover up this sexy.* Kamil looked surprised that I had been able to find something appropriate so quickly.

I had been appraising his ensemble as well and admired his cap. I had read that the Omani caps worn by the men were traditionally embroidered by a beloved family member. I asked him about this and he clarified, "Yes, they are made by a woman. A woman make for the man." I asked, "Who made yours?" He replied, "Oh, I just bought this one...but from a woman!" Ah, traditions.

⁓⁓⁓

The Grand Mosque was indeed grand. We had to remove our shoes to enter the prayer rooms. Kamil led us to the women's prayer room first, which looked lovely, with heavy wood-paneled walls and decorative chandeliers. Kamil informed us that the women's prayer room had a capacity of 750. He then told us that "Western women" he had toured around before were angry when they found out that the men's prayer room's capacity was six thousand. He continued on to say that Westerners just didn't understand that the Omani women didn't need a large prayer room because they should be home with the children. "This make Western woman more angry!" he laughed.

He looked pointedly at me when giving this explanation, but I just shrugged and said, "I'm living in Iraq right now. I'm used to it."

"Iraq?!" he blurted out, and then cocked his head as if looking at me in a new light. I seemed to be surprising Kamil right and left.

Kamil was proving to be a fairly boorish and obnoxious guide. He would bark orders in regards to which things he thought we should be photographing at the mosque, and then would huff in an exasperated manner when we would ignore his demands.

Upon exiting said Grand Mosque, we were handed several pamphlets on various facets of Islam in an apparent attempt to educate the Western infidels. My personal favorite was titled "Woman in Islam." If I wasn't entirely sure before that marrying a Muslim Kurd and converting to Islam wasn't such a bad idea, this cured me.

These were some excerpts from the "Twenty-Five Frequently Asked Questions":

1. Do men and women have equal rights in Islam?

> It is part of the mission of Islam to establish justice and harmony between the sexes with due consideration to the inherent natural differences. God has laid down certain rights and obligations for men and women,

each in accordance with the nature determined by his/her gender, and complementary to each other. If either departs from his/her specific nature, an unnatural "equality" will be forced.

So the short answer here would be "No."

5. Is a Muslim woman allowed to choose her husband herself?

Islam gives a woman the right to choose her own husband…It is, however, a wise custom among Muslims to involve the family in any important decision…

Translation: "No."

7. Is a Muslim woman allowed to marry a non-Muslim?

Marriage and family are particularly protected in Islam because, as the basic social unit, they guarantee the continued existence of the community. In order to work out, a marriage requires two partners to have a common basis and attitude. Thus it is naturally preferable for a Muslim to find a Muslim mate…A non-Muslim husband could limit his wife's religious practice. That is why a Muslim woman is not permitted to marry a man belonging to another religion.

Short answer: "No," but please continue for the absurd double standard.

The Qur'an allows a Muslim man to marry a woman from one of the communities of the "People of the Book"

(Jews and Christians). As societies tend to be patriarchal, a Muslim man married to a non-Muslim woman is considered to have the necessary social and family structure to protect him from being pried away from his faith.

I'm sorry...what?

8. How are we to understand the permission for polygamy in Islam?

Technically, Islam allows men to marry four women; however, there are certain conditions to be met. This is best understood from the following verse in the Qur'an: "...And if you have reason to fear that you might not act equitably towards orphans; then marry from among [other] women such as are lawful to you—[even] two, three or four; but if you have reason to fear that you might not be able to treat them with equal fairness, then [only] one—or [from among] those whom you rightfully possess." (Qur'an, 4:3)

I supposed I should first understand the "rightfully possess" thing to understand the permission for polygamy in Islam.

9. Why is a Muslim woman not allowed to marry several men?

I must say that while this pamphlet was shooting itself in the foot in its attempt to enlighten the non-Muslims, it was definitely answering all my questions.

Islam is the religion reflecting human nature. Generally

speaking, the marriage of one woman to several men is a rare occurrence throughout the world and hardly ever promoted. It can thus be assumed that it is not in accordance with the nature of a woman to be married to more than one man at a time. So it is not surprising that Islam is against it. One important factor is the fact that it is the man who is obliged to support his children. If there were more than one husband, the paternity of any particular child would be in doubt. This would lead to either quarrelling about the children or shying away from the responsibility. Clearly, it would not be practical for several men to be joint heads of the family. Alternatively, in the case of a matriarchal power structure, the experience in pre-Islamic time had resulted in a deterioration of discipline in society.

I would like to remind everyone at this juncture that the majority of my students no longer had fathers. Many of them had died in the wars and rebellions of the 1990s, and an entire generation was being reared by single mothers.

10. Is a Muslim man allowed to beat his wife?

This is a subject burdened with a lot of prejudice.

Yes, how unfortunate that there is prejudice against wife-beating.

[This] verse from the Qur'an makes it clear that the husband is required to apply three steps in any case: Admonition, separation in bed, and only thirdly beating. This means that beating in the heat of the moment is specifically forbidden...Furthermore, some scholars mention that this measure, i.e., beating, is only for such societies where it is an acceptable means of reform and likely to get results.

Oh good, at least they're clarifying. It is only acceptable to beat your wife after you've admonished her or placed her in a marriage bed time-out.

18. Why do women not pray side by side with men?

During an act of worship, participants should be able to concentrate fully. Were men and women to pray in an intermingled congregation, there would be distraction on both parts...women are normally allocated an area to pray either behind the men or in a separate section.

During one of my conversations with Awat, he was describing praying at the mosque during Ramadan. He said there were many people, all side by side, and I was picturing this very romantic, spiritual scene with the men all wearing long white smock things and white caps (precisely what the Omani men wore). I had excitedly asked, "What were you wearing?" and he had shrugged and said, "Jeans and a shirt." Oh. He then explained that all the people who were side by side were men. "Women pray in different room." Oh. "On second floor," he said. So I perked up and mischievously said, "Aha! Closer to God!" and just smirked while his smile tightened, and it appeared as though his head might explode.

The "Woman in Islam" pamphlet concluded by saying:

From an Islamic point of view the modern "Western" world presents women with the burdensome and unnatural stresses of having to glamourize herself to a media-projected fashion standard, to live as a "super-mom" earning a second family income or supporting a one-parent household (or, alternatively to marry late in life or not at all), vying with men in a cut-throat competitive work-place, in a materialistic society of "have's" and "have not's," where conscience and morals have lost their value.

This was irony at its most outrageous. I would think the ludicrous Islamic ideal of a woman's purity might be somewhat burdensome and cause "unnatural stresses." Also, that women are only permitted to show their faces (and hands) has led to a dramatic explosion of plastic surgery all across the Middle East. It's so much easier to go to the hair salon to get a blowout than to go to the hospital to have a face-lift.

If a woman in the Middle East fails to bleed on her wedding night, she can face shame, abuse, and even death. *That* is unnaturally stressful.[*]

It was hilarious to me that this pamphlet was printed with the intention of presenting Islam as a female-friendly way of life, when, in fact, it had the exact opposite effect. It merely

---

[*]A Chinese company called Gigimo was selling something called an Artificial Virginity Hymen, which was a small packet that would be inserted into the vagina and would release a small amount of fake blood "when your lover penetrate." My guess would be this is selling in slightly greater quantities in Islamic nations than anywhere else. They could put it right there on the shelf next to the Virginity Soap.

confirmed every previous stereotype, and even exacerbated several of the more controversial issues. What was truly tragic, however, was later doing a little research and discovering that there are similar ideas in the Bible and the Torah. It wasn't just a Middle East thing.

Before getting back in the car after the mosque visit, Kamil had to have a cigarette, so Josh and I waited. We then headed farther inland toward some market that was a feature of the tour. Kamil spent the majority of the drive trying to engage us in political discussion, and would say things like, "George Bush, he did a mistake! The people of Oman, we hope Obama does not do another mistake!"

Josh had been living in Australia for several years, and I had been in Iraq for almost a year. Neither of us was particularly political, and we were very uninterested in carrying on that particular conversation. When we wouldn't engage in discourse with him, Kamil would then expound on his own country's politics (which was fine, and somewhat interesting). According to him, 1959 was the last time Oman was involved in a war, the war with Yemen. Kamil said the Yemeni were "troublemakers." He said the border was where all the military were, and "Sultan controls the religious. You got the name, you got the oil, now shut your mouth." We interpreted this as the sultan doing an effective job of controlling the religious fanatics in the country.

Kamil took advantage of his captive audience at lunchtime to explain to us why Oman was the most superior of the Gulf States. "When driving in Bahrain, if you lose your way and ask directions? The people you ask will not be local. They are Indian or other thing and just tell you the wrong way. In Saudi if you ask directions, they say, 'How much will you give us?'" Josh and I hadn't been to Saudi Arabia, and I had really only been in Bahrain's airport, so we just had to take his word for everything.

Kamil spent part of the afternoon drive on his cell phone, yammering away in Arabic. He explained to us that he and his wife were trying to buy a house, and his wife's friend had a house in which they were interested. While Josh and I found this to be fairly unprofessional, we were just glad that he had stopped talking about George W. and all the mistakes he "did." There was some entertaining irony about how Kamil nagged on and on about "George Bush doing a mistake," since he was almost thought of as a hero to the Kurdish people. Warren had told me that it wasn't unheard of for random Kurdish restaurants to have a framed 8x10 glossy of W right alongside other framed photos of their political dignitaries. Although that *was* Warren talking.

On the most recent call, Kamil's wife had said something about her friend changing her mind about wanting to sell the property, so he said, "I tell her! Go and eat her brain! Find out!" I corrected him, "*Pick* her brain." I couldn't help it, it was the English teacher in me. But he ignored me and said "eat her brain" several more times that day, making for a very gruesome visual.

Josh was still being diplomatic and polite and was asking Kamil about the specifics of the house: have your kids picked out their rooms, etc. Kamil had two children, one boy and one girl. He explained to us that yes, his son had picked out a room, but, "The girl, she is a visitor in your home. When she grow up, she get married and move out of the house with her husband." That made me so sad. I couldn't imagine growing up with a family that only thought of me, really, as a temporary guest.

Being on a somewhat organized tour, we had the compulsory stop at a "typical" Bedouin tent, where Kamil introduced us to the Bedouin family and then brought us inside the spacious tent and subtly pressured us to buy ugly scarves that had allegedly been made by the Bedouin woman. The scarves were packaged inside neat plastic squares and did not appear to be handmade. Although he kept saying, "No pressure!" he would then continue with, "But this how they make their LIVING."

This typical Bedouin family had a late-model Jeep Cherokee parked outside of their tent, and the head male figure of the family had a very expensive-looking watch on his wrist, so I was guessing they were doing okay. All the same, Josh bowed to the pressure and bought a thin burgundy scarf with a faint beige plaid print. He wanted to wear it right away and had the quiet Bedouin teen-age boy wrap it properly around his head.

We walked back out to the car, and Kamil pressed the ignition button on his remote-control key chain. Josh exclaimed, "That's a fancy start button," to which Kamil responded, "Yes, all family. Brother, father, mother…" Listening was not his forte.

⌒⌒⌒

From the tourist trap of the Bedouin tent, we drove to our overnight destination of yet another tented camp in the Wahiba Sands desert. We were supposed to stay at the luxury tented camp that had been previously discussed with the Ministry of Tourism, but something had changed and Josh was informed that we would be staying at another tented camp, just a half mile down the desert from the luxury camp.

Boooo. I loved luxury. Having to spend all this quality time with Kamil was wearing on my good humor, and the luxury tented camp might have remedied that. Oh well, it was just for one night, and the normal camp might not be too bad.

We drove across the wide expanse of beautiful reddish sandy dunes and passed the luxury camp. I had my nose pressed against the window and whimpered as I noticed the camp's gleaming white canvases. We drove a half mile farther and arrived at the standard camp. There were four Bedouin men smoking shisha while sitting on large pillows, on a raised platform near the entrance to the camp. They did not stand up to greet us but merely sat and smoked until Kamil approached to shake their hands and pat them on the backs. These were our hosts.

The main Bedouin told us we would be in tent #11 and waved in the general direction of the dingy canvases off to his left. Josh and I took our overnight bags and wandered over to a canvas that had "#11" scrawled on the outside flap in black Magic Marker. The inside of the tent was a study in hodgepodge décor.

Kamil had been crowing on and on about the standard camp, saying how it was "real Bedouin camp" and a "real experience," all the while pooh-poohing the luxury camp. We did have a real orange plastic garbage pail in our tent, and there was real mold on the floral and plaid sheets that comprised the tent's interior. There was a Kelly-green plastic woven mat covering the floor (upon lifting this up, we found only sand underneath), and two black-framed single beds, the kind you might find in the aisles of Target, flanking each side of the tent. There was also a dusty, rickety, old electric lantern hanging in one corner.

Now, I prefer fancy, but nonluxury can be done well. Simplicity is charming when things are clean and well attended to. This camp was sloppy. It felt haphazard and had a film of griminess covering it. It just seemed like a few Bedouin dudes got together and were like, "Yeah, we'll bring tourists out here. They love the authentic experience. They'll pay our monthly expenses." I was sure that somewhere, there would actually be the ubiquitous grubby backpacker who would just inhale deeply and say, "Ahhhh, this is *great*! It's so *authentic*!" Just because something's "authentic" doesn't mean it's good.

℮〜℮〜℮〜

The big draw of desert camping was the desert itself. The scenery was stunning: miles and miles of reddish sand dunes, with the occasional flock of camels wandering through. Josh and I had arrived about an hour before the sun set, so after surveying the squalor of our tent, we wanted to get out of there and spend some time enjoying the *authentic* beauty of the Wahiba Sands. We were also dying to get away from Kamil, who had thankfully plopped himself down with the other men and fired up a shisha. We climbed up to the top of the closest dune, which took about fifteen minutes of trudging, then parked ourselves at the top, facing the descending sun. It was absolutely breathtaking. The air was silent, as there was no traffic anywhere nearby, and we could just barely make out the faraway voices of the shisha-smoking men.

⟶ ⟶ ⟶

We survived the night in the squalor, and the next morning I woke up and brushed a flying cockroach off my blanket, then got up and hurriedly packed my things. Josh and I made our way to the breakfast area to meet Kamil, who was having his morning tea and cigarette. Breakfast at this camp was appalling. Appalling meaning I could have made it myself. I don't cook. There were hard-boiled eggs, lentil mash, and two loaves of store-bought white bread. There was also a tray with one small jar of hot sauce, one jar of jelly, and one giant vat of mayonnaise. Seriously? This was an authentic Bedouin meal? I was so relieved we had been invited to the luxury camp for breakfast.

It was that day that I realized we had already spent exactly half of our vacation with Kamil. This made me rumpled and unhappy and so much less tolerant of his incessant yammering.

Kamil claimed to have once met, and had a brief chat with, Brad Pitt in the lobby of a Muscat hotel. He had been very impressed with Mr. Pitt, and began discussing his marriage with Angelina Jolie. He seemed surprised when Josh and I informed him that Brad Pitt and Angelina Jolie weren't married. "They not married?!" So Josh explained something he had read somewhere that Brad and Angelina had said they would only marry when it was legal for gay people to marry, because they thought it was very unfair that gays couldn't marry. This statement was met with stunned silence from Kamil. I vacillated back and forth between being thrilled we were finally able to shut him up and very badly wanting to hear him discuss that particular issue.

❧❧❧

Lunch was supposed to be included on the tour that day, but Josh and I had had enough of Kamil and asked to be taken back to our rental car in Muscat. We were both dying to go to the Muscat McDonald's to try something called the McArabia sandwich. Yes, it is somewhat of a travesty to eat at an American chain restaurant when you're overseas, but since we were both living away from America, we figured it was perfectly acceptable. Plus, nothing said "I'm lovin' it" more than time away from Kamil.

❧❧❧

The next morning we had to be up and ready by 9:00 a.m., per the instruction of the ever-demanding diva/tour guide. "Don't be late!" he had warned. He was just so unbearably arrogant. We enjoyed a leisurely breakfast, then strolled into the hotel's lobby at 9:10 a.m., and were rewarded with Kamil huffily standing up from his couch and pointedly looking at his watch. Josh and I stifled our immature, punchy giggles and climbed into the SUV.

Kamil took us to the Muscat Fish Market and to the main bazaar. By the time we had gotten to the bazaar, I was done with him. I could not bear the thought of being led through the bazaar stalls, with him pointing out the obvious, "This a silver shop. This

a dish-dash shop. This a sweet shop," and ordering us to pho-
tograph things. My suggestion to split up, and then reconvene
after a half hour, was met with an indignant and discourteous
"Fine." We shopped in blissful Kamil-free-ness and enjoyed the
sights, sounds, and smells of the souk. We laughed and took pictures of things Kamil would not have recommended, and finally
bought tacky tourist T-shirts that said "Oman" in cursive, with a
silhouette of a camel. When the half hour was up, we met back up
with Kamil, climbed into the car, and enjoyed a quiet ride back
to the Shangri-La. We would never have to see him again. It was
a happy day.

Dadyar picked me up, on time, at the airport. It was actually a
relief to return to Kurdistan, as it was far less conservative than
Oman had been. I didn't have to have my hair covered just to go
out driving in the car.

After unpacking, I needed to go to Ainkawa to pick up some
wine. Dadyar handed me the car keys and motioned toward
his Hyundai Santa Fe SUV, indicating that I could drive us to
Ainkawa. He climbed in the passenger side and said, "Ainkawa! I
need wine!" like he was me.

In the months since the airport fiasco, Dadyar had really put
forth more of an effort in his job and had grown on both Steve and
me. He wasn't the type of employee to show radical initiative, but
when we asked him to do something, he did it. He was reliable,
good-natured and good-humored, not in the least bit creepy, and

he didn't smoke. Based on what we had seen of other possible alternatives for drivers, we really couldn't have done much better. The fact that he suggested I drive to the produce stand just gave him a few extra points.

I had been there for so long that I found it strange when the locals stared at me as I drove along in the Hyundai. "What? I'm local. I live here now." I was still patiently waiting for those five-star hotels to be completed, but as I pulled out of the English Village gates, I looked to my right and gasped. There, literally within walking distance of our villa, was a Costa Coffee. It looked legitimate, unlike when I had started at the sight of a building with a dirty "Microsoft" billboard running along the rooftop. This Costa Coffee appeared to be the same Costa Coffee I had enjoyed at London's Gatwick Airport.

It was later confirmed, by people who knew things, that the Costa Coffee was indeed a legitimate branch of the international chain. If I was going to be stuck in Erbil, I needed to focus on the positives. Costa Coffee was a definite positive.

Chapter Thirty-seven

New Year, New News

Warren had all but physically left The Iraq. I hadn't heard anything from him since November and the Crazy Andy debacle, although I knew he was back in Suli. His most recent Facebook status update was "Dreaming of Maple Leaves."

The bad news in Erbil just kept coming. Steve and I had been back for an entire week, with no sign of Georgie Catstanza. I thought he would eventually "feel" that we were back and trot on over, but there was no sign of him. Katherine hadn't even seen him anywhere.

Mecca had also closed. The J&K Women's Fitness Center had been closed for good, at least the fitness center part of it. I had no idea if the closing was related to the rumor of ill-gotten funds, and I silently cursed the unscrupulous owners. The one bright spot was that the salon was still open, and I would still be able to get my pedicures from Sangela.

Married Ashton, the security guy who had been calling, had moved on to a beautiful Spanish girl who worked for an NGO. According to Katherine, they were having quite the raging affair. I was sorry for his Russian wife and wondered if she was as unhappy as he was.

෴

My visit to Psychic Sahar had cleared my head about the Awat situation. I found myself in a very secure, magnanimous place after my reading, and being at home, surrounded by family at Christmas helped to put things into perspective. I listened to the audio file of the reading a couple of times and spent a few days contemplating my entire relationship with Awat. When Sahar had said he wasn't the man for me, it was almost like she had pushed a secret "release" button, and instead of bemoaning the loss of my attachment to him, I felt clear. Once I was home, spending time with my family and connecting with my friends, I reached the point of thinking, "How could I have ever thought that situation was real?" Awat was truly a decent, funny person, and I was grateful for the friendship we had created, but a soul mate? Nuh-uh.

I was enjoying all the cheery, goodwill-toward-men Christmas-ness when I randomly came across something that made me think of Awat: a book about soccer star Cristiano Ronaldo, written by Cristiano himself, titled *Moments*. Cristiano Ronaldo was one of the world's best soccer players and was an icon even in Iraq. Awat idolized him. He would love the book. I decided to buy it for him as a birthday gift.

Since I hadn't had any communication with him for three months, I wasn't sure if he would want to see me, so I sent him an email:

Hey there,
I wanted to check in with you and see how you are doing.

Are you okay? Are things good?

I am so sorry about before. I really needed some distance between us to get my head sorted out. I was really having very strong feelings for you, which I thought was completely inappropriate on my part, and I wasn't able to just have a normal, platonic friendship with you. Again, my mistake, and I apologize.

Please let me know how you're doing.

Best wishes & hope you're well!

Gretchen

He sent a fairly subdued response one week later:

Hi ms gretchen

i am fine thank you for your asking…every thing good, i am working as a lawyer, dont being sorry, remember that your the best teacher i have ever had

best wishs to you and your family

This was not his usual happy-go-lucky tone. It seemed somber and professional. He may have been angry or upset about how I had ended things, I couldn't quite tell, but I was finally in a healthy mental space about the whole thing and selfishly wanted to give him the present. Giving special presents was one of my favorite things, and once I had the gift in my possession, it became a sort of hot potato that I couldn't wait to give away.

I'm so glad to hear you're working! That is great news, and I hope you are enjoying your job, although that leaves much less time for video games ;)

When I was home in the U.S. I bought you a gift. I was thinking I could give it to you as sort of an early birthday present (since your birthday isn't until March). It's nothing big, but it is something that I saw that I knew you would really like, and it will also help you with your English.

I am probably coming down to Sulaimani in a couple of weeks. Would it be okay to get together then, to give this to you?

It can just be quick—we could just meet at the coffee shop upstairs from Zara supermarket. You don't even have to talk to me at all, if you're angry with me—you can just take the present, but I want to see your face when you open it. That's me being selfish.

COME ON! LIFE IS SHORT! PRESENTS! Who doesn't want presents?! :D

If you say "No" I will be so sad and I might cry. You don't want to make me cry, do you? You're too nice for that.

That got a better response. No one can resist presents. And really, people hate to see me cry. It's sort of unsettling.

Subject: I will waiting for your gift

thank you very much my best teacher for your gift, yes you are right my birthday soon, be sure i never angry with you belive me ,i accept to meet you in zara beacuse i really miss you very much :) ,i am famous now :D i am kidding, how are you, are you still in erbile beacuse yeasterday i called you three times but you didn't anser me, until now i dodn't buy new enternet conection line thats cause to replay you late, please forgive me

Awat called me after sending the email, and we had a really nice twenty-minute phone conversation, where he told me he was working as a lawyer and that he had a new girlfriend. I was actually relieved to hear that.

> **Me:** Great! That is such good news.
> **Awat:** Yes!
> **Me:** But…you just have ONE girlfriend now, right? Not three, like before?
> **Awat:** *(laughing)* Yes, yes, just one.
> **Me:** And have you told your mother about her?
> **Awat:** YES!

So this sounded really good. He was becoming a grown-up. He had a job. He had just one girlfriend, and she wasn't even his cousin! Excellent news. I didn't ask if he was still sleeping in his mother's bedroom. That was no longer my problem.

We agreed to meet at the coffee shop located above Zara when I went down to Suli the following weekend. It would be great to see him, and I thought the meeting would provide some closure for me. He mentioned in an email that he had something important to tell me and asked that my driver not accompany us. That was intriguing, and since the driver never comes with me, that wasn't a problem. But I was so curious about the "important thing"! Maybe he was getting engaged to his new girlfriend?

I was kind of nervous, in that way you get when you haven't seen someone in a long time. I had stopped thinking of him in a romantic capacity, and I dressed as casually as possible, wearing my comfortable banana-colored Frye cowboy boots, so there wouldn't be any chance of anyone mistaking this as a date. There was no need for Wonder Woman today. Sirwan dropped me off at Zara, and I walked up the stairs to the coffee shop and looked around. I didn't see Awat, so I chose a booth, with my side facing the stairs so I could see him when he arrived.

As he walked up the stairs, I took in the visual. Awat was wearing a suit, which seemed odd, as Friday was a weekend day here. The suit was bad. Not at all like what he had worn to the party back in October. This was definitely a "Two Wild and Crazy Guys" suit, with its pastel colors and checked pattern situation. He was wearing the suit with a bright pink shirt and silver tie, and his pants were too tight. When he sat down, I could see out of the corner of my eye that there was a golf-ball-size hole in the crotch. He looked so different than I had remembered. I couldn't put my finger on what had changed. It was an overall feeling of *less*. He looked…really, just like any other Kurdish guy on the street.

I waved and we both said, "Hi!" in unison as he sat down across from me. When he was settled, I asked, "Why are you wearing a suit? Did you have to work today?"

"No, it is my day off!" he said.

"Is that all for me?" I asked him.

And he shrugged and said, "Yes!"

Well, the intention was very sweet, but he had this blue, plaid button-down that I really liked and… No, no, I reminded myself. We had finished with that.

Awat ordered two cups of tea from the waiter, and I pulled the bag with his book out from under the table and handed it to him. He reached into the bag and slid the book out and looked at the cover. I watched expectantly. The curiosity on his face broadened into a wide grin, and he looked at me with his hand on his heart and said, "Cristiano! Thank you very much!" I clasped my hands with glee and singsonged a "You're welcome." I loved a successful gift reception.

I tried to get him to tell me the "something important" immediately after he opened the gift, as he turned the pages and pointed at the photos of the soccer star, but he shook his head and said, "Maybe later." The Kurds use "maybe" when they mean "definitely," which I have tried to correct on numerous occasions. Like when I would ask a student, "Will you be in class on Sunday?" and they would say, "Maybe." So I would ask, "Why might you *not* be there?" and they always looked confused and said, "Yes, I be there!"

So I would wait until "maybe" later for Awat's grand announcement but thought I might be leading into it by asking him about his new girlfriend.

Awat: She is crazy about me!
Me: And you are crazy about her!
Awat: Maybe not as much.

Oh no. Maybe he hadn't grown up quite as much as I had hoped.

Me: Why?

Awat: I don't know. She know everything about me. She
       call me and text me every time!

He meant "all the time."

He then pulled out his cell phone to show me all the messages
and logged calls from her. I told him that I believed him, and then
continued prodding him about why he didn't like her as much as
she liked him. I think people should only be in relationships with
those they truly adore. They should want to be around them all
the time. They should be excited to see them. They should be
thrilled to hear from them. It shouldn't be a chore receiving texts
from them "every time."

The conversation wandered into even more bothersome terri-
tory when Awat complained, "My life so complicated. With job,
with school, with girls." I demanded, "What do you mean 'girls'?
I thought you just had the one girlfriend?" He went on to explain
that yes, he had only one girlfriend, but there were two other girls
who called him all the time. He got all worked up, whining about
how it was so inconvenient.

He continued to talk about these "other" girls who called him
and told him that they loved him and wanted to be with him. I
asked him how he would respond when they said things like that.
He claimed that he told them he did not return their feelings, but
they would just respond with "That's okay!"*

I found myself back in full teacher/lecturer mode and tried

---

*The university was always accepting donations of books, for the library. I was
going to donate *He's Just Not That into You*. These girls needed to read that.

to explain to Awat that he needed to take some responsibility for this. I said, "I think you *like* having these girls call you all the time. You *like* the attention." He tried to shake his head slowly to disagree, but I could tell he was considering what I said. I continued, "If you really don't want these girls calling you, block their numbers, or just don't answer the phone when you see it's them calling."

Honestly, this all just seemed like basic common sense to me. But where was all this common sense when I thought I was in love with him? I stared across the table, at the excessive hair gel, and the bad suit (carefully avoiding the hole in the crotch), and listened to him ramble on incessantly about how many women were in love with him, and thought, "Oh. My. God. Had I really thought *I* was in love with him?"

He was a good-hearted person, but he really was just a child. In countries where boys and girls are basically separated from each other from adolescence until their twenties, the emotional development is stunted. Men in their twenties here were similar to teenaged boys in Western countries. Even as we sat there, discussing other topics, at one point he stopped me in midsentence to point out to me that two girls, sitting at a booth behind me, were watching him. I tried hard to keep my eyes from rolling. My disappointment deepened.

> **Awat:** I meet my girlfriend for second time in car park [parking lot]. When no one looking she take my hand like this [he takes one hand in the other].
> **Me:** So you were holding hands?

Awat: Yes, holding hands, and then she do this. [He squeezed his hand.] What the word for this?

Me: Squeezed?

Awat: Yes! She squeezed my hand and say, "I want to kiss you."

Me: Wow, this girl is bold! I like it!

Awat: Yes!

Me: Did you tell her that you can't kiss her until you're married?

Awat: *(shrugging)* Maybe I kiss her.

Me: WHAT? I thought you said you wouldn't kiss a girl until you were married?

Awat: Yes, but I think I change my mind.

Me: WHAT?! But I thought that was very important to you! Because of your religion.

Awat: *(shrugging some more)* Yes, but I think maybe change my mind is okay. But I ask your advice. What is your advice?

Me: Noooooooooooo. No no no. You have to make that decision on your own. That is very personal, and I thought it was so important to you *because of your religion*.

What happened to him? His moral convictions had seemed so strong before. That was one of the things I had found so attractive about him. He had walked the walk. Oh, heavy sigh.

We had been sitting and talking for two hours and we were both starting to yawn, but I still hadn't heard the "big news" he had. It clearly wasn't that he was engaged. He paused, grinning at me.

> **Awat:** Big news is...I want to go United States.
> **Me:** Ohhhhhhhhhh. Huh.
> **Awat:** Yes, I want to go, and bring my family. I think I
> need sponsor, and I will pay them!

Oh wow. Did he mean me? This was a very different tune he was singing. When we used to have our after-class conversations, he would say that he hated Kurdistan and wanted to move to Europe. Then on other days he would talk about trying to find a bigger house in Suli. He was kind of all over the place with his future plans. The United States idea was a very new development.

> **Me:** Um...a sponsor? Have you researched this? I don't
> think the U.S. does that kind of thing.
> **Awat:** No, I don't know, but I think yes.
> **Me:** I think no.
> **Awat:** I think maybe, but I will check. I will pay the
> person for sponsor!
> **Me:** Okay, but do check into the specifics. I really don't
> think we do that.

I did not offer to help him. The creeping suspicion that his entire motivation for spending time with me was driven by ulterior motives made me feel ill. I suddenly realized that while I did care for him, I didn't want to *take care* of him. I had instant flashes of his whole family moving to the United States and being entirely dependent on me. It wasn't even as if they were refugees. Awat's family was one of the wealthier families in Suli, and from what he had told me, it sounded like they had a pretty good life. Where was this coming from? My head hurt. I felt dirty.

That last little bit of the conversation had kind of soured the afternoon for me; it was more disappointing than the crotch-hole suit. It really had been good to connect with him again, but I felt used. Embarrassingly, had that same conversation happened three months ago, in the throes of my delusion, I probably would have giddily (read: stupidly) considered it.

Awat paid for our tea and then walked me down the stairs and out to the street. I smiled, shook his hand, and said, "Good-bye." My crush on him was absolutely a thing of the past, and that conversation had guaranteed, 100 percent, that it would stay there.

Karzan pulled up in the Pathfinder, and I climbed in. We both waved to Awat as Karzan drove off toward the villas, and I thought, "There's closure, and then there's *cah-low-zhure.*" Three syllables.

Chapter Thirty-eight

Ethics, Schmethics

Since my Crocs class was learning the course material at a slower pace, we did not have enough time to complete Unit 10. However, it was still to be part of the final exam, so I wanted to introduce as much of the grammar as possible. It may or may not have been a coincidence that Unit 10 in the textbook was "Ethics and Values."

I passed out the Unit 10 exam and explained that we would go over the exam as a class, but then I needed everyone to return them to me when we were finished. We have to be very careful about keeping our exams, so they aren't leaked to other potential future students.

We spent all day Tuesday studying possessive pronouns: mine, yours, his/hers, ours, theirs. I flipped through the exam and found the pertinent sections, and we reviewed those multiple choice questions. At the end of class I collected the exams.

Wednesday I redistributed the exams, and we proceeded to attempt to tackle factual and unreal conditionals, and the concept of the moral dilemma.

Example:

> "If I eat too much, I gain weight." This was a factual
> conditional.
>
> "If I found a gold watch in the restroom, I would
> take it to the Lost & Found." This was an unreal con-
> ditional, and a perfect example of a moral dilemma.

The students took some time to understand the moral
dilemma, as they were confusing it with a standard dilemma/deci-
sion to make. I asked the class for an example of a moral dilemma,
and Hawall said, "If it is raining, I take umbrella."

Um, no. I mean, yes, you should probably take the umbrella,
but that—oh never mind.

I tried to expand on the idea by saying, "Usually a moral
dilemma is something that you wouldn't want anyone to know
about…" I then told them about the time I ordered the ski bag
from the company online, and how, when the package arrived
there were two ski bags inside. My *moral dilemma* was, do I:

1. Do the "right thing" and alert the company to the error
   (which would more than likely result in my having to go to
   the trouble of sending one bag back to them), or

2. Keep the bag and say nothing to the company.

I told my students I had just said "thank you" out loud to the
empty room where I had opened the box and gave the extra bag to
my sister, but I pointed out this was actually not the "right thing"
to do.

By the end of class, the students were exhausted and still mostly confused. They complained, "Teacher, we think Unit 10 no on test." I had to explain I couldn't control what was on the test, they were already printed, and that yes, Unit 10 would be on the final exam. They all appeared semidistraught.

After I dismissed them, everyone gathered their things to leave when Rabar said, "Teacher, you need this?" and held up his copy of the Unit 10 exam. I gasped. "YES!" and then looked accusingly at everyone else, who had all surreptitiously tucked the exams away in their respective belongings. On their faces were varying looks of sheepishness and annoyance (directed at Rabar). I was shocked, appalled, dismayed, and confused. In the first place, Rabar was the one student who would undoubtedly fail the class (his exam scores never exceeded 60 percent) and was in the most need of sneaking the exam home. In the second place, this was the Ethics and Values unit! We had spent at least fifteen minutes discussing moral dilemmas, and then here we had a real-life moral dilemma.

I should have lied about keeping the ski bags.

Moral dilemmas were clearly the theme of the day. Katherine called me to go running in the park and intimated that she had excellent gossip. We had finally discovered a large family park across the road from English Village. From the street it didn't look like much; however, once you made it beyond the gates and down one of the dusty paths, it opened into a lush, green, well-manicured extravaganza, which was the prime spot for many

Friday weddings and general family merriment. Only the occasional Westerner used it for exercise, so we were frequently the subjects of gawks and stares and pointing from children.

Katherine's gossip was good. Apparently Married Ashton had been home over Christmas break, with his "unhappy family" of beautiful Russian wife and one-year-old child. He suffered through the charade to keep up holiday appearances, but then rushed back to Erbil to be with his true love, the Spanish Gabriela. He had confided to Katherine that this time he was serious about Gabriela and was really going to ask his wife for a divorce. I was amazed. He had been complaining about his situation for such a long time, without actually making any changes or trying to do anything about it.

"Really?" I said. "Good for him!"

Katherine replied, "Just wait." She said that when Ashton called his wife, presumably to have the divorce conversation, before he could say anything, she told him she was pregnant with their second child. The child that had been conceived over Christmas break.

The ministry kids had concluded their semester of English study, and we had three days of final exams in which to chart their progress.

I projected the following up on the whiteboard, explained this was their final writing exam, and didn't anticipate any additional questions:

Choose two topics. Write an essay for your chosen topics, with at least three sentences each.

- Your favorite artist
- Your personal values
- Your personality type
- Your food passions

Straightforward, no? Even for low-level students.

But as soon as I put the essay topic up, at least four people raised their hands and started asking questions.

Azheen said, "Only two topics we choose?" Then she said, "Artist? Not art?"

Rabar asked, "Write one, two, three?" (I had explained, ad nauseam in class, what an essay should look like, and that no, it should not be three numbered sentences.)

Then Aryan asked, "You want we write one paragraph, then two?"

Solin asked, "For about artist, I tell you, and also explain?"

I had to explain, again, that part of the exam was being able to understand the instructions. And honestly, I don't think the instructions could have been any easier or clearer.

The following was a perfect example of the disparity in levels of the students in my class.

Dastan (who was at the appropriate level) wrote:

> My favorite artist is Julia Roberts, she is born in USA
> I think she is best acterses in Howllyood, she is winner
> award in Acadimic Oscar.

366 I Have Iraq in My Shoe

I'm crazy about Julia Roberts, and I like all his films, because when I see someone his films, realy I feel it is not film, it is real. I think all Julia Roberts films is fantastic.

If I have a time I'm watching to Julia Roberts films every day, because I'm Jilua Roberts films addect.

Grammatical mistakes? Yes. Creative spelling? Sure, but he gets his idea across effectively.

Rabar, on the other hand, wrote:

Your food passions.

I'm passions a chiken becouse for Healthey is good, and this food is not costly and for used is eassy, I am passions but know I don't too eatean becouse I'm tried and I hav'nt eatean Lot food becouse all piple this vaery good for disussion and confention.

What?

The ministry kids had varying results on their final exams. Some actually did well, others barely passed, and Rabar was a solid "fail." What was more disappointing was Warren and Jill's pro bono offer failed to produce the dubious result they had hoped for, and the ministry did not pay to re-enroll any students in the course.

From: Warren

Sent: Friday, January 29

Subject: Transition

Dear CED,

As I have discussed in the past, CED is poised to go through an administration transition at the positions of Director and Deputy Director. Very shortly, I will be leaving Iraq after almost 3 years of working for the university...

[And this continued on for several paragraphs.]

I expelled a heavy, yet unsurprised, sigh. Warren was leaving his contract early, just because he was sick of Iraq. He was supposed to stay until May.

I wondered if I could add a few concrete blocks to his packed hockey bags.

Chapter Thirty-nine

My Villa/Hotel/Office

From: Jill

To: Gretchen

Subject: Wednesday night

Hey, Gretchen,

You will have two visitors Wednesday night. I will be staying in the small room, and Tom in Warren's room. He will not be arriving until 9 or even 10 p.m., and we will both be out of there before 3:30 a.m. Sorry about this, but he is traveling back to the U.S. and since there is a prof staying in the men's villa, there's no choice (plus, he's the Chancellor). This will also be a very good opportunity for me to point out to him the lack of privacy in the villas. They're already on board with a move to a new place, which will offer both more privacy and also greater room for expansion, so consider this icing on the cake.

Thanks for your understanding,

Jill

Jill and I had very different ideas on how to ice a cake, and she was mistaken about my understanding. Forget the Iraq War, forget the War on Terror; we were still engulfed in the War on Gretchen's Privacy. Distress ran through me like Indian food. Who thought this was a logical idea?

Tom Pappas was not staying in my villa. There would be no bathroom sharing, and *no* chance encounters in the hallway in tighty-whities, possibly with Tom playing his guitar and crooning a ballad about fighting lionesses. My hair was standing on end and I was close to hyperventilating as I carefully typed back a response to Jill. It said, "Please do not offer my villa as an option for Tom. I am not comfortable with that arrangement."

I could not believe that I was the only person to recognize how totally inappropriate that was. This was a Muslim region, where unmarried men and women were hardly permitted to be seen together in public, much less have sleepovers at one another's houses. I had Kurdish neighbors. This was a university building. Why was there absolutely no concern for how that would look? If I had been a Kurdish female employee, the subject would never have been brought up. If I had been the daughter of one of the board members or faculty, this idea would have been considered an offense. And "plus, he's the chancellor"? Was that some sort of ultimate trump card that could be pulled at any moment? Where was the line drawn with that? "I'm sorry, but yes, you have to wear this gag ball and rubber dominatrix catsuit. *He's the chancellor.*"

                                       ꙮꙮꙮ

The next morning my cell phone rang and it was Jill. My stomach tightened and I rolled my eyes as I answered. She was there at the villas and wanted to speak with me. I went downstairs and across the deck to Steve's villa, where Jill was waiting. She began with, "There will not be any overnight guests." My relief was hesitant, and I was still wary. She continued on to explain that, after our emails, she sat down and thought about the situation. She said, "I realized *I* didn't want to be running into Tom in the middle of the night in the hallway!"

Yes! Finally, we had some perspective! No matter that it took Jill actually having to almost be in my shoes to understand this; we were there. I think Jill's common sense must have temporarily broken, but she managed to fix it. She then went on to explain that she called both the chancellor and the provost and told them Tom couldn't stay in my villa, and now they were both very angry. The provost threatened, "Jill, you'd better talk to Gretchen, or I will."

I was aghast that both were "angry" about the situation, and I told Jill, "I will *gladly* have a conversation with the provost, gladly!" *Why did they not get this? What was wrong with these men?*

Jill said that wouldn't be necessary, and the issue had been resolved, but the tension was still there.

The following week I received something a little closer to cake icing:

> From: Awat
> Subject: I miss you
> To: Gretchen
> Hi,Miss gretchen how are you? Are you fine? I miss you very much...

That is how you ice a cake. I didn't care if he wanted to use me as a sponsor to get his family to the United States. I was just grateful to have someone ask how I was doing. The only other person who was sympathetic and understanding was the Citibank agent on the phone, when I called to yell about the fraud alerts that kept shutting down my card when I was trying to use it. After they transferred me several times, I had to talk to a hard-nosed manager, who was difficult up until the point where I exhaustedly said, "I'm in Iraq, and it is impossible to have to keep calling about this!" She was immediately profusely apologetic and uber-sympathetic, and I realized she probably thought I was in the armed forces, keeping our country safe and whatnot. I didn't correct her; I really needed the sympathy.

ᕲᕮᕮᕲ

The Erbil living situation was exhausting me. I had less privacy than ever. The university hired a part-time administrative assistant and had turned the downstairs bedroom into her office. A large copy machine had also been placed at the bottom of the staircase. This was horrible feng shui, I was sure, or possibly one of those weapons of mass destruction everyone had been wailing about.

The new admin was a short, plain, guarded Kurdish woman who wore T-shirts and jeans to work. She was also a tattletale and complained to Jill that Steve and I weren't always in our classrooms. Jill wanted Steve and me to be sitting in our classrooms "during working hours," which meant pretending we actually had eight hours of work to do. Warren hadn't cared if we spent part of the day upstairs in our villas. Jill was less flexible. Whatever slight perks there had been in the Erbil villas were slowly being taken away.

My newfound contentment with Dadyar was short-lived. I had to have an awkward conversation with Jill regarding other "complaints from the staff," which meant either Dadyar or Vana. Jill said that Vana was "incredibly intimidated" by me, and she proceeded to recount a story in which the innocent, put-upon heroine (Vana, who I then decided was like the stupid, incompetent Prissy in *Gone with the Wind*) had been diligently scrubbing away in the kitchen when the wicked and ruthless Scarlett happened by and disgustedly wiped a fingerful of dust in poor Vana's/Prissy's face. This was absurd, and I had thought Jill might have been joking, except when I said, "Oh my God, are you joking?" she said unsmilingly, "No. That was what I was told."

Vana had complained to her boyfriend Dadyar, who then complained to his cousin Rana, the HR director, who then complained to Jill. I could only imagine the story becoming more and more sinister as it passed from person to person. Ellen informed me that Jill and Rana had adjoining offices at the university and were frequently seen talking and laughing together. This was not good news.

Of course Vana was intimidated by me. I knew about the torrid, illicit love affair! She knew I knew! It was like *The Young and the Restless*, except no one was particularly young. I had long passed the point of caring about the infidelity of "the staff." It was none of my business. I just didn't care. I was so disappointed in this turn of events, however, as I had gone out of my way to be nice to Vana. Each week she would drag her bucket and mops into the villa, and I would give her my most winning smile and say, "Hi, Vana! How are you?" And I had warmly welcomed her back from her three-week trip to Ethiopia by saying, "We're glad you're back! We missed you!" I didn't understand how any of that could have been misunderstood to be intimidation. These were the few people involved in my day-to-day life, and I couldn't trust them. From the moment I set foot outside my bedroom in the morning, until 5:00 p.m. when the staff left, I had to be on my guard. All of that nonsense, combined with the fact that Katherine had gone back to Australia to begin her diplomat training, and most of the other people I knew in Erbil had finished their respective contracts and left to go on to bigger and better things, equaled me really wanting to go back to Suli.

The teachers in Suli had recently been moved from the isolated villa compound to a high-rise apartment complex, with beautiful, spacious, brightly lit apartments. They had designated one entire apartment building for the university staff. The top floor had been made into an all-purpose recreational area, with a Foosball table, movie-screening room, and workout room. Ellen had moved in with Carey, who had brought even more crap than I had and whose apartment could have been featured in a special homesick-themed issue of *Elle Décor*. Once you set foot in the apartment, you may as well have been back in the United States. Carey had generously offered for me to live with them, in the pretty *Elle Décor* apartment, where Ellen was still channeling Betty Crocker and Mrs. Fields. I wanted to be in Suli.

In spite of the deluxe new accommodations in Suli, things with the school were slowly unraveling, and morale was low. Jill had explained to our department that despite what Warren had told us (that we were wildly profitable, and making "millions" for the university), we were actually in fairly dire financial straits. Warren had lied about all the money that was coming in and left Jill with an enormous mess to clean up. An image of Jill's baby-sitting days unfolded in my head. I saw Warren as a misbehaving seven-year-old, guiltily caught standing in the middle of a jumbled pile of crap, with Jill, hands on hips, standing over the pile, ruefully shaking her head. This was bigger than broken Legos or spilt Cheerios, though. Everyone began worrying about losing their jobs.

Even though things with the CED were bad, I still wanted to be in Suli. I explained this to Jill, who claimed she would do her best to bring me down there, depending on whether or not she could find another female to trade places with me. All of the female teachers in Suli knew how bad the Erbil living situation was, and none of them wanted any part of it. Hey! Who wants to live where they work, and be subjected to unfair rumor-spreading and constant privacy invasions? Anyone? Are you sure? No one? Bueller? I was stuck. I knew I was teetering on the edge of insanity when, after everyone left the villa at the end of the day, I would rush around, slamming and locking each door and yelling, "MINE!" with the click of each lock.

Chapter Forty

Reality Bites

One sunny Saturday morning I woke up at 11:00 a.m. and thought, "Wow, it is late," and then proceeded to lazily stay in bed, reading. At 11:15 the doorbell rang. I had developed a Pavlovian response to the unwelcome doorbell-ringing and door-knocking that occurred on the weekends, when I was supposed to have my perpetually diminishing me-time. My immediate response was to quietly say, "No. Fuck off," to the empty room and then return to whatever it was I had been doing when the interruption occurred.

The doorbell rang again at noon, a double-ring this time, and again I responded without thinking, "No. Fuck off." I then heard the door handle rattle. MOTHERFUCKER! Are they trying to get in? It was the bedraggled, unscrupulous Union soldiers, descending on Tara to pillage and plunder and steal Mrs. O'Hara's rosewood sewing box. I silently cursed Jill for not bringing me down to Suli. No one in Suli ever had to deal with potential students or Union soldiers knocking on their doors in their deeeee-luxe apartment in the sky.

I was in my room, clad in nothing more than somewhat transparent, pink summer shortie pajamas. It was hot. Was it Steve?

Or Dadyar? Both had keys to the villa. Although they would have at least tried to call first, wouldn't they? My cell phone was on the dresser, silent, sans any indication of missed calls or text messages. I then heard chatter outside my window. I couldn't discern whether it was English or something else over the whir of my air conditioner. I crept to the window and carefully peeled back one of the hanging vertical blinds to peek out at the shared deck between the villas. There, at one of the deck tables, sat a Kurdish man, woman, and ten-ish-year-old child, who had made themselves comfortable. There were papers on the table, and I momentarily wondered if they were here to take a placement test? But I would have been told about that beforehand—wouldn't I? I looked around for Steve but couldn't see anyone else. Someone was now aggressively knocking on my front door. *Dammit!* Whoever it was they were being fairly relentless, considering all the villa blinds were closed: kitchen, living room, classroom.

The large billboard out in front clearly stated, "If interested in English courses, call the number below." It did not say, "If interested in English courses, please aggressively ring doorbells and knock on the villas, especially on the weekends."

So, I continued to answer, "No. Fuck off," to the knocking, and decided to abandon ship for the day. In the past, I would have had no place else to go. But now? Ha HA! Costa Coffee! I could walk there! I could escape the forced entrapment of "my" villa, while Kurds rang my doorbell incessantly. I didn't care why they were there. I hadn't been advised of any official school business happening today, and it was Saturday for crying out loud. I needed my weekend!

I quickly pulled on yoga pants and a billowing Maximall top, and tucked a few necessities into my purse: money, sunglasses, sunblock, and my little writing pad and pen. I crept down the stairs, past the hulking copy machine, carrying my flip-flops, so as to approach the door stealthily, like the Pawnee hunting Tatonka. The last knock had rapped roughly five minutes ago, so I deduced the coast was clear. I swiftly unlocked the door, whipped it open, and immediately closed it behind me and locked it again. No Kurds. The deck was on the opposite side of the house, so I could quickly stroll down the driveway before turning a sharp right into the street and away from the villa. I made it. During my escape I noticed three unfamiliar cars now parked in front of the villa. What was going on here today?

I continued slowly down the street, walking through the oppressive, ovenlike heat of midday, turned right, and walked the remaining three blocks to Costa Coffee, every step releasing a bit of the tension and anxiety that had built up with each ring of the doorbell, each aggressive knock on the door.

Ahhhh, Costa Coffee. I heart you. This was clean, untainted air-conditioning. Smoking was not allowed. The men had to go outside and stand under the overhang with their cigarettes. Traditional coffee shops in Iraq had the unwritten rule of being men only. They were starkly furnished and usually packed with cigarette-smoking men. This coffee shop was identical to other Costa Coffees, with the comfortable living room chairs and cherry wood tables, and the glass counter full of paninis and muffins. It was heaven. Heaven's prices were fairly high, in that you'd drop $12 on a sandwich and froufy coffee drink, but it was absolutely worth it.

I took my BBQ chicken quesadilla and coffee mocha frescato and parked myself in one of the overstuffed, striped chairs, next to an Iraqi girl who was busily typing away on her pink Mac laptop. I had only been sitting and writing for a few minutes when the Iraqi girl stood up and leaned over my table. "Hello!" she said pleasantly. "Hello," I answered, smiling. "Is there anything I can do for you?" she asked. I knew she didn't work for Costa Coffee, so my resulting facial expression must have said "Hanh?" She explained herself, "You looked a little lost, and I just wanted to know if you needed anything." Her name was Heba, and she was from Baghdad. I asked why she was in Erbil, and she happily replied, "I'm on vacation! Just for the weekend." She was very cheery and friendly. I wanted her to have a better vacation option. She went on to tell me that she worked for such-and-such company (something I had never heard of and quickly forgot the name of) and asked what I did. I said I taught English for the university, and she seemed excited. Heba explained that she was interested in getting her MBA, so I wrote down the school's website and my email address and said there would be a link to the MBA program on the site. She thanked me, then went back to her little pink Mac. There were Kurds sitting and having conversations, in English, and Westerners enjoying snacks, and best of all, no one was smoking. It felt familiar and safe.

It finally dawned on me that the only things that made me happy here were things that reminded me of home. I no longer wanted to read *The Kite Runner*, or *The Poet of Baghdad*, or *A Thousand Splendid Suns*. I had completely lost my objectivity and my political correctness. It took an observation from a total stranger, a woman from Baghdad, for me to acknowledge that I really was lost. I didn't want to be in Iraq, or Kurdistan, or Erbil, or really even Suli. I wanted to be home, and home wasn't here.

ⅇↄⅇↄⅇↄ

The very next week, when I went down to Suli to do my banking, Jill called me into her office and quietly informed me that I had to be laid off.

Ever since Warren left, and we were made aware that CED was losing money, being laid off had been a distinct possibility. We had all been living on pins and needles for a while, and the overwhelming sense of foreboding was something everyone tried to ignore. I was the first to go. The one with the highest salary, who was a "pain in the ass" of the chancellor and the provost, was an easy first choice, and my recent "rebellious" uncooperativeness was probably just the extra shove they had needed.

After being told I would have to be out of the Erbil villa within a week, I went into a bit of a tailspin. My Excel budget spreadsheet wasn't ready for me to go, and the daunting task of making spur-of-the-moment travel plans from Iraq was not easy, but I did not make a dress out of living room curtains and go swanning into the administrative offices in order to manipulate or guilt them into keeping me on. Mostly because the living room curtains were cheap Venetian blinds. There was no begging, or attempted manipulative guilting, but there might have been some crying, some hyperventilating, some hand-slapped-to-the-forehead wailing coupled with despair.

There was maybe a half hour of the above before there was some clarity. I didn't want to be there. That was the bottom line. Four hours after my conversation with Jill, I was sitting in Carey and Ellen's *Elle Décor* living room, with at least six other Americans and Canadians, wearing shorts, playing Cranium, and drinking a strong vodka cocktail that Carey had lovingly poured for me. The vodka helped quell the vacillating emotions of relief and wistfulness.

In life, it is important to find where you fit in, where you feel comfortable, where you feel home. I was not home in The Iraq. While I never expected to stay longer than my original signed contract, I also hadn't expected to so desperately need to be somewhere I was openly accepted and welcomed. I longed to be back in a place where bacon was consumed freely, and out in the open, and where I could drink a glass of wine without worrying that the waiters were judging me, or that I was sitting in the "wrong" section of the restaurant. I longed to be back in a place where the TV series *Dirty, Sexy, Money* was not censored down to *Dirty Money*, and where *Mad Men* and *Big Love* were not considered to be lifestyle recommendations. I longed to be back in a place where kissing scenes were aired in their entirety and where smiling in photographs wasn't considered a "stigma." I longed to be back in a place where I would only be considered a whore when I wore provocative clothing *and* asked to be paid for sex. There was a lot of longing. I didn't care about the loss of salary; I didn't need any more shoes. I needed to be *home*.

The university worked with the Qalawa Refugee Camp and would periodically take donated goods to the families in need. I wanted to donate a good portion of the clothing I had brought, including some of my completely impractical footwear. The camp was composed of roughly forty to fifty families of Iraqis who migrated to Kurdistan from Baghdad in 2007 and was located just outside of Suli. I wasn't sure they would actually benefit from platform espadrille wedges or grommetted stilettos, so I spoke with Dashnye, a British-educated Kurdish woman at the university, who coordinated the donations. I explained, "I want to donate some shoes, but most of them are silly, impractical high heels. Would the refugee camp even want these?" Dashnye assured me that there were a number of young girls at the camp who would be thrilled with high heels. Just because people are displaced doesn't mean they don't want pretty footwear. Plus, variety is the spice of wardrobe. I donated nine pairs.

If nothing else, Miss Teen South Carolina 2007 would be pleased. I had helped The Iraq with their education system and had also helped with their fashion sense. Never judge a person until you have walked a mile in her shoes. Or, if you have more than enough of your own shoes, let the person walk a mile in the shoes you donated. That's a lesser-known idiom, sure, but just as true.

One of my students had once said to me, "Teacher, I must know how you think about Kurdistan? What you think of the city, the people, the place?" It was sort of unfair for me to truthfully answer a question like that. I had seen some astoundingly spectacular things. According to the "Where I've Been" feature on Facebook, I had been to over 182 cities in 41 countries, now including Turkey, Greece, and The Rest of Europe. I could say I loved the mountains or that the city was...sprawling? Or that the place was exotic-ish? I could say I found the mosques beautiful, or the markets entertaining, but the physical aspect of Kurdistan was not what had most impressed me. What most impressed me was the people. Their sense of community, their resiliency, their collective sense of humor, and their capacity not to take anything too seriously. While they seemed frustratingly lazy or apathetic at times, the silver lining of that was an admirable carefree attitude that corresponded to a preferred coping strategy for tougher times. Everything will work out, inshallah.

My initial impressions of the Middle East were not far from the mark. It is a completely male-dominated society, and what I found most disconcerting was how deeply the sexism was ingrained. Women are not respected and have centuries of cultural conditioning to overcome. What was encouraging was seeing potential for change and the desire to balance tradition with an ever-changing world. What I found interesting on a personal level was how easy I thought it would be to dislike the men for their aggregate misogyny, but I found that my students, like anyone else, were human. Some of the women were shy and tentative, but others were surprisingly bold, passionate, and brilliant. More than one of them thanked me for teaching them "so much more" than just English, and I was glad to have done that, however unwittingly. Many of the men exhibited textbook sexism toward their female classmates, and usually when speaking of women in general, but at the same time they treated me, their female teacher, with the utmost respect. The overall experience was exhausting, enlightening, frustrating, rewarding, and best of all, really fun. They were my kids, and I felt endlessly grateful for having had the opportunity to teach them and to know them.

It was rather poetic that my last semester class was composed of only two men. Just two. It ended as it began. Adel and Idres both worked as drivers for one of the Western companies in English Village. Adel (the tall one) and Idres (the portly one) were very eager but very elementary Level 1 learners. The Level 1 book was even too advanced for them at times, and we plodded through some challenging classes. When I told them I was leaving to return to the United States, both fiercely protested. Idres even went so far as to say he was "very angry" with this new development, and shook his head in obvious disgust. Adel generously offered to drive me to the airport. At first I brushed him off, saying, "Oh no, that is really nice, thank you but no." When he protested, I thought, "Why not?" and he seemed so pleased and so proud to be able to take me.

After all my things had been packed into Adel's SUV, and we were on our way to the airport, he said, "Miss Gretchen, thank you so much for your teaching. I am happy to learn more English!" As he was effusing, his cell phone rang, and he answered in Kurdish, then handed the phone to me. It was Idres, calling to say good-bye and wish me (and my family) well. When I said, "Hello?" he immediately crowed, "Miss Gretchen! What are you wearing?" I burst out laughing at the absurdity of the question, which, if overheard by an innocent eavesdropper, might have seemed racily inappropriate, but one of our last lessons had been articles of clothing and describing them. I informed Idres I was wearing a brown sweater and blue jeans, then let him talk some more while my eyes welled up with tears.

৩৩৩

Crying a little, yes, but no longer sobbing into my apron. Having survived more than a year in The Iraq, and having paid off over $40,000 of debt, I was leaving. And while I had told Idres I was wearing a brown sweater and jeans, in my head I was triumphantly clad in my chain-mail tunic, fierce metallic headband, and my green Marc Jacobs platform sandals, dragging my overweight suitcases in a long, slow-motion walk up to the airport check-in counter; the luggage scale just sitting there, waiting for me. It would be worth it, though. My mom promised BLTs for lunch upon my return.

Epilogue

I managed to make it home, in spite of one airline canceling a leg of my flight. I managed to receive the stupid hockey bag I had shipped home, despite the shipping company trying to extort more money from me after I had paid them and left my precious cargo in their care. I'm sure it was just my karma coming back from the ski-bag incident. And, finally, I managed to spend some time reflecting on my experience and my astounding accomplishments in The Iraq:

- Grand total spent on overweight luggage: $4,880

The shipping company charged me $1,010 to ship one stupid hockey bag home. All things considered, $5,000 was a small price to pay to have the comforts of home with me.

- Debt eliminated: $41,745

All of it. All the debt was gone. There would be no mocking credit card statements waiting for me in the mailbox. And, more importantly, Suze Orman would be proud. I even had enough left over to send my parents to Europe, first class.

- Countries traveled: 9

Austria, France, Croatia, Greece, Turkey, Sweden, Italy, Jordan, Oman. It was an amazing, fulfilling potpourri of cultures, languages, food, and, of course, shoes.

• Pairs of shoes purchased: 20

This seems excessive; however, since I donated nine pairs, and gave two pairs to my sisters, I really only purchased nine for myself, right? Or is that creative shoe math?

• Soul mates met: 0

My "great, big, core-connecting, fate-fulfilling, gotta-have-it earthquake love" was not to be found in Iraq. However, Psychic Sahar assured me I would have one in this lifetime. Inshallah.

• Cultural tolerance level: 5

My initial rating remained true. I won't sugarcoat it. While there were definitely things I could appreciate about the Middle East, the glaring inequities between men and women were too great to ignore. Five is average. It's not the murky bottom, but it leaves plenty of room for improvement. Girls should not be thought of as "guests" in their own families. Women should be allowed to roam about as freely as men, without chaperone or the threat of being labeled a whore. Coffee shops and restaurants should not be gender restricted. The menstrual cycle, while annoying and mostly inconvenient, is not a "hurt" or a "pollution." And Virginity Soap will always be bullshit.

After returning to the United States, I had a serious "aha!" moment, which, no offense to Oprah, I would really prefer to call my "holy shit" moment. In watching an HBO documentary on Gloria Steinem, I saw what I thought were shocking examples of widespread and generally accepted sexism in the United States. From hideous newscaster opinions to vitriolic sign-carrying protesters, to a Chicago restaurant that had a men-only section—and this was only forty years ago. Chicago! That's where I grew up!

How could it betray me like that? I was thankfully born too late and was too busy reading *Free To Be You And Me* and *Our Bodies, Ourselves* to have experienced any of it firsthand, which makes it near-impossible to believe it happened. Like when I try to explain to teenagers that cursive writing is not a pretend language I made up myself, and it really used to be taught in school. My mom confirmed that some things had, indeed, been a little grim for women. That documentary both horrified me and made me re-assess my somewhat harsh perspective on the Middle East. Maybe it's just a matter of time…

I am now older, wiser, and completely debt-free. While Warren and I have gone our separate ways, I am still grateful for the crazy opportunity he provided. I am also grateful for the experience, which proved to me that people are just people, no matter where you go.

At the end of *Gone with the Wind*, Scarlett O'Hara was alone and jobless too, but did she wallow? Did she whine? No, she did not. She focused on the comforting and encouraging thoughts of home and the future, and the new boxes from YOOX waiting in the closet. Herb, purring loudly, winds his way around the open hockey bag as I sit on the hardwood floor unpacking in the spare room at my parents' house. I reach into the bag and pull out one red suede Wonder Woman boot, and a clump of red Iraqi dirt, not unlike the red clay of Tara, falls off one of the soles. Snickering to myself, I pick up the clump, raise it triumphantly in the air, and boldly declare aloud, "Tomorrow is another day!" Herb is startled at the outburst and looks momentarily confused, before resuming his purring and nuzzling the hockey bag that is being, finally, unpacked. The bag, it seems, has a familiar smell.

Acknowledgments

Gracias, Obrigado, Merci, Danke schoen, Tack, Grazi, Efcharisto, Spassiba, Spass, Shukran, Didi mad lo ba, Domo arigato, Kamsa ham-nida, multsumesk, kap kun kaa, and thank you to:

- Scooter-Pooter McCoubrey, who loaned me Wade Rouse's hilarious *At Least in the City, Someone Would Hear Me Scream,* where I stalked his agent from his acknowledgments page.
- All my other Iraq friends and coworkers, whom I am reluctant to name for fear of inadvertently leaving someone out, like in an Academy Awards speech, and then everyone would just be talking about it for weeks and weeks, and we'd probably get divorced over it.
- Wendy Sherman (stalked agent), for helping me whip the book proposal into shape, and for just ignoring any of the offensive language she asked me to tone down, that may or may not have made it into the book.
- Shana Drehs for humoring me throughout all the edits, and for trying to understand why I hate footnotes.*

---

*I mean, it's just a nuisance. There you are, happily reading along when you hit a footnote, and you have to leave your current, comfortable paragraph and drag your eyes all the way down to the bottom of the page, and when you've finished

- Kerry Rupp, the first person to pay me for writing.
- All my other friends who encouraged my writing (just not with money).
- Piers Drysdale, for letting me stay in his villa after being kicked out of mine in The Iraq.
- Piers's mum, Mrs. Drysdale, for letting me stay in the flat in Notting Hill, London, on my way home.
- My step-class teachers: Dan J., Casey, Michelle D., and Nancy at the Portland, Oregon, Hollywood 24-Hour Fitness for keeping me sane, and fitting into my pants, while I was living with my parents and finishing the book. I was the one in the back row who consistently refused to do squats and jumping jacks.
- All the people whose names I've changed in the book, for not taking it too personally. You're all three-dimensional people, and I probably just experienced one of the dimensions.
- My family: Little Nolan, Ellie, Pete, Jessie, Dad, and especially Mom, who did her own bit of editing in between yelling encouragement into the megaphone and waving the pom-poms.
- Tina Fey and Seth MacFarlane.
- Mrs. Gentry, my eleventh-grade typing teacher, for the most worthwhile class I've ever taken. "A, a, a, space, a, a, a, space, a, a, a, space, return."

---

reading the footnote, you have to drag your eyes back up to try to find the place where you left off. I'm exhausted just talking about it.